Praise for *Trust Your Gut*

'From the first page Eugene Sadler-Smith provides a hugely engaging book, packed with fascinating stories, top academic research, and the practical wisdom of global names on the subject of decision making. By the end of the book you will have a firm understanding of how to improve your decision making, when to "use your gut" and, just as important, when not to! A must-read for company executives.'

Richard Williams, former Global MD, Mott MacDonald

'This book is dense with fascinating, and usable, insights. Eugene explains clearly what intuition is and isn't and under what conditions it's useful. I wish I'd had this knowledge much earlier in my life. I'd have relied less on "sensing" when I should have been relying on "solving", and vice versa. A riveting read.'

Sally Bibb, author of *The Strengths Book*

'*Trust Your Gut* epitomises Professor Sadler-Smith's extraordinary dedication to studying intuition, which had a tremendous impact on the academic and practitioner worlds. Trust your gut and read this book; it will explain, in wonderfully captivating language, that we know more than we think and that learning to feel that is the ultimate power for navigating an increasingly complex and ever-changing world.'

Professor Marc Stierand, PhD, Director, Institute of Business Creativity, EHL Hospitality Business School, Lausanne, Switzerland

'Thanks to *Trust Your Gut* I can now explore an intelligence we've always had, and with so many practical takeaways I can coach people to apply their intuitive intelligence to improve the speed and quality of decisions, not just at work but in their personal lives too. Highly recommended to leaders, coaches and anyone interested in improving the quality of their life through better decision making.'

Richard Thorp, Founding Partner, Wiseheart

'Our ability to understand when and when not to listen to our intuition often determines the difference between success or failure. This book provides clear guidance on when to "trust your gut". A must-read for leaders who want to improve their decision-making processes.'

Dirk Verburg, Management Consultant and Executive Coach; Producer and Host of 'Leadership 2.0' podcast, Switzerland

'Professor Eugene Sadler-Smith makes a powerful case that artificial intelligence is already augmenting sense and decision making; that alongside our "intuitive knowing" it will create a powerful hybrid intelligence that will change the way leaders lead. "Feeling the way" will become synonymous with "leading the way".'

Dr Garry Hargreaves, Director, NATO Communications and Information Academy (NCI Agency)

'Intuition is a tricky aspect of decision making, being both a huge source of bias and a way we subconsciously process valuable information. Drawing together a rich body of research on the psychology of intuition, this immensely accessible book explains how we can navigate this tension, harness its benefits and avoid the pitfalls, to make better decisions.'

Jonny Gifford, Principal Research Fellow, Institute for Employment Studies

'This book is an endorsement of how human abilities can complement the growing reliance on artificial intelligence and offers business leaders practical advice on how to harness intuition for better decision making. A compelling read!'

Thomas Morineaux, Director, Alix Partners

Trust Your Gut

Pearson

Trust Your Gut

Go with your intuition and make better choices

Eugene Sadler-Smith

Pearson

Harlow, England • London • New York • Boston • San Francisco • Toronto • Sydney
Dubai • Singapore • Hong Kong • Tokyo • Seoul • Taipei • New Delhi
Cape Town • São Paulo • Mexico City • Madrid • Amsterdam • Munich • Paris • Milan

PEARSON EDUCATION LIMITED
KAO Two
KAO Park
Harlow CM17 9NA
United Kingdom
Tel: +44 (0)1279 623623
Web: www.pearson.com

First edition published 2024 (print and electronic)

ISBN: 978-1-292-46216-5 (print)
          978-1-292-73033-2 (ePub)

British Library Cataloguing-in-Publication Data
A catalogue record for the print edition is available from the British Library

Library of Congress Cataloging-in-Publication Data
Names: Sadler-Smith, Eugene, author.
Title: Trust your gut : go with your intuition and make better choices /
   Eugene Sadler-Smith.
Description: First edition. | Harlow, England ; New York : Pearson, 2024. |
   Includes bibliographical references and index.
Identifiers: LCCN 2024033231 | ISBN 9781292462165 (paperback) | ISBN
   9781292730332 (epub)
Subjects: LCSH: Decision making. | Intuition.
Classification: LCC HD30.23 .S196 2024 | DDC 658.4/03--dc23/eng/20240719
LC record available at https://lccn.loc.gov/2024033231

10 9 8 7 6 5 4 3 2 1
28 27 26 25 24

Cover design by Kelly Miller

Print edition typeset in 10/14 Charter ITC Pro by Straive
Printed in the UK by Bell and Bain Ltd, Glasgow

NOTE THAT ANY PAGE CROSS REFERENCES REFER TO THE PRINT EDITION

Contents

—

While we work hard to present unbiased, fully accessible content, we want to hear from you about any concerns or needs with this Pearson product so that we can investigate and address them:

- Please contact us with concerns about any potential bias at https://www.pearson.com/report-bias.html

- For accessibility-related issues, such as using assistive technology with Pearson products, alternative text requests, or accessibility documentation, email the Pearson Disability Support team at **disability.support@pearson.com**

The opinions and perspectives presented in this book are solely those of the authors and do not represent the positions or viewpoints of any affiliated organisations or institutions.

About the author

Eugene Sadler-Smith is Professor of Organisational Behaviour at Surrey Business School, University of Surrey, UK. His research interests are intuition (in decision making) and hubris (in leadership). He is the author of numerous research articles and books on these topics including *The Hubris Hazard, and How to Avoid it* (Routledge, 2024) and *Intuition in Business* (Oxford University Press, 2023). Prior to becoming an academic he worked in industry for the best part of ten years.

Acknowledgements

—

My sincere gratitude goes out to all those friends, family members, students and colleagues, too numerous to mention, who've supported me in my pursuit of 'intuitive intelligence' over the years. I'm very appreciative of the work of the fantastic team at Pearson who helped turn the intuitive intelligence idea into a reality and am especially grateful to my editor at Pearson, Eloise Cook. Thank you.

Introduction

———

How intuition saved the world, and why you should read this book

On 26 September 1983, one man's intuition may have saved the world from nuclear Armageddon. That man was Stanislav Petrov, a 44-year-old lieutenant colonel in the Soviet Air Defence Forces. His job was to monitor the possibility of a nuclear attack on the Soviet Union by the USA. If such an attack were to be detected, he was required to alert his superiors immediately, who would then order a retaliatory strike and mutually assure the destruction of both the Soviet Union and the USA.

Early in Petrov's shift on 26 September, the alarm sounded and the unthinkable appeared to be happening: the computer system detected a missile launch from the West Coast of the USA aimed directly against targets in the Soviet Union. Initially, Petrov surmised that it was a computer malfunction. Surely it was unlikely that the USA would launch only one missile. He dismissed it as a false alarm. Then, a few minutes later, the situation went from bad to worse: the computer system was showing that four more missiles had been launched.

Had Petrov stuck to the procedures, he'd have alerted his superiors who would have automatically launched a retaliatory all-out nuclear assault against the USA and the chances are we might not be here today. Data from the satellite early warning system was the only hard information he had to go on; by the time Soviet radar was able to pick up the missiles once they came over the horizon it would be too late. But Petrov had a nagging feeling that all was not as it seemed with the data. He chose not to inform his superiors immediately. He waited, and waited, for what seemed a lifetime. After five nerve-racking minutes, Petrov judged all five missiles to be a genuine false alarm. He was proven right. No missiles materialised because none had been launched. No Soviet cities were going to be engulfed in a nuclear holocaust. The early warning error was caused by the satellite mistaking the reflection of sunlight from the top of the clouds for a missile launch.

Petrov later explained that it was a gut decision, at best '50:50'. He told the BBC that he 'couldn't move, I felt like I was sitting on a hot frying pan'. He told *The Washington Post* that 'I had a funny feeling in my gut' that it was a false alarm. He put it down to his training *and* his intuition.[1] Petrov has been described as 'the man who saved the world'; perhaps more accurately he's 'the man whose intuition saved the world'.

If, like Stanislav Petrov, decision making is part of your job, then *Trust Your Gut* will help you to develop a new and powerful tool in your decision-making toolkit: *intuitive intelligence*.

Who is this book for?

Trust Your Gut will help anyone, at any level of a business, to take decisions, large or small, that affect both themselves (for example their job performance, relationships with colleagues, career prospects and progression, etc.) and their organisation (for example its productivity, effectiveness, reputation, sustainability, etc.).

The advice in *Trust Your Gut* isn't aimed at any particular type of job or industry; it applies across the board because intuition is found everywhere in business, whether that's in sales, marketing, HR, finance, innovation, operations, strategy, or any other aspect of any business large or small.

Although the main focus in *Trust Your Gut* is on business decision making, the principles it promotes and the tools and techniques it teaches can be applied equally to decision making in your personal life; for example which course to study, where to study, which car to buy, which job to take, where to live, etc., as well as important decisions in friendships, family matters and personal relationships.

If you're not sure that intuition is for you because you've been schooled in the 'analytical' method – which, let's face it, most of us have – then *Trust Your Gut* is definitely for you because, as we'll discover, no one has the luxury of choosing between intuitive and analytical approaches to decision making in life or in business: effective decisions involve a blend of *both* intuition *and* analysis. *Trust Your Gut* shows you how to get the best out of the intuitive half of the equation. In other words, *Trust Your Gut* is aimed at people just like you.

In *Trust Your Gut* I define intuition as follows:

'Intuition is a quick, automatic judgement based on unconscious processing of information and recognition of patterns; it's a product of learning and experience which reveals itself as a "gut feeling".'

I've written *Trust Your Gut* because I want more people to appreciate the marvels and acknowledge the flaws of intuition; I want them to be able to use its strengths and avoid being sabotaged by its weaknesses. My aim is to make intuition powerful, not perilous, and turn it into your decision-making friend, rather than your foe, so that it'll help rather than hinder decision making, both in your professional and personal life. Ultimately, I want people to be able to use their intuitive intelligence to take better decisions and improve their own and other people's lives and, even if it's only in a small way, make the world a better place.

How does this book work?

Trust Your Gut takes you on a seven-step journey towards intuitive intelligence, which I define as:

> **'The capacity to be aware of, understand, interpret and manage intuitions in yourself and in others and hence make better judgements and take more effective decisions.'**

Along the way you'll discover how to build intuitive 'muscle power', how to get in touch with your gut feelings, how to know when, and when not, to use your intuition, how to think without thinking, how to tune in and translate your gut feelings into action, how to de-bias your intuitions and how to continuously hone your hunches. The journey begins with a basic question of 'what is intuition?' and concludes by asking what role human intuition will play in the age of artificial intelligence (AI).

Each chapter begins with a power quote from a major public figure in arts, business, sports, science, etc., on the importance of intuition to them. In each chapter you'll find 'Spotlights' which highlight some of the key ideas from the science of intuition; you'll also find 'Big thinkers' dotted about: these are the remarkable people whose insights have built the science of intuition over the past half-century. Every section in each chapter ends with a 'Takeaway' and, at the end of each chapter, there's an 'In a nutshell' which captures the main point. In the 'Dig deeper' section, I'll signpost you where to go to find out more about the topics covered in each chapter. Each chapter ends with 'Workouts' that will help you to apply the ideas to decisions you're currently facing and build your intuitive intelligence; these can be used individually or in intuitive intelligence training sessions. Along the way you'll be invited to stop and think about the ideas that are being introduced and reflect on how they apply to you in your professional and personal life. I've kept facts and explanations as simple and clear as possible, steered clear of dumbing down and not shied away from using technical terms (usually in brackets and 'single quotes') albeit in a user-friendly way.

Intuition is a rich but untapped source of decision-making power that's inside each and every one of us. *Trust Your Gut* will help to unleash that power by showing you how to use intuition to improve both your professional and your personal effectiveness.

That's it by way of introduction; let's get started.

I hope you enjoy the book.

Eugene Sadler-Smith

Note

1 Chan, S. (2017) 'Stanislav Petrov, Soviet Officer who helped avert nuclear war, is dead at 77', *New York Times* 18 September 2017. Available online at: https://www.nytimes.com/2017/09/18/world/europe/stanislav-petrov-nuclear-war-dead.html.

part 1

What is intuition?

'Listen to your inner voice. Trust your intuition. It's important to have the courage to trust yourself.'

Dawn Ostroff (former Spotify and Condé Nast executive)

This chapter will help you to understand what intuition is (and isn't) and to distinguish between two different types of intuition; it also introduces the idea of 'two minds in one brain'.

Knowing without knowing how or why you know

Like Henry Ford, who once remarked that if he'd asked people what they wanted they'd have said 'a faster horse', Steve Jobs had a knack for intuitively 'reading things that aren't yet on the page'. Instead of relying on mountains of market research, Jobs somehow seemed to know, without knowing how or why he knew, what customers wanted. For example when he first saw the icon-based graphical user interface, which is now the standard on smartphones and laptops, 'every bone in his body' told him 'it's going to be great, and people are going to realize that and buy it'.[1] Jobs's 'intuitive intelligence' was the driving force behind many of Apple's remarkable innovations.

Oprah Winfrey is living proof of the power of positive thinking and pursuing purpose. In most of her major life moves, Oprah has, in her own words, taken in 'all the available information, listened to proposals and advice' but then created a space for her intuition – she calls it her 'inner GPS' – because it helps her to know, without knowing how or why she knows, where her 'true North' lies.[2] Oprah's intuitive intelligence has helped to make her into not only a global media icon but also one of the most respected and influential women in the world.

For Jobs, 'intuition is a very powerful thing – more powerful than intellect'. For Oprah, 'learning to trust your instincts, using your intuitive sense of what's best for you, is paramount for any lasting success'.[3]

Like Steve Jobs and Oprah Winfrey, have you ever 'just known' with knowing how or why you knew? It can be 'just knowing' in an important professional decision such as which course to study, which university to go to, which job to take, what direction to take your current business in, or whether to change jobs, retire or start a new business. 'Just knowing' also figures prominently in big personal decisions (for example where to live or which car to buy) and in friendships, relationships and family matters (for example when you 'just know' something's not right with your child or partner). It can even be suddenly just knowing not to go down a poorly lit shortcut on the way home or digging a little deeper into a yarn that someone has spun that somehow doesn't stack up. Often, when people have a 'just knowing' experience, even when pushed, they can't put their reasons into words: they 'just know'. This is intuition.

People who have a magical view of the world like to think of intuition as a sixth sense: 'the voice of [your] guardian angel', 'a curious telepathy' and 'a message from the soul'.[4] For those who are more inclined towards a 'muscular' view of intuition, it's a potent decision-making 'superpower' that, like any 'muscle', can be pumped up by exercise.[5] The 'magicals' and the 'musculars' have one thing in common: they both believe in the power of intuition. On the other hand, intuition has its fair share of sceptics and doubters who see 'going with your gut' as a surefire way to sabotage sound judgement and decision making. So, is intuition magical or muscular, powerful or perilous?

Based on what I've read and researched, and experienced directly, my view is that intuition:

- isn't magical but it's definitely muscular
- can be both powerful and perilous.

This book aims to offer a balanced view of when you should and when you shouldn't trust your gut. Also, I think the best way to harness the power of intuition is to unravel if, why and when it should be trusted. But before we do that we need to define what it precisely is that we're trying to unravel. So, what is intuition?

It's tempting to dumb intuition down to a sound bite such as 'knowing without knowing how or why you know', but because intuition is one of the most complex aspects of human psychology we shouldn't shy away from being a bit wordy in pinning it down. Scientists agree that intuition is:

- based on *fast, unconscious processing* of information and the *recognition of patterns*
- experienced *automatically* as '*gut feelings*'
- a product of *learning* and *experience* (Figure 1).

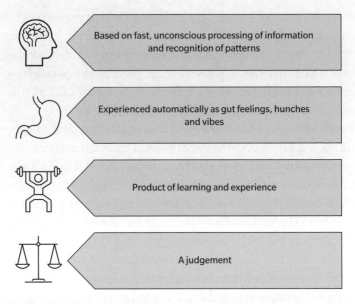

Figure 1 Intuition

When all of this unconscious mental work comes together it is perfectly possible to 'know without knowing how or why you know'. This 'just knowing' can then be used to take decisions, but it comes with no absolute guarantee of success because, at the end of the day, an intuition is a *judgement*.

These four key points come together in this book's definition of intuition:

> **'Intuition is a quick, automatic judgement based on unconscious processing of information and recognition of patterns; it's a product of learning and experience that reveals itself as a "gut feeling"'.**

The rest of this book unravels the science behind these various aspects of intuition. Intuition isn't an infallible sixth sense but, when it's used in the right way, it can be a source of decision-making power in personal and professional life. On the other hand, if it's used in the wrong way, it can sabotage sound judgement and good decision making. Before we get into the science of intuition, we need to take a step back and look at the 'rationality myth' as part of a bigger decision-making canvas on which intuition and analysis are often depicted as competing with each other when, in actual fact, they complement each other.

Takeaway

Intuition is: (1) a quick, automatic judgement based on unconscious processing of information and recognition of patterns; (2) a product of learning and experience that reveals itself as a 'gut feeling'; (3) the counterpart to rational analysis.

The myth of the rational approach

The rational approach to decision making is the go-to method in business schools and on management training courses. It might come as a surprise therefore to discover that some psychologists claim that the rational approach a 'myth' in the sense not that it's wrong or bad, but that it's not how people *actually* take decisions.[6]

Benjamin Franklin (1706–1790) was a US writer, historian, scientist and diplomat. He's recognised widely as one of the founding figures of the USA and its constitution. It's his image that adorns the US Treasury's $100 bill. He's celebrated for various aphorisms such as 'an ounce of prevention is worth a pound of cure' and also famous for 'Franklin's method': a well-known technique for taking decisions which, in his own words more or less, goes like this:

'Divide a sheet of paper by a line into two columns writing over one Pro and the other Con. Then over a period of three or four days list the pros and the cons for the decision in question and assess the importance of each of the pros and each of the cons. Then having pondered sufficiently, work out if the pros outweigh the cons, or vice versa, then come to a decision and act on it.'

Franklin's method is a prime example of the rational approach (sometimes called the 'classical approach') to decision making.

A version of the rational method is shown in Table 1 (it's technical name is 'multi-attribute utility analysis'). Maybe you've tried this when taking a big decision. In the example of choosing between two job offers, Alternative X and Alternative Y, the winner is Alternative Y, but only just. A table like this can be a very useful tool for taking a big decision with a rational hat on.

Table 1 Example of the rational approach

		Job offer X		Job offer Y	
Attribute	**Weighting (1–10)**	**Score (1–10)**	**Weighting × score**	**Score**	**Weighting × score**
Location	3	4	12	9	27
Prospects	6	7	42	8	48
Salary	8	8	64	7	56
Benefits	2	4	8	1	2
Colleagues	1	7	7	1	1
Total			**133**		**134**

As an approach it's simple, straightforward and systematic. In general, it goes like this:

- Step 1: List the options (for example electric versus petrol vehicle).
- Step 2: Figure out a set of attributes (for example running costs, range, environmental friendliness, etc.).
- Step 3: Weight each attribute (by giving each one a numerical value on, for example a 1–10 scale).
- Step 4: Score each alternative (for example electric versus petrol vehicle) on each attribute (for example running costs).
- Step 5: Do the arithmetic.
- Step 6: Pick the one with the highest score.

Table 1 shows how to set it out. It can be a reassuring grab rail in the face of risky and uncertain decisions because it's based on 'hard' data (more on that later). On the downside, it can take time, it's a big consumer of brain power and isn't as objective and bias-free as it seems at first sight; for example not only can the final 'score' be sometimes less than helpful (as in the closely tied example) but how many times have you done this and the result was 'wrong', meaning that it didn't fit with what you really wanted the outcome to be, in other words, what your gut was guiding you to do?

Notice also that there isn't a row in the table for how you feel about each alternative. Feelings, including gut feelings, are hard to pin down and quantify, so they tend to get factored out in the rational approach. But just because something can't be quantified doesn't mean to say it's not important.

When we try, with the best of intentions, to use this kind of cool, calculative approach, it can reveal something pretty basic about how we take big decisions, whether it's where to live, which job to take or who to partner with: gut feelings are hugely important and hard, if not impossible, to leave out of decisions, big and small. That's why there's often the temptation to tweak the scores in the table so that the figures and our feelings get 'fixed'. We can then go for what we *felt* all along was the right choice.

The bottom line is that the rational approach works well on simple decisions under controlled, stable conditions, like in psychology decision labs where much of the research evidence for it has been gathered. It works less well for decisions in the real world because:

- we can rarely, if ever, have full knowledge of all of the alternatives and, even if we did, our brains might struggle with the calculations; for example I might accept a job not knowing the full facts about my own, or my potential employer's, situation and prospects

- we don't know how the factors that we take into account today (including our own preferences) are likely to change over time; for example it's impossible for me to know whether my likes and preferences for the kind of work I want to be doing now will be the same this time next year or in five years' time

- if we're taking a decision with other people or one that affects them (which, let's face it, most decisions do), it's unlikely that everyone involved will agree on the weighting or scoring of the attributes; for example gaining a promotion might be a good reason for me to take up a job offer, but it might be less important to other members of my family who might be much more interested in other factors, for example proximity to family, friends and schools.*

Although the rational approach is often held up as best practice, it can have only limited traction in a world that's as messy, muddled, complicated and confused as ours is. The rational method's drawbacks have led some well-known decision scientists to claim that 'the whole [rational] thing is a myth';[7] again, not in the sense that it's bad but because it isn't the panacea that it's sometimes portrayed to be.

So, if the rational model isn't all it's been cracked up to be, then how *do* we take many of our most important decisions in our professional and personal lives?

The answer, of course, is 'intuition'.

Takeaway

The rational (sometimes called the 'classical') approach to decision making is a useful tool, but it isn't the panacea that it's sometimes portrayed to be.

Intuition as 'automated expertise'

Firefighting is a high-risk occupation. Firefighters have to take quick decisions in uncertain, fast-moving and time-pressured situations.

---

* Nobel laureate Herbert Simon, whose work we'll meet shortly, is one of the critics of the rational or classical approach. He described rationality as 'bounded', hence 'bounded rationality', the concept for which he's most famous. These three bullet points are the things that make rationality 'bounded' (or limited).

In firefighting, the rational approach is on the back foot from the word go because there isn't likely to be enough time to come up with multiple options and weigh up the pros and cons. The decision-making expert Gary Klein was both sceptical of the rational approach and fascinated by how experienced firefighters take the high-stakes, life-or-death decisions in the extreme circumstances they meet on a daily basis.

In his research, Klein came up with the reasonable proposition that in fighting a fire the recommended rational approach to take your time, identify multiple options, ponder the pros and cons for each, weigh them up and then go with the best one is impractical, to say the least. It could even be downright dangerous. Klein's alternative and, at the time (this was in the late 1980s), radical hypothesis was that experienced firefighters wouldn't compare multiple options; instead, they'd narrow it down to just two choices, compare them, then select the best one and act on it.

But Klein's two-option hypothesis was wrong. In fact, the experienced firefighters he interviewed – over 30 of them with many decades of experience between them – came up with only one option in over 80 per cent of incidents. This shocked and surprised Klein but led him to an unexpected and deep insight into how intuition works in the real world outside of decision labs.

Klein's surprising finding was that, most of the time, the firefighters he studied didn't consider two options; they came up with *one* only, and invariably went with it if they thought it'd work. If, after an instant's reflection, they figured that it wouldn't work, they'd come up with a next-best option and go with that if they thought it'd work, and so on. A comment from one of the firefighters, which astonished Klein who'd spent his whole career studying the psychology of decision making, was that 'we don't make decisions!'

Klein studied numerous life-or-death decisions and, in the vast majority of them, most of which were taken in less than a minute, the firefighters had no time to work out what might be going on. Instead, they had to sense intuitively and work out unconsciously what to do to save life and property.

These groundbreaking discoveries led Klein to develop the 'recognition-primed decision' (RPD) model of how intuition works in practice. In a typical situation, RPD goes like this.

1 Situation (such as a fire) generates *cues* (such as smoke, sound, etc.).

2 Cues cause an experienced decision maker (in this case a firefighter) to instinctively recognise *patterns*.

3 Patterns automatically activate *action scripts* (these are 'recipes' for action, for example 'douse the flames').

4 Action scripts are used spontaneously to affect the situation (if they're judged likely to work).

This is the conventional way in which intuition as an 'automated' response works.

'Action scripts' are those things that an experienced firefighter, or any other expert for that matter, could reasonably expect to work based on their experiences of similar situations. For example an action script for an experienced driver could be how to use the brakes and steering to avoid aquaplaning on a wet road; for a paramedic it could be how to administer CPR in a cardiac arrest. In each case, there's no conscious weighing up of pros and cons; instead, as in the firefighting example, the situation generates cues that help an experienced driver or paramedic to recognise a pattern, and this activates an action script that they then use to affect the situation, for example by avoiding a car crash or saving a life. This is the intuitive part of the recognition-primed decision-making process. It's called 'recognition-primed' because an experienced person's *recognition* of the key features of the situation (the cues) kicks off (*primes*) the *decision-making* process.

In some of the incidents that Klein studied, an extra step was used at the action script stage: firefighters would check quickly, by fast-forwarding events in their heads, to 'see' if the action script would work. This bit of the process is analytical because it's in their conscious awareness; they know what they're thinking and they're in control of it. If they judged that the script wouldn't work, they'd go to the next-best option and so on.

This is the analytical part of the recognition-primed decision-making process.

In fact, Klein found that in most situations the fast-forwarding (the technical name is 'mental simulation') isn't always necessary because in highly familiar situations it often can be dispensed with.

This is a good example of the intuition (which comes up with the action script) and analysis (which checks if it'll work) working together to provide an optimum solution by complementing each other.

For experienced decision makers in familiar situations, following the action script would likely solve the problem and result in 'job done'. This was how many of the firefighters Klein interviewed had dealt with hundreds of such fires in the past. This is a typical way in which intuitive decision making works: cues match patterns that activate action scripts that normally work to fix the problem. This is *automated expertise*.[8]

Automated expertise is one of the ways in which intuition works; it involves unconsciously accessing information that's been stored in the experienced decision makers' long-term memory (LTM) database and then replaying past learnings based on recognising a familiar pattern.[9] Automated expertise is like an autopilot system that's been trained over many years in how to handle familiar situations. It's worth pointing out that 'automated expertise' and what comes next ('holistic hunch') are a reinterpretation of Klein's work; they aren't terms that he used but were suggested by other researchers sometime later.

Intuition as 'holistic hunch'

One incident in particular that Klein studied illustrates another, and a somewhat different, way in which intuition works. In it, the firefighter led his team into the kitchen area at the back of a burning building where the source of the fire seemed to be located. Having found it, they drenched the flames with a high-velocity jet of water. But to the firefighter's surprise and consternation, the water didn't have any effect. He ordered the 'nozzleman' to back off and then hit it again, but to no avail.

His automated expertise didn't seem to be working. This threw him momentarily.

At the same time, the firefighter also noticed that this fire was 'odd' in that it was intensely hot and unusually quiet. He told Klein afterwards that he had no idea what was going on: 'It was different enough, it didn't react normally. If you cool something down, it becomes cool and this didn't. The quietness got me. There was something wrong.'[10] His experience of this fire was out of kilter with his expectations of how it ought to have reacted. It made him feel jittery and uneasy. He needed to act. All he had to go on was his gut reaction. He decided there and then to evacuate the building immediately.

Within seconds, the floor he and his team had been standing on collapsed. As it turned out, the fire was in the basement beneath them. They had no idea of this at the time, but this explained why the water had no effect and why the fire was so hot and so quiet.

All this happened in less than a minute.

In the heat of the moment, the lead firefighter didn't have the time or the conscious mental capacity to figure out exactly what might be going on. Nonetheless, his unconscious appraisal of the totality of the situation – what decision researchers sometimes refer to as 'situation awareness' – told him that he had to get everybody out.

When asked to explain why he did what he did, the firefighter was adamant that it was down to his 'sixth sense'. But it wasn't ESP: the explanation for what happened in the basement fire was much more intriguing and plausible. This firefighter's intuition was muscular not magical.

Without consciously thinking it through, the firefighter's experience gave him the ability to quickly, subconsciously and automatically parallel process an incompatibility between his expectations (that the water would dampen down the flames) and what actually happened (the fire was becoming hot and quiet). This mismatch gave him a powerful sense that something wasn't right, and that an immediate and drastic action was required. When Klein explained that it wasn't ESP, this unnerved the firefighter; he'd come to depend on what he thought of as his paranormal 'sixth sense' to get him out of many tricky situations over the years after it saved the day in this incident.[11]

On reflection, and only afterwards, under forensic questioning from Klein and his colleagues, was the firefighter able to make sense of what happened: the mismatch that gave him a bad vibe about the whole situation. The cues that set off his anomaly detection system came to light during the questioning process:

1 The situation generated three significant cues: a hot, quiet fire that didn't respond to the 'douse with water' action script.

2 The cues didn't fit an established pattern: fires are usually cooled by water, are not so hot and are noisier.

3 The mismatch between expectations and outcomes gave the firefighter a bad vibe about the situation: 'The quietness got me. There was something wrong'.

4 The bad feeling activated a different action script as a response to the anomaly: the recipe in this situation was to evacuate.

5 The action script affected the situation and led to a positive outcome: the firefighters' lives were saved.

This is the other way in which intuition works: when things are out of kilter, there's a 'mismatch', an anomaly is detected and, as a result, an experienced decision maker gets a 'bad vibe' about something or someone. The typical script in this situation is 'avoid'; it often helps to get us out of tricky situations. This is a *holistic hunch*.[12]

Not all situations are as time pressured as fighting a fire. When the pressure is off and a holistic hunch creates a bad vibe, the sensible thing to do is to dig deeper to find out what the source of the unease might be. It's something that would be familiar to the fictional detective and master of the intuitive inference, Sherlock Holmes, who said: 'Intuitions are not to be ignored. They represent data processed too fast for the conscious mind to comprehend.'[13] Travellers on trains in the UK will be familiar with the standard safety announcement that urges passengers to be on the lookout for bad vibes and go with their gut: 'If you see something that doesn't look right, alert British Transport police on 61016: *see it*, *say it*, *sorted*.' Passengers in their hundreds of thousands every day on trains in the UK are being urged to trust their gut.[14]

In holistic hunches there's no conscious weighing up of pros and cons; nonetheless, they often tell us when things don't stack up. This gives a strong signal that we should *avoid* an object (for example a house purchase or a suspicious package on a train), person (for example a potential business or life partner) or situation (for example a job offer). But holistic hunches also work the other way round: when things do stack up, for some at-the-time unknown reason, this can be a signal to *approach* an object, person or situation.

The originators of the term 'holistic hunch' (and of 'automated expertise'), management researchers Chet Miller and Duane Ireland, describe holistic hunches as being the product of information that's stored in long-term memory becoming combined subconsciously in complex ways resulting in a judgement or a choice that *feels* right.[15] Holistic hunches often involve novel approaches, creative actions or decisions that run counter to prevailing wisdom. Another intuition researcher, Roy Rowan, referred to these holistic hunches as the 'vapour' of past experiences: 'If the subconscious mix causing this vapour is right it can result in the glimmer of a new idea.' Tentative connections are made between things that, on the face of it, seem to be unrelated but are there, nonetheless, to be *sensed* by those who are prepared to do so. The process involves a faint detection at first followed by a stronger 'homing in'.[16] These signals can be faint at first, therefore it's easy for them to become blocked or jammed by incoming 'noise', hence the importance of getting in touch with your gut feelings (Step 2 of this book) and then tuning in and translating them (Step 5).

Spotlight on intuition
Intuition and the 'Spidey-sense'

The 'Spidey-sense' is one of the comic book superhero Spider Man's superpowers. It's his holistic hunch, originating as a tingling feeling at the back of his head. In the language of parapsychology (the study of all things psychic) the Spidey-sense is 'precognitive': it helps Spider Man to detect danger before it happens and take the necessary evasive action. He can also use it to dodge physical attacks, navigate, detect evil and find missing objects.

Of course, Spider Man's intuitive Spidey-sense is a product of Marvel Comics' author Stan Lee's and illustrator Steve Ditko's creative imagination and a work of pure science fiction. But this didn't stop the US Office of Naval Research (ONR) in 2017 investing almost $4 million in a project to investigate whether US naval personnel could deploy their 'sixth sense' premonitions for operational use in combat zones and fighting terrorism.

The project originated from reports from battlegrounds going back to the Vietnam War in the 1960s where certain soldiers seemed able to intuitively sense the presence of land mines and booby traps set by their enemy, the Viet Cong, without consciously analysing the situation or being able to explain how or why they 'knew'. Similar reports emerged about certain US Marines' abilities to detect, through an unexplained feeling of danger, the presence of improvised explosive devices (IEDs) in Afghanistan and Iraq.

The Navy wanted to understand whether these abilities were real or imagined. The ONR itself branded the phenomenon as a 'Spidey-sense for sailors and marines'. The headline in *Time* magazine ran 'The U.S. military believes people have a sixth sense'.[17] In spite of the headlines, the US Navy wasn't pursuing research into the paranormal. The scientists didn't believe that some psychically gifted sailors and marines literally have a sixth sense. It was based on the principle that seasoned combatants, through their hard-won experiences, develop gut instincts for where booby traps and IEDs might be. The Navy's aim was to understand the psychological processes behind intuitive pattern recognition and anomaly detection that might make the Spidey-sense something they could capture and use.

➤

If they could prove that the Spidey-sense was real and understand how it works, it might be possible to train marines how to use it to outwit their enemies in combat zones and in the fight against terrorism. The aim was to 'weaponise' intuition.

The phenomenon that the ONR aimed to get a better understanding of was the ability, acquired over many years of learning and experience, of some marines to detect and act on complex patterns of cues in volatile, ambiguous, uncertain and time-restricted contexts without consciously and intentionally analysing the situation. This unconscious ability to connect the dots and see patterns is the basis of experienced marines' intuition – their metaphorical 'Spidey-sense'.

Holistic hunches don't always create a bad vibe. When they give us the sense that things *do* stack up, they're telling us that it's okay, and may be to our advantage, to approach an object, person or situation; for example when an entrepreneur's 'intuitive alertness' spots a business opportunity that others have missed. This is how many successful business ventures and projects have started out. It was how Brian Chesky and Joe Gebbia used their 'entrepreneur instinct' to come up with the idea of building their own Airbnb website rather than relying on established platforms such as Craigslist.[18] The intuitive part of the process is sensing the opportunity; the analytical part of the process is making sense of and exploiting it. Holistic hunches help to explain how some alert entrepreneurs are able to creatively spot, make sense of and make money out of business opportunities that others can't see. Some exceptional people, including remarkable scientists such as Einstein, artists, musicians such as Mozart, inventors such as Thomas Edison and business people, seem to have been blessed with the gift of 'creative intuition' which helps them to think outside the box and see things that others miss.

Table 2 summarises the differences between automated expertise and holistic hunches.

Table 2 Automated expertise and holistic hunches

Automated expertise	Holistic hunch (negative)	Holistic hunch (positive)
Cues match patterns	Expectations violated	Connections sensed
Patterns activate action scripts (recipes) that normally work	Strong feelings that things don't stack up	Strong feelings that things do stack up
If necessary run mental simulation to check if script is likely to work	Bad vibe about object, person or situation	Good vibe about object, person or situation
Replaying past learnings based on feelings of familiarity	Signal to avoid object, person or situation; investigate problem	Signal to approach object, person or situation; investigate potential

To sum up: holistic hunches can be positive (when things do stack up) or negative (when things don't stack up). Positive holistic hunches give scientists, inventors and innovators a sense that a novel idea might work. Steve Jobs's decision to develop the iPod, which helped transform Apple from being just another computer maker to the world's most valuable company, was based on a series of holistic hunches that went beyond market research.[19] In the words of his biographer Walter Isaacson, Jobs was sometimes, for better or worse, his own 'one-person focus group' in which his intuition based on 'accumulated experiential wisdom' gave him an ability to read things that weren't yet on the page and have an uncanny sense for customers' 'desires that have not yet formed'.[20]

The Columbia Business School professor William Duggan calls this kind of holistic hunch 'strategic intuition': it's where a clear shining thought 'cuts through the fog of your mind'; it works best in new situations where novel, mould-breaking ideas are needed.[21] It gives entrepreneurs, as well as inventors, scientists and business strategists, a sense of direction. These intuitions are, as Oprah Winfrey described them, an 'inner GPS' which helps you to locate your 'true North'.

Big thinker
Gary Klein

Gary Klein is a cognitive psychologist who pioneered the study of naturalistic decision making (how people take decisions in the real world as opposed to decision labs) and developed the recognition-primed decision (RPD) model. Klein believes in muscular intuition – the kind that can be developed through the right kind of practice – rather than magical intuition – the kind that's claimed by clairvoyants and mystics. Here are three insights about intuition from Klein's 2003 book, *Intuition at Work*:

1 'We are all intuitive decision makers ... we would never get through the day if we had to analyse every decision. Intuition is an essential, powerful, and practical tool.'[22]

2 'Analysis has its function, and intuition isn't perfect, but trying to replace intuition with analysis is a huge mistake.'[23]

3 'I don't think you can make effective decisions without developing your intuition.'[24]

Klein's research has revealed the strengths, rather than the shortcomings, of intuition. His aim is to help people take better decisions by leveraging intuition as a source of decision-making power in their professional and personal lives.

> ## Takeaway
>
> Intuition works in two ways: through automated expertise and holistic hunch; both rely on a finely tuned situation awareness. Automated expertise comes with a 'plug-and-play' action script, whereas holistic hunch involves an inexplicable feeling of 'rightness' or 'wrongness', signalling approach or avoid.

The two minds model

Daniel Kahneman, who passed away in 2024 at the age of 90, was one of the world's most famous psychologists. His work shone much-needed light on the perils and the powers of going with your gut. Kahneman, who was awarded the Nobel Prize in 2002 for his research on how human beings take decisions in uncertain situations, was best known for two big ideas as far as intuition is concerned:

- Intuition leads to errors of judgement when it's used under the wrong circumstances.
- Even though we have one brain, we have, metaphorically speaking, two minds in one brain (the technical name for this psychological theory is 'dual-process' or 'dual-system' theory).

Kahneman brought these ideas to a wide audience in his bestselling book *Thinking, Fast and Slow* (2011). He sat firmly on the fence on whether intuition is good or bad, describing it as simultaneously 'flawed and marvellous'.[25]

The clue to Kahneman's model of the human mind is in the title of his bestseller. Inside our heads we have two minds: one, which I'll call the 'analytical mind', is the slow effortful thinker, it's a 'serial processor', its workings are conscious, it sees fine details and communicates what it thinks to us in words. Kahneman, and others, call it 'System 2'.

The other mind, co-existing alongside and complementing the analytical mind, is its fast-thinking counterpart, which I'll call the 'intuitive mind'. As well as being faster, the intuitive mind also requires minimal effort, it's a parallel processor, its workings are non-conscious, it sees the bigger picture and communicates what it thinks to us in feelings (Table 3). It's also called 'System 1'.

Table 3 The two minds model

System 1 (intuitive mind)	System 2 (analytical mind)
Quicker	Slower
Lower effort	Higher effort
Non-conscious	Conscious
Parallel processor	Serial processor
Sees bigger picture	Sees fine detail
Communicates via feelings	Communicates via words
Old mind	New mind

The intuitive mind is good at sensing patterns. In fact, it's so good at pattern recognition that it sometimes sees patterns where none exists. When this happens, it 'puts 1 and 1 together and makes 3', metaphorically speaking. As a result, its inferences can sometimes lead our thinking up the garden path to serious errors of judgement, including bias and prejudice (more on this in Step 6 on how to 'de-bias' our intuitions). For example, imagine you're at a job interview, and the candidate comes across as confident and charismatic. Your gut feeling might be that they're highly qualified and capable for the position simply because they present themselves so well. However, this intuitive inference could be false because confidence and charisma don't always correlate with competence. Making false inferences based on potentially misleading information is one reason why intuition can be both powerful and perilous.

Incidentally, the split between the intuitive mind (System 1) and the analytical mind (System 2) is nothing to do with the 'neuromyth' of intuition being in the right brain (it isn't). It does however fit with the idea that much of our thinking is conducted off-stage and offline by a system that is essentially unconscious. Also, this has nothing to do with the neuromyth that we only use 10 per cent of our brains (we don't).

Spotlight on intuition
Old and new minds

Another name that some psychologists give to System 1 (the intuitive mind) is 'old mind'; they also refer to System 2 (the analytical mind) as the 'new mind'. This is because the analytical mind (System 2) is thought to have evolved in human beings not that long ago. It's been described as a recently acquired 'download' estimated to have occurred somewhere in the region of 60,000 years ago.[26] Up until this time, Neanderthals are thought to have been the dominant hominid species in Europe and are believed to have been eradicated by us, *Homo sapiens*.

System 2 (the analytical mind) is uniquely human. However, some psychologists have speculated that as well as having a 'very long evolutionary history', System 1 may also 'operate in nonhuman as well as in human animals'.[27] Animals don't have intuitions as such, but they do have powerful instincts that help them to survive and thrive in their natural environment. This is one of the differences between instinct and intuition: intuition is learned, whereas instinct (unless it's being used as metaphor for intuition, as in 'gut instinct') is innate.

Over the course of evolution it appears that nature has equipped us with two minds (metaphorically speaking) that sometimes conflict, but that can be used to complement each other because the intuitive mind *senses* while the analytical mind *solves*. Of course the picture is more complex and nuanced than it's been presented here, but this 'duality' of intuition and analysis is at the heart of how we make sense of the world.

Whether we have 'two minds in one brain' is debated hotly by psychologists and neuroscientists. Kahneman has gone on record as saying that 'System 1 [intuition] and System 2 [analysis] ... are fictitious characters ... and there is no one part of the brain that either of the systems would call home.'[28] Nonetheless, the two minds model is a helpful metaphor (Kahneman called it a 'useful fiction') for two very different, but complementary, ways of thinking. The workings of the analytical mind are conscious and it's adept at *solving*, although machines can be much better at this than humans. That's one reason we've outsourced calculations to machines – a process that began with the abacus 3,000 years ago and has come right up to date with artificial intelligence. On the other hand, the workings of the intuitive mind are non-conscious, it's good at seeing patterns and is adept at *sensing*. We haven't yet managed to outsource human intuition to a machine (more on this in the final chapter).

The intuitive mind's sensing capabilities are behind the faith that Reed Hastings, founder and CEO of Netflix, puts in 'just knowing': he said that even though big decisions 'always start with the data ... the final call is always gut'. Arianna Huffington, founder of the new US website Huff Post, is on the same page as Hastings: 'We've all experienced it: a hunch, an inkling, our inner voice telling us to do something or not to do something. We hear the message, and it feels right, even if we can't explain why.' This is intuition.

At the end of the day, taking better decisions relies on using each tool for the things it's good at. Like any tool, each is designed with a particular job in mind and, as the old saying goes, 'if the only tool you have is a hammer, you tend to see every problem as a nail'. For example, in the quick-fire world of speed dating, rational analysis isn't likely to be feasible or socially acceptable: for example asking 'Would you mind if I compiled a list of your strengths and weaknesses and then did a quick calculation?' isn't likely to go down well. On the other hand, taking an intuitive approach when filing a tax return is definitely not recommended: for example a plea to the tax authorities that you used your intuition isn't likely to cut any ice.

Intuition isn't inferior to analysis even though it can sometimes lead to biases, but neither is analysis right 100 per cent of the time. As the former governor of the Bank of England Mervyn King and the Oxford economist John Kay point out, seeing it any other way would be as though 'God has given two legs ... but made one leg shorter than the other'.[29] The intuitive mind isn't the shorter of the two legs; they're both as long, and as potentially useful, as each other. The key point to come out of all of this is that nature has equipped us with two equally powerful and complementary pieces of kit in our mental tool-box. The challenge, and the art, of good decision making is knowing if, when and how to use each of them for what they're good at.

> ## Takeaway
>
> We have two minds in one brain, the intuitive mind (System 1) is a fast, low-effort, parallel-processing system, its workings are non-conscious, it sees the bigger picture, is good at sensing, it communicates what it thinks to us in feelings and it complements the analytical mind (System 2).

Dig deeper

Gary Klein's *Intuition at Work* (2003, published as *The Power of Intuition at Work* in the USA) offers a muscular rather than magical view of intuition, 'demystifies' the role that intuition plays in the workplace and gives readers 'permission to trust [their] instincts'.

In a nutshell, what is intuition?

Intuition is a quick, automatic judgement based on unconscious processing of information and recognition of patterns, it's a product of learning and experience and operates in two ways: automated expertise and holistic hunch.

Workout 1: Apply the rational approach and understand its limitations

1 Choose a consequential decision that you're currently faced with, for example a house or car purchase, which course to study at which university, whether to apply for or take a job, etc.

2 Write down the alternatives that you need to choose between (for example to choose between a petrol-powered car (Alternative A) or an electric-powered car (Alternative B). In this example, it's a choice between one of two alternatives; if there are more than two alternatives, simply add more columns to the table.

3 Write down a list of things (attributes) that are important for you in taking this decision, for example how much each alternative would cost to buy, its running costs, practicality, environmental friendliness, etc. Add more rows to the table, if necessary.

4 Give a weighting for how important each attribute is to you from one (low) to ten (high).

Table 4 Blank table for choosing between Alternatives A and B using the rational method with N attributes

		Decision			
		Alternative A		Alternative B	
Attribute	Weighting (1–10)	Score (1–10)	Weighting × score	Score	Weighting × score
Attribute 1					
Attribute 2					
Attribute 3					
Attribute 4					
Attribute N					
Total					

5 Then score each of the alternatives on each attribute on a scale of one (low) to ten (high).

6 Multiply the attribute scores by the weighting for each attribute.

7 Add up the totals of weighting times score and choose the one with the highest number of points.

8 Which one comes out on top? How do you feel about this outcome? Does the result echo what you *feel* is the right thing to do?

9 If the numbers and your gut feelings are out of kilter, what will you do?

10 How useful has the rational approach been in helping you with your consequential decision? When do you think the rational approach is likely to be most useful to you when taking decisions?

Workout 2: Know the difference between automated expertise and holistic hunch

Check your understanding of automated expertise versus holistic hunch by considering the following questions:

1 What sophisticated actions do you carry out without having to think them through every time? Can you think of any examples of this in your personal or professional life?

For me, it's delivering a lecture, something that I've done for the best part of 30 years. I've done it so often that my hard-won expertise in lecturing has become automated; I can multitask, don't have to think about what I'm going to say next, and I can deal with most issues as they come up, and rarely get wrong footed. The fact that I'm experienced enough to be on autopilot much of the time gives me the headspace to read the road ahead and deal with any challenges if and when they arise.

2 What about situations where things didn't stack up, you know something's not right and you then have to work out why and

what to do? Can you think of any examples of this in your professional or personal life?

This has happened to me on appointment panels – and contrary to HR best practice – where my judgement has been swayed negatively by a gut feeling about a job candidate based on something they did or didn't say, how they said it, etc. On a more positive note, my holistic hunches have worked well in situations such as buying a house: the places where I've enjoyed living most have been the ones where I just knew they were right the minute I walked through the door.

This begs the question of 'If intuition is related to experience, then how can buying a house, for example, be intuitive because we don't have very many experiences of buying houses?' It's true that we don't have very many experiences of buying houses (or apartments), but what we do have is a lot of experience of living in a house (or apartment), which means that we know intuitively what works for us.

Notes

1 Isaacson, W. (2012) 'The real leadership lessons of Steve Jobs', *Harvard Business Review* (April). Available online at: https://hbr.org/2012/04/the-real-leadership-lessons-of-steve-jobs.

2 Castrillon, C. (2019) '3 ways entrepreneurs can tap into intuition to get that extra edge', *Forbes*, 29 May 2019. Available online at: https://www.forbes.com/sites/carolinecastrillon/2019/05/29/3-ways-entrepreneurs-can-tap-into-their-intuition-to-get-that-extra-edge/.

3 Winfrey, O. (no date) 'What Oprah knows for sure about trusting her intuition', *Oprah.com*. Available online at: https://www.oprah.com/spirit/oprah-on-trusting-her-intuition-oprahs-advice-on-trusting-your-gut (accessed May 2024).

4 Kansikas, F. (2023) 'Intuitions & premonitions: Messages of the soul', *Medium*. Available online at: https://medium.com/@kansikas.f/

intuitions-premonitions-messages-of-the-soul-fdbaeaa20abc; Burnham, S. (no date) 'A curious telepathy', *Guideposts*. Available online at: https://guideposts.org/angels-and-miracles/angels/a-curious-telepathy/ (accessed May 2024); Sadler-Smith, E. (2011) 'The intuitive style: Relationships with local/global and verbal/visual styles, gender, and superstitious reasoning', *Learning and Individual Differences*, 21(3), 263–70.

5 Browne, S. J. (2021) '4 ways trusting your intuition is a superpower', *Forbes*, 2 October 2021. Available online at: https://www.forbes.com/sites/womensmedia/2021/10/02/4-ways-trusting-your-intuition-is-a-superpower/.

6 Klein, G. A. (2003). *Intuition at Work*. New York: Currency Doubleday, p. 10.

7 Klein (2003).

8 Miller, C. C. and Ireland, R. D. (2005) 'Intuition in strategic decision making: Friend or foe in the fast-paced 21st century?', *Academy of Management Perspectives*, 19(1), 19–30.

9 Miller and Ireland (2005) p. 22.

10 Klein, G. A., Calderwood, R. and Clinton-Cirocco, A. (1988) *Technical Report 796; Rapid Decision-Making on the Fire Ground*. US Army Research Institute for the Behavioural Sciences, p. B-8.

11 Klein, G. A. (2017) *Sources of Power*. Cambridge, MA: MIT Press, p. 33.

12 Miller and Ireland (2005).

13 Gatiss, M. (2016) *Sherlock Series 4: Episode 1 – The Six Thatchers*. Hartswood Films. Available online at: https://www.bbc.co.uk/writersroom/documents/sherlock-s4-ep1-the-six-thatchers.pdf.

14 South Western Railway (no date) Our trains. Available online at: https://www.southwesternrailway.com/travelling-with-us/our-trains (accessed May 2024).

15 Miller and Ireland (2005).

16 Rowan, R. (1987) *The Intuitive Manager*. Aldershot: Wildwood House, p. 37.

17 Jacobsen, A. (2014) 'The U.S. military believes people have a sixth sense', *Time*, 3 April 2017. Available online at: https://time.com/4721715/phenomena-annie-jacobsen/.

18 Brown, M. (no date) 'Airbnb: The growth story you didn't know', *GrowthHackers*. Available online at: https://growthhackers.com/growth-studies/airbnb/ (accessed May 2024).

19 Isaacson (2011) *Steve Jobs*. New York: Simon & Schuster, p. 384.

20 Isaacson (2011) p. 97.

21 Duggan, W. (2013) *Strategic Intuition*. New York. Columbia Business School Press, p. 2.

22 Klein (2003) p. xvi.

23 Klein (2003) p. xx.

24 Klein (2003) p. 3.

25 Popova, M. (no date) 'How our minds mislead us', *The Marginalian*. Available online at: https://www.themarginalian.org/2013/10/30/daniel-kahneman-intuition/ (accessed May 2024).

26 Sadler-Smith, E. (2023) *Intuition in Business*. Oxford: Oxford University Press, p. 111.

27 Epstein, S. (1994) 'Integration of the cognitive and the psychodynamic unconscious', *American Psychologist*, 49(8), 709–24, p. 715.

28 Kahneman, D. (2011) *Thinking, Fast and Slow*. London: Allen Lane, p. 29.

29 Kay, J. and King, M. (2020) *Radical Uncertainty*. London: Bridge Street Press, p. 154.

part 2

—

Seven steps to intuitive intelligence

step 1

Build intuitive muscle power

'Champions keep playing until they get it right.'

Billie Jean King (former world no. 1 tennis player and winner of 39 Grand Slam titles)[1]

- -

This chapter will help you to understand how to develop your intuitive 'muscle power' through both quantity and quality of practice.

- -

How intuition imitates chess

Garry Kasparov is one of the greatest chess players of all time. He became the youngest ever world champion aged 22 and held the title from 1985 to 2000. He was ranked number 1 in the world for over 20 years (255 months, in fact). He was beaten by IBM's chess-playing computer, Deep Blue, under tournament conditions in 1997.

In his book, *How Life Imitates Chess* (2007), Kasparov estimated that the number of conceivable moves in a game of chess is 1 with 120 zeros after it.[2] That's more than the number of seconds that have passed since the beginning of the universe; about as many zeros as the number of letters in the previous sentence. Chess is a game of almost infinite possibilities played out on an 8 × 8 board with 32 pieces to a strict set of rules. How can a human being navigate successfully through the ocean of options that this creates? Kasparov's answer is simple: gut feelings.

It's tempting for outsiders to think of the game of chess as being the epitome of rational analysis with no room for intuition. But, according to many grandmasters, and contrary to common sense, at the highest level, chess is highly intuitive.

How can this be so?

To find out why, we need to wind the clock back over half a century. The idea of chess as an intuitive game was centre stage in the work of the Dutch psychologist and chess grandmaster Adriaan de Groot (1914–2006). De Groot captured his insider's view on how to play tournament-level chess in a famous book called *Thought and Choice in Chess* (1965).[3]

De Groot studied chess not only by reflecting on his own experience, but also by asking other chess grandmasters to think aloud when they were making particular moves. He wanted to understand what was going on inside their heads and, in particular, how they decided on the best next move.

He discovered that chess grandmasters got a 'feeling for a position' by scanning the board and intuitively sensing the situation for possibilities.[4] Switching mental gears to analyse what their intuition was telling them was useful only in that it usually confirmed their gut feel for the best next move rather than changed it. As with Klein's firefighters from Part 1, the first move that came to mind was invariably the best.

The Norwegian chess grandmaster, five-time world champion, number 1 in the world since 2011, and the highest rated chess player of all time, Magnus Carlsen, described chess as being 'mainly about intuition and instincts'.[5] In a TV interview in 2021 following a rare defeat, Carlsen remarked dolefully that 'I do feel that I missed quite a lot of chances, and the frustrating part is that at several points I did not trust my intuition.'[6]

Carlsen doesn't try to reason through the possible moves and often can't explain why he feels a move will or won't work. Instead, he trusts the gut feeling that he's developed for the best next move through thousands of hours of practice. Consequently, Carlsen has built up a vast memory bank of how certain moves make him *feel* based both on the mistakes he's made and the successes he's had. This is how he's built up his intuitive muscle power for chess.

Spotlight on intuition
The muscular view of intuition

To the best of my knowledge, it was Gary Klein, author of *Intuition at Work* (2003), who first coined the term 'muscular' when talking about intuition. At the heart of this view is the idea that intuition is a developable skill and the more you exercise, or more 'reps', you do, the stronger your intuitive muscle gets. The bottom line is that for intuition in work and professional life, as in the gym, 'results come through reps', hence the idea of 'intuitive muscle power'. As in the gym, the best results come from doing your 'reps' using proper techniques and as part of a systematic training programme. That said, we're not always aware that we're doing the necessary reps because learning isn't always conscious or explicit (more on this below). You can think of Klein's book, and the one you're reading now, as a 'fitness programme' for intuition.

Going back to chess, here's how gut feelings figure in this process.

'Associative learning' is one of the main ways in which the intuitive mind registers connections between experiences (for example particular chess moves) and outcomes (for example winning or losing). Perhaps the most famous example of associative learning is Pavlov's dogs where the Nobel Prize-winning Russian physiologist Ivan Pavlov (1849–1936) trained dogs to salivate at the sound of a bell. He did this by associating the bell with the appearance of food and then withdrawing the food so that the dogs salivated automatically when the bell rang even when no food was on offer.

The intuitive mind is an 'associative learning system'.[7] It automatically and unconsciously associates cues with outcomes, as in the case of a firefighter linking the sound, colour and smell of a particular type of blaze with an action script that's proven to be effective in the past for extinguishing fires of that particular type.

The intuitive mind also associates feelings (positive or negative) with outcomes (good or bad). The link is strong and non-conscious. Here's an analogy: have you ever had an instinctive aversion to a food which, through a random incident of contamination, made you sick. People who have this experience often struggle to dissociate the food from the bad feeling. I can't help associating chicken with norovirus, even though I've only ever had one unpleasant experience; nonetheless, it always causes me to pause, and usually take evasive action, when chicken is on the menu.

Associative learning is not only simple, it's also quick in that the linkages don't take long to form, especially when the outcome is bad, and it's 'sticky' in that associations, especially negative ones, are hard to dislodge once they've been formed. This makes good sense from an evolutionary point of view. Where passing on our genetic material is concerned it's always better to be safe than sorry. Therefore, having a system that is good at automatically identifying things that might be bad for us, and could even kill us, is likely to have been advantageous in the survival stakes in our species' dim and distant past.

Associative learning is also at work when blunders on the chess board get 'tagged' with negative feelings, while good moves get tagged with positive feelings. Over time, these positive and negative vibes become associated unconsciously with accurate intuitions about which moves are likely to work and which ones aren't.[8] The same is true of significant experiences in work and personal life. Intuition in chess, as in other walks of life, is a storehouse not only of accumulated successes and failures, but also the feelings that go with them.[9]

Carlsen, in common with other grandmasters, 'just knows' which moves will and won't work without necessarily knowing how or why he knows. In this respect, life does indeed imitate chess. Significant experiences, whether they're in a burning building or the board-room, get tagged with positive or negative feelings. Next time we meet a similar situation, one of the first things that pops into our head is a gut feeling for the situation. This is then taken as a signal to 'approach' or 'avoid' someone or something.

In life, as in chess, intuition can be quicker and more accurate than analysis when it's based on many years' experience of 'playing the game'.[10] Chess players' intuitive muscle power gets built up over many years of successes and failures. Likewise, in personal and pro-fessional life, the same principle applies.

Garry Kasparov extrapolates directly from chess to life: he says that 'intuition is the bedrock of our decision making especially in the quick-fire decisions that make up our daily lives'.[11] This is why, in his view, it always makes sense to tune in and ask the intuitive mind what it 'thinks'.

Takeaway

Through the process of associative learning, bad experiences get tagged with negative gut feelings that signal 'avoid', while good experiences get tagged with positive gut feelings that signal 'approach'.

Analysis frozen into habit

Intrigued by de Groot's original research of the 1950s, the Nobel Prize-winning decision researcher Herbert Simon conducted a famous experiment in the 1970s to dig down into why chess experts are able to go with their gut in deciding on the best next move.[12]

Like many of the best scientific experiments, Simon's research was simplicity itself.

First, present a chess grandmaster (an expert) and a chess novice with 25 chess pieces arranged on the board as they're likely to be in an actual game (Simon called this the 'meaningful pattern' condition). After five seconds, remove the board and ask the expert and the novice to reproduce it from memory.

How many pieces do you think the experts were able to recall correctly? What about the novices? The answer is in the footnote.*

Next, follow exactly the same procedure but this time arrange the pieces randomly (this is called the 'non-meaningful pattern' condition). As before, remove the board and ask the experts and novices to reproduce it from memory.

What do you think the result will be? The answer is in the footnote.†

This surprising result told Simon that the ability of the experts to remember virtually all of the positions in the meaningful pattern condition wasn't because of some remarkable photographic visual memory that the experts might have had (otherwise they'd have performed just as well in the second condition). Instead, it was a result of their accumulated knowledge of what typical arrangements of pieces on a chess board look like acquired through the long, hard slog of decades of learning and experience.

In fact, the experts weren't recalling the location of individual pieces. They couldn't because psychologists have known for a long time that working memory – the temporary workspace for the things that we're currently thinking about – can only hold about seven

---

* In the meaningful pattern condition, the expert usually gets at least 24 of the 25 pieces in the correct position. The novice can replace only about 6 out of 25 pieces.
† In the non-meaningful pattern condition, the novice is still only able to get 6 out of 25 pieces in the right place. But so is the expert.

items at any one time.[13] Remembering the position of 25 pieces is impossible because it would massively overload working memory's physical capacity. Instead, the experts were recalling half a dozen or so familiar patterns, their relationships to each other and their potential significance in a game. Simon concluded that that as a result of experience we come to see the world in terms of patterns and that this is the basis of expertise.

The experts were flummoxed by the non-meaningful pattern because there was no intelligible arrangement that could be recognised, recalled and reconstructed. For them, there was nothing to make sense of. One of the experts in the experiment told Simon that the non-meaningful patterns troubled him because they looked 'unreasonable' and that he couldn't get the 'sense' of their positions.[14] By being out of kilter they didn't make sense and made him feel uneasy.

The non-meaningful arrangement of pieces was simply 'noisy'. This 'not making sense' is true of random situations in general: they just don't make sense, either intuitively or analytically.

Spotlight on intuition
Noise and unbridled intuitions

Daniel Kahneman, along with his co-authors of *Noise: A Flaw in Human Judgement* (2021) Olivier Sibony and Cass Sunstein, illustrated the concept of 'noise' with the analogy of rifle shooting. When the shots are clustered systematically, for example in the bottom left of the target, they are *biased* (towards the bottom left). There might be a good reason for this, for example the sight on the rifle being miscalibrated. On the other hand, when the shots are scattered all over the target with no obvious pattern, they are *noisy*.[15]

As far as decision making in the real world is concerned, Kahneman and his colleagues give the example of personnel hiring decisions: these are noisy when interviewers give wildly different assessments of the same candidate. Likewise, medical decisions are noisy when doctors come to different diagnoses of the same patient. Asylum decisions in the USA are noisy: some judges grant asylum to as many as 85 per cent of applicants, while for others the figure is only 5 per cent.[16]

Intuitive decisions can be noisy when you're in unfamiliar territory or when intuition is being used for the wrong thing. This is why it's important to try and take steps to de-bias our intuitions. Techniques for doing so are discussed in Step 6.

Noisy situations where intuitions aren't challenged and as a result become 'unbridled' can be a breeding ground for overconfidence and hubris. There are plenty of examples of hubristic leaders in business and politics whose feelings of rightness in noisy situations overwhelmed any better judgement they might have had, and whose unbridled intuitions led to negative consequences and nasty surprises.

Returning to the much less noisy world of expertise in chess: in the non-meaningful condition, the experts, like the novices, were limited to recalling seven items plus or minus two. This is the limit to working memory mentioned above. Seven-plus-or-minus-two is important. It's the fundamental rule discovered in the 1950s by psychologist George Miller that the human brain has a working memory capacity of between five and nine items. This puts an absolute limit on our ability to process information consciously. But our brain has found a way round Miller's rule.

In the meaningful pattern condition, the experts weren't recalling seven *individual pieces* plus or minus two, they were recalling seven *patterns* plus or minus two. Simon called this 'chunking'; it's one of the ways in which intuition works. It sees patterns in the bigger picture. The experts could recall the patterns that they'd built up over the years through learning. The novices, on the other hand, didn't have any patterns to recall.

Because the meaningful condition in Simon's experiment contained patterns, it wasn't noisy; instead, it had an internal structure and logic that made sense to expert players but not to novices.

When someone has played enough chess, once a pattern is recognised it brings to mind the associated feelings (positive or negative) and the best next move for that pattern of pieces. This is their intuitive muscle power in action. Intuitive experts see things that others don't.

Simon estimated that chess masters have a repertoire of between 50,000 and 100,000 patterns stored in long-term memory acquired over a decade or more of serious play. Memory for patterns of pieces is the secret source of chess experts' intuition. It's this that tells them to approach or avoid certain moves.

But what's all this got to do with decision making in the real world?

Likewise in life, a negative gut feeling can be interpreted as a signal to avoid a particular object, person or situation while a positive gut feeling can be interpreted as a signal to approach. However, in life, as in chess, gut feelings aren't infallible; they're a judgement and don't come with any guarantee of success.

This 'pattern matching principle' was why Herbert Simon called intuitions 'analyses frozen into habit and the capacity for rapid response through recognition'.[17] In other words, what was once accomplished by slow, conscious, analytical thinking can, after enough successes and failures, be arrived at by fast, unconscious, intuitive thinking. Under the right conditions and given enough time, knowledge gets shunted from the analytical mind to the intuitive mind. This is how we build intuitive muscle power.

The other side of this of course is that we should avoid using intuitions in unfamiliar areas where we don't have enough knowledge or experience to justify trusting our gut feelings. Unfortunately, this means that while the ability to acquire intuitions is innate (in that we're 'soft wired' for intuitions), intuitions themselves aren't a transferable skill. For example intuition in chess or firefighting doesn't cross over into intuition in management.

Over the years, this idea of intuition as 'analysis frozen into habit' has been found in lots of different areas of high-level performance – from management to musicianship, surgery to sports, etc. Intuition is like a muscle; it can be developed through the right kind of exercise and, when developed sufficiently, like a muscle, it can be a source of decision-making power.

Big thinker
Herbert Simon

Herbert Simon (1916–2001) was Professor of Computer Science and Psychology at Carnegie Mellon University in Pittsburgh for 52 years. He was awarded the Nobel Prize in economic sciences in 1978 for 'his pioneering research into the decision-making processes within economic organisations'.[18]

Simon is famous for his concept of 'bounded rationality'. This is the idea that in the real world (in other words outside of psychology decision labs) people have to make judgements on limited amounts of information without knowledge of what the consequences of their decisions will be. Simon also realised that our ability to be rational when we take decisions is limited by our brain's computing power and the information that is available in the situations that we find ourselves in. Here are three insights from Simon about intuition from a milestone article he published in 1987:

- 'The intuitive skills of managers depend on the same kinds of mechanisms as the intuitive skills of chess masters. It would be surprising if it were otherwise.'

- 'Experts often arrive at problem diagnoses and solutions rapidly and intuitively without being able to report how they attained the result ... this ability is best explained by postulating a recognition and retrieval process that employs a large number of chunks or patterns stored in long-term memory.'

- 'Every manager needs to be able to analyze problems systematically [and] every manager needs also to be able to respond to situations rapidly, a skill that requires the cultivation of intuition and judgment over many years of experience and training.'[19]

Simon's most famous book is *Administrative Behaviour* (first published in 1947 and still in print). The foreword to its first edition was written by Chester Barnard (1886–1961), a business executive (he was president of the New Jersey Bell Telephone Company) who was also a scholar of decision making and an advocate for intuition.

In his own book, *The Functions of the Executive* (first published in 1938 and still in print), Barnard distinguished between what he called 'logical mental processes' and 'non-logical mental processes', which he described as a 'complex and rapid mental process not capable of being expressed in words or analysed by the person within whose brain it takes place'. This is intuition. He also wrote that 'both kinds [of thinking] together are better than either alone'.[20]

This automated, unconscious knowledge that so fascinated the chess grandmaster and psychologist de Groot, the business executive Barnard and the decision researcher Simon is called 'tacit knowledge' (from the Latin *tacere*, meaning 'silent'). Tacit knowledge is the stuff that we know but we find hard, and sometimes impossible, to put into words. More on this anon.

One of the big ideas to have emerged from research into how experts take decisions is that, contrary to what people used to think, complex, high-level mental work isn't something that's the sole remit of the analytical mind. The intuitive mind can do this kind of mental work as well. For example chess is very high-level mental work, but chess grandmasters often are unaware of how or why their intuitive mind generates the best next move. But what they have come to appreciate is that, based on their knowledge and experience, the first option that comes intuitively to mind has a good chance of being the best.

Takeaway

Our brain optimises the use of scarce mental resources by performing a wide range of tasks intuitively based on pattern recognition. The ability to do so is an outcome of associative learning and experience. This is how intuitive muscle power is built up.

Intuition and unconscious competence

We discovered in Part 1 that intuition is based on fast, unconscious processing of information. We've also discovered in this chapter that intuition is a skill that's developable under the right conditions through learning and experience.

The ideas of consciousness, unconsciousness, competence and incompetence (where competence is 'the knowledge and skills appropriate for a specific task') come together in the four-stage 'Ladder of Competence' developed by Noel Burch at Gordon Training International way back in the 1970s.[21] Here's how Burch described the steps on his ladder from lowest to highest (Figure 2).

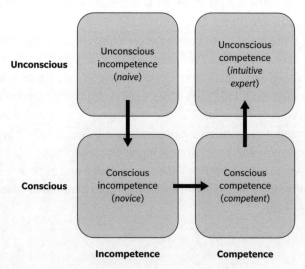

Figure 2 Journey from naivety to intuitive expertise

Unconsciously incompetent: people who are unconsciously incompetent are inept and unaware of their ineptness; for example the clueless boss who's utterly unempathetic and totally unaware of precisely how unempathetic they are. This is the naive stage; although it can be tempting to do so, here is definitely not the place to go with your gut.

Consciously incompetent: people who are consciously incompetent are still inept but their saving grace is at least they know they're inept; for example the unempathetic boss at least realising how clueless they've been and how unempathetic they are even if they can't yet do anything about it. This is the novice or beginner stage. Novices at least have some idea of what they need to do to become competent.

Consciously competent: people who are consciously competent are skilled in that they're no longer inept, but to perform competently they need to think about what they're trying to achieve and work hard at it. Practising a complex skill such as 'being empathetic' can take up a lot of emotional energy and brain power. It can make multitasking a challenge, it's easy to be wrong-footed and, when things don't go to plan, they have to be consciously thought-through. For example the previously unempathetic boss moves forward by deliberately, consciously and successfully practising empathy, but the ability to do so only comes through hard mental and emotional labour. Competence is the halfway house between novice and expert.

Unconsciously competent: people who are unconsciously competent are skilled and no longer need to think about the skill they're using – it's habituated to the extent that it's second nature to them. For someone who's unconsciously competent, the complex interpersonal skill of empathetic communication has been delegated to their intuitive mind which then frees up the analytical mind's scarce resources for other more complex tasks as and when they come along. For example the experienced empathetic boss is able to be intuitively empathetic with employees. This is the expert stage, and it's where you can justifiably go with your gut.[22] In the unconscious competence stage, we often don't consciously know how we're able to do what we do, we just do it.

When we reach the zone of 'personal mastery', our actions become automatic, peak and intuitive. On rare occasions, we may even get into a 'flow' state.[23] Flow, as described by the renowned Hungarian psychologist Mihaly Csikszentmihalyi (pronounced 'Me-hi Cheek-zent-me-hi'), is a state of effortlessness and ease where our attention is fully absorbed, where high levels of skill meet high levels of challenge, and everything 'just clicks': we're 'in the zone', 'on the ball', 'peaking' and 'in the groove', like the expert Formula 1 racing car driver who becomes 'at one' with their vehicle, or the expert pilot who feels like *they*, not the plane, are flying.[24] Intuition contributes to flow and, according to Csikszentmihalyi, cultivating flow can help to make many types of work intrinsically rewarding.

Takeaway

The incompetence zones (naive and novice) are hazardous places for going with your gut; on the other hand, the unconscious competence zone (the expert level) is the safest and most satisfying space for doing so.

Practice, practice, practice

A tourist in New York, who got lost on their way to a concert being held at Carnegie Hall, asked a passer-by who happened to be carrying a violin case: 'Excuse me ma'am, can you tell me how to get to Carnegie Hall?' The musician smiled and replied: 'Practice, practice, practice.' The same is true for building intuitive muscle power, but with one important caveat: as far as intuition is concerned, *quality* of practice is as important as *quantity* of practice.

In the 1980s, the educational psychologist Benjamin S. Bloom conducted a famous study of how exceptionally talented individuals – such as musicians – acquire the skills that make them stand out from the crowd. The subjects of Bloom's study included concert pianists, sculptors, scientists, medics and sportspeople. Bloom wasn't claiming that almost anyone could become a concert pianist, but what he was claiming was that we all have enormous, and often untapped, potential that can be released through the right amount and right kind of practice under the right kind of guidance.

It's one reason why, under the right conditions, 'ordinary' people can become intuitive experts in their professional and personal lives. The reverse is also true: without a long and intensive process of learning and feedback it's impossible to attain the levels of skill necessary to become an intuitive expert.[25] This idea echoes Klein's muscular view of intuition.

The bottom line is that intuition is developable, and the thing that correlates with success across many fields, barring some sports where physical prowess is essential, is the quantity *and* quality of practice. This idea that the journey from the swampy lowlands of novice performance to the lofty heights of expertise requires 'struggle, sacrifice, and honest, often painful self-assessment' and is not 'for the faint of heart or impatient'[26] is captured succinctly in the well-known, but sometimes overinterpreted, 10,000-hour rule. It supports the saying that 'experts are made not born'.

Spotlight on intuition
The 10,000-hour rule

The 10,000-hour rule was made famous by the Swedish psychologist K. Anders Ericsson (1947–2020). It can be stated simply as: expertise is achieved through deliberate and stretching practice for around 10,000 hours, which equates to roughly ten years.

➤

Ericsson based his conclusion on groundbreaking research he carried out at one of Germany's top music schools. He found that the violinists who would go on to reach the pinnacle of their profession had accumulated over 10,000 hours of deliberate and stretching practice. He also found that there are few, if any, shortcuts to attaining these heights.

The 10,000-hour rule definitely isn't the same as saying 'anyone can do anything'. This was one of the big criticisms of this research when it was popularised by the journalist Malcolm Gladwell in his best-selling book *Outliers* (2008).[27] The bottom line is that the figure of 10,000 hours isn't a precise number or absolute law, it's simply an approximation that varies across different fields, people and situations.

Bill Gates, in an interview with his father William H. Gates Sr in 2010, made the point that it's not as simple as 'if you spend 10,000 hours doing something you'll be super good at it ... you have to be lucky enough *and* fanatical enough to keep going.'[28]

Asking 'How many hours will it take to become intuitive?' is like asking 'How long is a piece of string?' It all depends on:

- Who you are, what strengths and talents you have and what motivates you. As the author of *The Strengths Book* (2017), Sally Bibb reminds us that knowing what these are will 'change your life because if you keep trying to be someone you're not you'll always be frustrated'.[29]

- What it is you're trying to learn because some things are intrinsically more difficult than others, for example pizza making is, I can assure you, easier than piano playing.

- The situation in which you're learning it and the feedback you get along the way, for example having sufficient time creates the space and having a coach speeds things up.

There are no hard-and-fast rules for how long it takes to build intuitive muscle power; more practice isn't necessarily better and, anyway, personal mastery is a journey, not a destination. In a world where the only constant is change, the person who thinks they've arrived and doesn't have anything else to learn is likely to come unstuck. Thomas J. Watson, chairman and CEO of IBM from 1914 to 1956, thought of success as a journey, not a destination: 'We have not made a success, but I do feel IBM is *succeeding*. We want you [IBM employees] to feel that you are aiming for success but are never going to catch up with it, for if you do, you are finished.' If we agree with IBM's Watson, then success isn't a state of *being*, it's a state of *becoming*.

Notwithstanding the saying 'practice, practice, practice', the bottom line is that *quality* of practice is as important as *quantity* of practice in building intuitive intelligence. Quality practice not only takes you outside your comfort zone, it also requires feedback so that you can see *when* and *how* you're getting it right and getting it wrong; coaching so that you can understand *why* you get some gut calls right and others wrong.

Personal trainers provide feedback and coaching to help gym members build bodily muscle power. In professional life, the feedback and coaching needed to build intuitive muscle power can come from workmates, managers and mentors; in personal life, it comes from friends and family, as well as from professionals such as counsellors.

Quality practice is also *deliberate*; in other words, like working out in the gym, it means purposely using the right piece of kit and pushing yourself outside of your comfort zone rather than just doing the same thing over and over again. We'll discover more about how to do this throughout this book.

The inevitable conclusion is that there are few, if any, shortcuts to success. It's likely to take a substantial number of years of hard slog with the right kind of support to become an intuitive expert. As the tennis ace Billie Jean King said: 'Champions keep playing until they get it right.' The path can be smoothed, and even accelerated, with the right type of practice, feedback and support.

Knowledge and experience are the foundations not only for intuition but also for wisdom. In Aristotle's philosophy, 'practical wisdom' gets formed out of knowledge and intuition. It's the highest intellectual virtue and gives us a 'profound understanding' of situations. Aristotle's idea of practical wisdom also applies to management: a good manager has a knowledge of the rules of management but also knows that they don't give definitive guidance in all situations. Intuitive managers rely on a 'feeling' for each situation that takes them beyond the rules that they've learned.[30]

Takeaway

Expertise is achieved over a protracted period of learning that involves high-quality, deliberate and stretching practice. Moreover, becoming an intuitive expert is a journey, not a destination.

Dig deeper

K. Anders Ericsson (1947–2020) was a Swedish psychologist and professor at Florida State University. He was the internationally recognised expert on expertise. He also worked with this chapter's Big thinker, Herbert Simon. His 2016 book with Robert Pool, *Peak: Secrets from the New Science of Expertise* shows how to nurture the 'seeds of excellence' that are within all of us.

In a nutshell, building intuitive muscle power

Intuitive muscle power is built up over a period of time through the right amount of high-quality practice under the right circumstances.

Workout 1: High-quality practice

1 According to the famous nineteenth-century French chemist Louis Pasteur, chance favours the prepared mind.

2 Whether '10,000 hours' is too little or too much preparation is debated. What isn't in doubt though is that the time spent in preparing should involve deliberate practice, whether it's on the sports field, on the concert platform or in the workplace.

3 This means that time simply spent carrying out a task isn't likely to be the most efficient way to become an expert.

4 Practice time needs to be carefully choreographed and managed to stretch you outside of your comfort zone.

5 The table below, based on the online resource in Scott (2023), offers ten tips for high-quality practice that will give you the experience necessary to become an intuitive expert (Table 5).[31]

Table 5 Ten tips for high-quality, deliberate practice

1 Know your destination	There's a saying that 'if you don't know where you're going, you're liable to end up someplace else'; be clear about what skill you need to develop and why
2 Make it relevant	The skill needs to be important and useful to you, otherwise motivation and perseverance will be challenging
3 Enjoy the journey	There's a saying that 'it's better to travel than arrive': as far as skill development goes, you need to enjoy the journey as well as the destination
4 Take small steps	Break the skill down into small, manageable steps (micro-skills) and get some quick wins; this will help not only with progress but also with motivation
5 Use the teach-back technique	A good way to practise your skills and to check on your level of performance is to teach someone else some of the micro-skills you've picked up

➤

Table 5 continued

6 Create the time	Set aside time on a regular basis not only to practise your current level of skill but also to extend your level of skill beyond your current capability
7 Work with your body clock	Work with, not against, both your body clock (depending on whether you're a 'lark' or an 'owl') and your routine, otherwise practising will be an uphill struggle
8 Focus on quality not quantity	Focus on producing quality outputs in the first place; if quantity is important, that will follow
9 Get a role model	Find someone who you can work with and who's willing to be your role model, who will share with you their story, and pass on the tips and techniques they've picked up in their journey
10 Be open to criticism	There's a saying that 'your harshest critics are your best friends'; criticism can be painful but it is invaluable in highlighting your weak spots

6 The final piece of advice is to be patient: even if it doesn't take '10,000 hours', it'll nevertheless take time to become an intuitive expert. There are few, if any, shortcuts; if there were, someone would have found them already. The journey should be hard work but enjoyable, and the destination should be relevant and rewarding.

Notes

1 Pope, K. (updated 6 February 2024) '50 powerful quotes from women about strength and empowerment'. *Good Housekeeping*. Available online at: https://www.goodhousekeeping.com/life/g38335193/strong-women-quotes/.

2 Kasparov, G. (2007) *How Life Imitates Chess*. London: Arrow.

3 De Groot, A. (1965) *Thought and Choice in Chess*. Amsterdam: Amsterdam University Press.

4 Sadler-Smith, E. (2023) *Intuition in Business*. Oxford: Oxford University Press, p. 165.

5 RoaringPawn (2020) 'Carlsen, Tal, Kasparov, Kramnik, Anand, all in unison: Chess is about intuition', Chess.com, 3 August. Available online at: https://www.chess.com/blog/RoaringPawn/carlsen-tal-kasparov-kramnik-anand-all-in-unison-chess-is-about-intuition.

6 Carlsen, M. (2021) 'Magnus Carlsen: "I didn't trust my intuition!"'. Available online at: https://www.youtube.com/watch?v=pxo_9qSuESQ.

7 Epstein, S. (2014) *Cognitive Experiential Theory*. Oxford: Oxford University Press, p. 13.

8 Ashton Smith, M. (2010) 'How making mistakes & intuition made Magnus Carlsen chess no 1', *Mindware*, 3 February. Available online at: https://www.highiqpro.com/brain-fitness-peak-performance/how-making-mistakes-builds-intuition-expertise.

9 Chess Grandmaster Garry Kasparov – Trust Your Gut. *Goalcast*. 13 March 2023. Available online at: https://www.goalcast.com/chess-grandmaster-garry-kasparov-let-intuition-guide-you/; RoaringPawn (2020).

10 Kasparov (2023).

11 Kasparov, G. (2007) *How Life Imitates Chess*. London: Random House, p. 160.

12 Chase, W. G. and Simon, H. A. (1973) 'The mind's eye in chess'. In *Visual Information Processing: Proceedings of the Eighth Annual Carnegie Symposium on Cognition*, held at the Carnegie-Mellon University, Pittsburgh, Pennsylvania, 19 May 1972, pp. 215–81. Cambridge, MA: Academic Press.

13 Miller, G. A. (1956) 'The magical number seven plus or minus two: Some limits on our capacity for processing information', *Psychological Review*, 63(2), 81–97.

14 Chase and Simon (1973).

15 Kahneman, D., Sibony, O and Sunstein, C. (2021) *Noise: A Flaw in Human Judgement*. London: William Collins.

16 Kahneman *et al.* (2021).

17 Simon, H. A. (1987) 'Making management decisions: The role of intuition and emotion', *Academy of Management Executive*, 1(1), 57–64.

18 Sadler-Smith (2023), p. 10.

19 Simon (1987).

20 Barnard, C. (1938) *The Functions of the Executive*. Cambridge, MA: Harvard University Press, p. 302.

21 Adams, L. (2021) 'Learning a new skill is easier said than done', *Gordon Training International*. Available online at: https://www.gordontraining.com/free-workplace-articles/learning-a-new-skill-is-easier-said-than-done/.

22 Dreyfus, H. L. and Dreyfus, S. E. (2005) 'Peripheral vision: Expertise in real world contexts', *Organization Studies*, 26(5), 779–92.

23 Järvilehto, L. (2016) 'Intuition and flow'. In Harmat, L. *et al.* (eds) *Flow Experience: Empirical Research and Applications*. Dordrecht: Springer, pp. 95–104.

24 Biasutti, M. (2011) 'Flow and optimal experience'. In *Encyclopaedia of Creativity*, 2nd Ed. (Vol. 1, pp. 522–8). Academic Press; Csikszentmihalyi, M. (1997) *Flow: The Psychology of Happiness*. London: Rider.

25 Bloom, B. S. (1985) *Developing Talent in Young People*. New York: Ballantine Books, p. 3.

26 Ericsson, K. A., Prietula, M. J. and Cokely, E. T. (2007) 'The making of an expert', *Harvard Business Review*, 85(7/8), 114–22.

27 Gladwell, M. (2008) *Outliers*. New York: Little Brown.

28 FORA.tv (2011) 'Bill Gates on Expertise', *92Y An Open Door to Extraordinary Worlds*. Available online at: https://www.youtube.com/watch?v=CsGihiSE6sM&t=188s.

29 Bibb, S. (2017) *The Strengths Book*. London: LID Publishing, p. xi.

30 Hutchinson, D. S. (1995) 'Ethics'. In Barnes, J. (ed.) *The Cambridge Companion to Aristotle*. Cambridge: Cambridge University Press, pp. 195–232, p. 206; Hartman, E. (2013) *Virtue in Business*. Cambridge: Cambridge University Press, p. 52.

31 Scott, S. J. (2023) '10,000-hour rule: A simple rule for mastering a skill', *Develop Good Habits*. 13 August. Available online at: https://www.developgoodhabits.com/10000-hour-rule/

step 2

Get in touch with your gut feelings

'More of a feeling than a voice – a whispery sensation that pulsates just beneath the surface of your being.'

Oprah Winfrey (author and broadcaster, on what intuition is like for her)[1]

- -

This chapter will introduce you to a number of practical tools and techniques for getting in touch with your gut feelings.

- -

Funny bone feelings

In the 1950s, an US paper cups-cum-food mixer salesman bought into a fast-food restaurant franchise. He put everything he had into the deal and helped build it into a thriving business. However, there was one not-so-small problem: he was handing over more than a quarter of the turnover to the two brothers who owned the business and keeping less than 2 per cent of it for himself. In a bold move in 1961, he offered to buy out the owners. The asking price – $2.7 million dollars – was a significant sum of money even by today's standards; back then it was astronomical. Whether the buy-out would fly or flop was uncertain, and no one could put a figure on the probability of success or failure. His lawyer warned him not to take the deal. It was a clear make-or-break judgement call. He later recalled: 'I'm not a gambler and I didn't have that kind of money, but my "funny bone" instinct kept urging me on. So I closed my office door, cussed up and down, and threw things out the window. Then I called my lawyer back and said, "Take it!"'[2] The gamble paid off: six decades later, the business, now headquartered in Chicago, has over 40,000 restaurants in over 100 countries worldwide, employs over 150,000 people and has a revenue in excess of $25 billion.

The food mixer salesman was called Ray Kroc. The fast-food business was owned at the time by the McDonald brothers, Richard and Maurice, who'd opened the original McDonald's restaurant in San Bernardino, California, in 1940. They hired Kroc as their franchising agent in 1954 until he bought them out in the 1961 'Big Mac' deal. Kroc's giant leap from selling paper cups via milkshake mixers to building the world's largest fast-food empire is the stuff of intuition, and business, legend.

But what did Kroc mean when he claimed that his 'funny bone instinct' kept urging him on? What's it like to have this kind of feeling in your 'funny bone', your 'gut', or anywhere else for that matter?

To try and find out more, I conducted a research project in 2016 with a sample of over 100 managers. I was interested in their first-hand experiences of intuition. I asked them a straightforward question: 'What happens when you intuit?'[3] Before reading about what I found, try answering the question for yourself by completing the statement below.

'When I intuit ...'

The only stipulation is that your response should be a sentence and make grammatical sense. (For example 'When I intuit I get a funny feeling that things just don't stack up.')*

Given that I can only know what intuition is like for me, the managers' answers were revealing because they uncovered, second-hand, what it's like to be in someone else's shoes when they have that 'funny-bone feeling'. It gave me a glimpse into the private world of the intuitive mind.

Here's what I found.

Quite a few wrote about their 'gut feelings', for example: 'When I intuit I get feelings in my stomach.' Others had a physical sensation but it wasn't in their gut, for example: 'When I intuit I get a whole-body feeling' and 'When I intuit my hands tingle.'

Others placed it in their head rather than in their body, for example 'When I intuit I get a picture in my mind,' 'I see it in my mind's eye' or 'I listen to that still small voice in my head.' One manager was quite adamant that it's all 'upstairs' and there's 'nothing going on below the neck'. Others were quite vague and unspecific: 'When I intuit there is something under the surface,' 'When I intuit I have a hunch that something feels right' or 'When I intuit I experience something you can't necessarily explain.'

What's it like for you?

Incidentally, this technique is known as 'de-nominalising': the noun ('intuition' in this case) is replaced with the verb ('intuit'). This encourages the person answering the question to 'go inside' and

---

* In 'de-nominalising': the noun ('intuition' in this case) is replaced with the verb ('intuit'). This encourages the person answering the question to look inwards and focus on their subjective experience of the phenomenon of interest. I'm grateful to Neurolinguistic Programming (NLP) expert Dr Jane Mathison for bringing this method to my attention.

focus on their experience of the thing you're interested in getting to grips with. De-nominalisation is a useful technique for getting people to talk about their 'internal states' that are otherwise difficult or impossible for an outsider to access.

A word cloud of the managers' responses is shown in Figure 3 below.

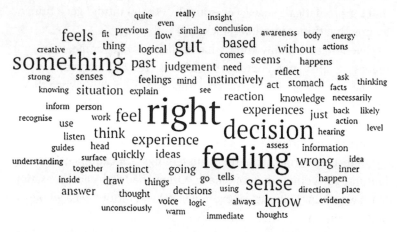

Figure 3 Wordcloud of what happens when HR managers intuit

This research revealed a number of things about intuition:

- It's different for different people: for some it's a gut reaction, for example 'an excited buzz in my stomach'; for others it's a hunch, for example 'I sense an unsaid'.

- It can be a 'bad vibe': it can be a warning signal, for example 'When I intuit I know something is wrong' which could be interpreted as a signal to avoid an object, person or situation.

- It can be a 'good vibe': it can be positive and provide an affirmation, for example 'When I intuit I get a feeling that something is right' which could be interpreted as a signal to approach an object, person or situation.

It's also clear from these data that 'gut feeling', 'gut reaction', 'gut instincts' and probably Kroc's 'funny bone instinct' as well are used sometimes as metaphors for intuition. They might not refer literally to a gut feeling; and, even if a feeling is involved, it's not necessarily in the 'gut'. Incidentally, the funny bone that Kroc seems to have been referring to isn't a bone at all, it's where the ulnar nerve runs along the outside of the elbow and creates a painful sensation when it gets knocked against the bones of your upper arm. This adds to my suspicion that his funny bone feeling was metaphorical, not literal.

Spotlight on intuition
A 'second brain'?

There are approximately 100 billion neurons in the human brain. But it's also been estimated that there are approximately 500 million neurons in the human gut. There are more nerves in the human gut than in the spinal cord or the entire peripheral nervous system.[4] For this reason, some scientists have nicknamed the gut our 'second brain' (its technical name is the 'enteric nervous system'). The emerging evidence suggests that the relationship between our brain and our gut (the so-called 'gut–brain axis') is important because there's a 'cross-talk' between the brain and the gut. For example 90 per cent of the neurons in the vagus nerve (which controls a number of vital functions including digestion, heart rate and breathing) carry information *from* the gut *to* the brain, not the other way around. As a result, signals generated in the gut may influence the brain and from there affect how we think, feel and act.[5]

The managers' data also shows that even though many of us have been educated into believing that rational analysis is the best and sometimes even the only way to take decisions – and in many situations it undeniably is – there's no doubt that managers use gut feelings when taking business decisions even if they don't always admit to it in public.

This echoes the results of a 2015 survey by PwC and the Economist Intelligence Unit in which 1,300 managers (half of whom were C-level) were asked, 'Which of the following inputs did you place most reliance on for your last big decision: intuition and experience; data and analysis; advice and experience of others?' There was a roughly three-way split between intuition and experience (30 per cent), data and analytics (29 per cent) and advice and experience of others (28 per cent) (see Figure 4).[6] Students in my MBA classes invariably give much the same response.

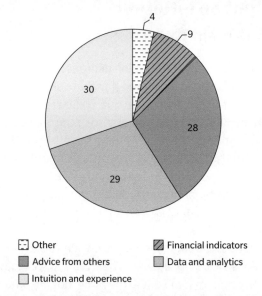

Figure 4 How a sample of 1,300 C-suite managers took important decisions

In the PwC research, in a follow-up interview, one respondent described intuition as providing insights that you get from having 'feet on the street, which the data may not tell you'. A marketing executive commented that gut feelings are critical for big decisions because even though 'data will tell you what *has* happened' intuition could tell you 'what *will* happen'. In a world that's volatile, uncertain, complex and ambiguous (VUCA), working with what's likely to happen is much more useful than knowing what's already happened. When I used this same question with a group of over 200 Italian managers, the results were even more in favour of intuition: 65 per cent of them said that they relied most on intuition and experience in their last big decision.

You might be forgiven for thinking of Bill Gates as an embodiment of the analytical mind. But this is a stereotype. In an interview with CNN in 2002, he was asked if he had 'some sort of sounding board you use, for when you see something that strikes you as a good idea, but you're not really sure if this is going to catch on'. Gates replied: 'Well, if I think something's going to catch on, I trust my own intuition.' CNN: 'And you're never wrong?' Gates: 'No, I'm often wrong, but my batting record is good enough that I keep swinging every time the ball is thrown.'[7]

Decades of research with managers and executives allied to anecdotes from some of the world's top business people point to the inescapable conclusion that gut feelings aren't a nuisance to be factored out of decision making; instead, they're an essential data point in many, if not most, big decisions. The data bear this out, and the higher that managers climb up the business hierarchy, the more important their intuition appears to become. Figure 5 shows managers'

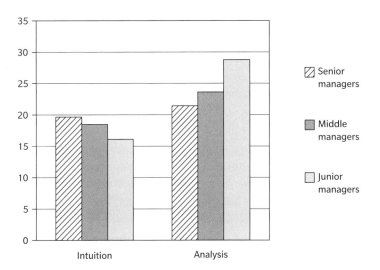

Figure 5 Preferences for intuition versus analysis by job level

Source: Hodgkinson, G. P. and Sadler-Smith, E. (2003) 'Complex or unitary? A critique and empirical re-assessment of the Allinson-Hayes Cognitive Style Index', *Journal of Occupational and Organizational Psychology*, 76(2), 243–68.

preferences for intuition versus analysis in terms of job level. Senior managers are more intuitive for sure, but they also have a more balanced thinking profile than the middle or junior managers (you can check your preference for intuition versus analysis, your Intuition Quotient, using the survey in the Workout section of this chapter).

Spotlight on intuition
Intuition in Eastern philosophy

People in many Western cultures have been educated to trust in their analytical intelligence more than their intuitive intelligence. On the other hand, many non-Western cultures and traditions give much more recognition to intuition.

For example, in Hinduism and Buddhism *pragya* or *prajña* (प्रज्ञ in Sanskrit) is transcendent knowledge that arises from a deep spiritual connection to the universe. It's a direct, and therefore intuitive, perception of truth and reality that's not been 'tainted' by analysis.[8] Yogis claim to have methods for developing intuition through meditation, mindfulness and other practices.

Vipassana ('seeing things as they really are') is one of the most ancient techniques of meditation, practised by Gautama Buddha in India over 2,500 years ago. Meditation is a tried-and-tested technique for quieting the restlessness of the analytical mind and creating a space for the voice of the intuitive mind to be heard.

In the world of business, research reported in *Harvard Business Review* asked 3,400 business leaders how important they believe certain attitudes are in management and leadership. Eighty-five per cent of leaders in Asian countries believed that intuition is important compared to only 54 per cent in Europe. The article concluded that intuition, and the competitive edge that it gives in areas such as creativity, could be the difference between getting ahead as an innovator and getting left behind.[9]

Steve Jobs was influenced by *prajña* wisdom. On his return to the USA following his time in India in the mid-1970s, he commented that in the Indian tradition people relied much more on their intuition than people in the West did. Based on these experiences, Jobs advocated meditation as a way to calm the restlessness of the analytical mind to create room for more subtle thoughts to emerge into consciousness. He said when you do that, 'that's when your intuition starts to blossom and you start to see things more clearly and be in the present more'. Jobs's connection to Buddhism led him to the belief that intuitive intelligence can be more significant for creativity in business than analytical intelligence alone.[10]

Meditation in its various forms has been suggested as a way to quiet the rational mind, activate our intuitions and 'get in touch with the wisdom that's stored in our bodies'.[11] It's not just for Buddhists and yogis. I've used mindfulness meditation to help MBA students tune in to their gut feelings and develop a stronger and deeper connection with their intuitive mind.[12]

In the bigger picture, there's more to human intelligence than intellectual intelligence alone: there's 'emotional intelligence' which is based in the brain's limbic system and was made famous by Daniel Goleman in his book of the same name; there's 'analytical intelligence', which Daniel Kahneman and others refer to as 'System 2' thinking, and there's 'intuitive intelligence', which is sometimes called 'System 1' thinking (Figure 6). The bottom line is that evolution has equipped human beings with an innate potential for analytical, emotional and intuitive intelligences. Together they form a complete package and, as a consequence, we've not only survived as a species, but up until now thrived.[13] Whether adding artificial intelligence to the mix heralds a new dawn or signals humanity's demise remains to be seen (more about this in the final chapter).

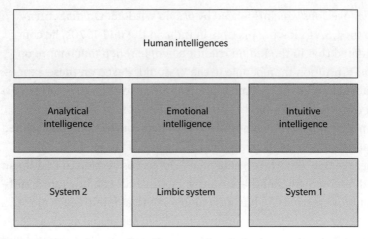

Figure 6 Three human 'intelligences' (analytical, emotional and intuitive)

Takeaway

'Gut feelings', 'hunches' and 'vibes' are both literally and metaphorically the 'voice' of our intuitive mind. It's a voice that a majority of managers appear to listen to when taking big decisions and, with the right training, can be developed.

The body knows

Imagine you're an interviewer on an appointment panel. There are several candidates to choose from. On paper, Candidate A checks all the boxes. Their answers to your questions are exemplary; their references are glowing. But there's something about Candidate A that sets you on edge and makes you feel uneasy; you feel that you 'just know' that something doesn't stack up; they give off a hard-to-pin down 'bad vibe', which is difficult to resist in your evaluation even though doing so may be contrary to HR best practice.

But what does it mean to 'just know'? Are you simply being biased, consciously or unconsciously, against this person? Do the other members of the panel feel the same way? How will you explain how you feel when asked to give your views? Even more worryingly perhaps, how will you document it in the HR paperwork? Should you go with your gut and recommend they not be offered the job, or just ignore what your gut might be trying to tell you? More fundamentally, is what's going on merely imagined, or is there something biological and real to these kinds of bodily experiences?

According to the eminent neuroscientist Antonio Damasio, the answer to this last question is 'yes': our body has evolved to generate physiological responses that help us to take decisions automatically, quickly and non-consciously. Damasio called these signals 'somatic markers' (from the Greek *soma* meaning 'body'); they're referred to colloquially as 'gut feelings', 'hunches' or 'vibes'.

In his work as a clinical neurologist, Damasio has day-to-day contact with patients who are unable, for very good physiological reasons, to experience 'gut feelings'. As a result, their decision-making capabilities can be seriously debilitated. It's as though their intuitive mind has been disconnected and switched off. The backstory is that, as a clinician, Damasio was intrigued by the question of why some patients he dealt with made consistently bad decisions in their personal and professional lives. One thing that many of them had in common was that they'd had the misfortune to incur damage through disease or injury to part of the brain's frontal cortex called the 'ventromedial prefrontal cortex' (VMPFC) (it's in the middle of your head just above and behind the eye sockets) (Figure 7).

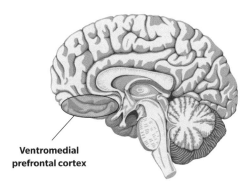

Figure 7 Approximate location of the ventromedial prefrontal cortex

Damasio explains this phenomenon with the compelling story of one of his patients, 'Elliot'. Elliot had the misfortune of having had a type of brain tumour called a meningioma. It was removed some years previously from the middle-front part of his brain near where the VMPFC is located. Luckily, the tumour was benign but, as sometimes happens in such cases, the surgery inadvertently damaged some of the surrounding brain tissue. The peculiar thing was that, after the operation, Elliot's personality changed profoundly while his intelligence remained intact. Prior to the operation, Elliot had been a good husband, father and employee. After the surgery, Elliot, in Damasio's words, 'was no longer Elliot'. The root of Elliot's problem was that he'd lost the ability to take effective decisions.

Two things seem to have happened. First, Damasio noticed that all of Elliot's decisions boiled down to a cold, calculated trade-off between as many pros and cons as he could think of. As a result, he developed the annoying habit of producing a myriad of options for even the most trivial decisions. For example, in work, he'd spend hours trying to decide how to categorise paperwork: should it be by date, size of document, importance, etc., such that he got very little done. He was hyper-rational to the extent that he became too systematic and diligent for his own good. Elliot was tormented by Benjamin Franklin's pros-versus-cons method 'on steroids'. Things got so bad at work that he eventually got fired from his job.

Second, it seemed as though Elliot was unable to produce any gut feelings that would help him to discriminate between options that might be beneficial to him that he should approach versus those that might put him in jeopardy and ought to be avoided. For example, without a regular job, Elliot drifted into obsessive collecting behaviours (mostly junk), he divorced his wife and left his kids, teamed up with disreputable people in failed business ventures, lost all his money as a result, entered into a bad second marriage and got divorced again.

Damasio put this plague on Elliot's personal and professional life down to the fact that Elliot could not, as a result of his brain injury, attach any feelings to the choices he was faced with to give them an 'oomph'. The brain injury left Elliot bereft of any way to sway his choices one way or the other and towards a path that might benefit him in the long term. In Damasio's words, Elliot's decision-making landscape was 'hopelessly flat'. Bizarrely, because he could *only* use analysis, Elliot's decision-making abilities had been seriously diminished and his previously normal life had been all but destroyed. In two-minds terms, Elliot's System 2 (his analytical mind) went into overdrive without System 1 (his intuitive mind) to hold it in check or tell him what it thought. Elliot became a victim of analysis paralysis.

Big thinker

Antonio Damasio

Antonio Damasio is Professor of Psychology, Philosophy and Neurology at the University of Southern California. The main idea behind the somatic marker hypothesis is that people who've incurred damage to the VMPFC make poorer decisions because they're no longer able to generate the gut feelings that speed up decision making by refining the number of options and discriminating between signals for a potentially good or bad outcome. Here are some insights from Damasio on somatic markers and intuition:

- 'This covert mechanism [somatic markers] would be the source of what we call intuition, the mysterious mechanism by which we arrive at the solution of a problem without reasoning toward it.'[14]

- 'When the bad outcome associated with a given response option comes to mind, however fleetingly, you experience an unpleasant gut feeling.'[15]

- 'Wisdom, if you choose to accept it, is what happens when you accrue lots of somatic knowledge in your life.[16]

Damasio is keen to point out that he uses the term 'somatic' to refer to the whole body, not just the viscera; this is consistent with the managers' data shown in Figure 3 above. In other words, somatic markers include hunches and vibes, as well as gut feelings.

By studying people with brain damage, like Elliot, and by carrying out laboratory experiments to understand the neurology of what exactly was going on, Damasio and his team of researchers concluded that when people with an intact and functioning VMPFC face a big decision (for example, to buy or sell, invest or gamble, take up or decline a job offer, buy the right house, marry the right person, etc.), they automatically and unconsciously use their gut feelings to accept or reject certain courses of action. On the other hand, people with damage to the VMPFC are unable to decide properly because, in Damasio's words, they're able to '*know* but they cannot *feel*'[17] and, as far as decisions are concerned, if 'we *feel* nothing we tend to *do* nothing'.[18]

Why should a lack of gut feelings mess up decision making so much? Damasio explains their role as follows.

Feelings don't think for us, but they do shine the spotlight on how we might feel about potential future scenarios associated with the alternatives that are in front of us, for example 'Can I imagine myself being happy in this house?', 'Can I imagine myself enjoying working with Candidate A?', etc. If a bad vibe (the technical term is a 'negative somatic state') springs to mind at the thought of working with Candidate A, it helps enormously in rejecting the option of employing Candidate A. This judgement could of course have been contaminated for some reason by bias and prejudice against Candidate A. If it's a good vibe ('positive somatic state'), then the reverse is true. The thing is that we might not even be aware of the influence that our gut feelings are having over us. It's as though the body knows before the brain does, and when this happens the body sometimes takes charge without the brain having much of a say in it.

Spotlight on intuition
Knowing before you can tell

The neuroscientist Joel Pearson in his book *The Intuition Toolkit* (2024) tells the story of two experienced pilots who were practising for an air show. It was the job of the pilot in the following plane to mirror in perfect synchrony what the lead plane was doing. But, as they came out of a barrel roll, something went tragically wrong. The lead plane was flying too close to the ground. The lead pilot called out 'Pull up, pull up!' But for him it was too late. His plane crashed into the ground and he was killed instantly. But, mysteriously and miraculously, the following pilot found that he'd already pulled back on the joystick *before* the lead pilot gave the emergency call and even before he knew it himself.

Pearson explains this as follows: the cues that the following pilot's brain was processing unconsciously led it to conclude, within milliseconds, that something wasn't right with the manoeuvre. His intuitive mind bypassed his conscious awareness and instructed his body to respond; it knew that he needed to bring the nose of the plane up just in time. His intuition ended up saving his life.

Pearson defines intuition as 'the learnt productive use of unconscious information to improve decisions or actions'. He calls this phenomenon of unconscious information automatically making its way into our actions and guiding our behaviours 'blindaction'. It's analogous to 'blindsight': the remarkable ability in people who are cortically blind to respond to visual stimuli they're not consciously aware of.[19]

Sometimes, we're unaware of the unconscious signals that our bodies are responding to (as in the example of the air show pilot); our bodies may 'know' before we do. At other times, we're aware of them as gut feelings, hunches and vibes. In this situation, somatic markers help with 'shortlisting' both literally and metaphorically. They're a biological mechanism that preselects alternatives, examines the available options and allows only one, or at most a few, to present themselves for final consideration.[20] In general: positive somatic states, or 'good vibes', signal 'approach' (Damasio calls this a 'beacon of incentive'), whereas negative somatic states, or 'bad vibes', signal 'avoid' (Damasio calls this an 'alarm bell').[21]

The intuitive mind has evolved to be able to sense what might be good or bad for us, but because it's a part of a non-verbal system (System 1) it has to have an alternative to words to tell us what it 'thinks'. It tells us what it thinks, or more precisely what we should do, in the language of gut feelings.

An object, person or situation becomes 'tagged' with positive or negative feelings as a result of associative learning.[22] It's like the chess grandmasters we met in Step 1 who, over thousands of games, had unconsciously tagged good or bad vibes to particular patterns of pieces based on previous experiences. They're then able to make their best moves intuitively even though they don't always consciously know why they preferred one move over another. All they know was that their gut appears to be guiding them.

Gut feelings are part of an automated anomaly detection system. It probably evolved to protect us against the downsides of certain objects, people or situations; as such it would have erred on the side of caution. This makes sense: it would have aided our ancestors' survival because, in the face of a threat, avoidance is better than approach. Our ancestors have passed on the genes for this automated alarm system to us.

Takeaway

Gut feelings, hunches or vibes in the form of a 'negative somatic marker' signal 'avoid' whereas a 'positive somatic marker' signals 'approach'.

Getting in touch with your 'gut'

The body has been described as the 'theatre' in which the drama of our gut feelings is played out.[23] The experience of having a gut feeling has been likened to a subtle shift in the internal contours of the 'body landscape'. It's not the same as the upheaval we get with primary emotions such as anger, disgust, fear, happiness, sadness or surprise; this is why intuitive feelings shouldn't be equated with emotional feelings. If we're to make intelligent use of our intuitions, rather than following them blindly and being sabotaged by them, we need to 'hear', and also heed, what these changes in the internal 'bodyscape' are telling us.

The technical term for an awareness of the internal state of our body through the perception and detection of bodily signals, such as heart rate, breathing and gut feelings, is *interoception*.[†] Interoception can be measured in various ways, including our ability to detect accurately our own heartbeat. But does being consciously aware of what our body might be trying to tell us have any bearing on the quality of our decision making?

Spotlight on intuition
Gut feelings and financial folklore

Researchers based at Addenbrooke's Hospital at the University of Cambridge explored whether City of London hedge-fund traders' heartbeat detection scores bore any relationship to their ability to make money. They studied 18 male traders who were involved in high-frequency trades lasting typically a few seconds or, at most, minutes. The time pressure that the traders were under meant that they didn't have the luxury of being able to analyse their options and come up with reasons for their choices; instead, a bit like Klein's firefighters, they had to go with their gut. The researchers made a number of significant discoveries:

- Heartbeat detection was positively associated with profit and loss (P&L) over the previous year; traders with higher heartbeat detection scores made more money.

➤

[†] Interoception is different from *exteroception* (the perception of the external environment) and *proprioception* (sensing of the body's position in space).

- Heartbeat detection was associated with the number of years that traders had 'survived' in one of the most challenging of financial markets.

- Experienced traders had higher heartbeat detection scores than junior traders.

The researchers speculated that financial markets might actually be 'selecting' (via the number of years' survival in the industry) those traders who had, for whatever reason, the ability to detect what their bodies were telling them to do. Those who couldn't tune in to and decipher their gut feelings would be 'eliminated' by not being able to make enough money to survive and thrive in the hyper-competitive world of hedge-fund-trading.

Subtle changes in the traders' internal bodyscape provided cues that helped them to select 'the one that just "feels right"' from a range of possible trades. This research suggests there may be something to the financial folklore that good gut feelings and the ability to have good *interoceptive awareness* are important for selecting profitable trades.[‡24]

Although this kind of research is in its infancy, it suggests that rather than gut feeling being just another figure of speech, perhaps there may be something going on biologically in the form of bodily processes and sensations that guide decision making in risky and uncertain situations. It seems likely that these bodily signals are communicated along various pathways in the body, including the vagus nerve, to *interoceptive centres* in the relevant parts of the brain, including the part that had been damaged in patients such as Elliot (in his case the VMPFC).[25]

---

‡ The researchers acknowledge that because their study was field based, not laboratory based, they have not been able to establish causation; for example it could be that as traders become more successful their heartbeat detection ability improves for some as yet unidentified reason.

Research also suggests that there might be differences between people in their ability to generate, notice and interpret bodily signals. Some people might be able to readily tune in to their body while others are metaphorically deaf to what it might be trying to tell them. If this is the case then this would mean that some people have better interoceptive awareness than others, which could help them to tune in to and use their gut feelings. As a result they'd have a head start in the intuitive intelligence stakes.

A problem for many people who are accustomed to, or prefer, analysis over intuition is that the incessant chatter of the analytical mind can sometimes drown out what Oprah Winfrey refers to as the 'still, small voice of intuition ... a whispery sensation that pulsates just beneath the surface of your being'.[26] Becoming more aware of the signals that our body is communicating is a crucial step on the road to becoming intuitively intelligent. Tuning in to, and then translating, gut feelings is a skill in itself; there's more on how to tune in and translate in Step 5.

Takeaway

Gut feelings are a biological phenomenon and can be a reliable source of data when taking complex and consequential decisions.

Dig deeper

Antonio Damasio's *Descartes Error: Emotion, Reason and the Human Brain* (1994) is a classic of the intuition literature. In it Damasio demonstrates that gut feelings are neither fictitious nor mysterious; they're explicable and essential to effective decision making.

In a nutshell, getting in touch with your gut feelings.

Gut feelings, the 'voice' of the intuitive mind, can be a reliable signal for 'approach' or 'avoid' when taking complex, consequential decisions in uncertain situations.

Workout 1: Coin flip

How in touch are you with your gut feelings when it comes to consequential decisions? A straightforward way to appreciate the power that your gut feelings have over your decisions is to do the following:

- Toss a coin next time you're confronted by a consequential choice;
- Call heads or tails (for example heads take the job offer, tails turn it down).
- Then notice how you feel if the coin comes up heads (take the job).

What did your body tell you? Were you delighted or disappointed? If you were delighted, perhaps your intuition is telling you to take the job, hence the good vibe at the result of the coin toss. On the other hand, if you were disappointed, perhaps your intuition was to not take the job. Your immediate reaction to which side of the coin comes up could be a good indicator of how you really feel about the choice that you're confronted with. However, it's worth remembering, at the end of the day, intuition is only a judgement that comes with no guarantee of accuracy or success.

You can try a similar technique with any consequential decision. For example, imagine that the decision is whether or not to change jobs. Now imagine that you've turned up at your office and your key won't open the door. How do you feel about the fact that you can't get in: good or bad? If you feel elated, perhaps it's because your intuition is telling you that to leave is the right decision and it's time to go; if you feel down-hearted that you can't get in, perhaps your intuition is telling you that you should stay put. You can adapt this technique to all sorts of consequential decisions in your personal and professional life using the symbols of keys, red and green traffic lights, stop and go flags, thumbs up or thumbs down, etc., or anything that can be used as a clear signalling device.

Workout 2: Thinking style

How comfortable are you with going with your gut versus analytics? The brief survey below will help you to get a feel for your preferences for intuition versus analysis (Table 6).

The minimum score for analysis or intuition is zero and the maximum is 20 points (five questions for each, times a maximum of four points per question).

People who prefer analysis tend to: do a lot of fact finding before deciding; research the facts and make lists of the pros and cons, read a lot and consult experts, take their time because they're concerned that the decision needs to be 'right' and aren't very likely to change their mind once they've assembled all their reasons. People who prefer intuition tend to use their overall impression and feelings to come to a quick decision, they may not always be able to explain their 'reasons why' but they're in touch with their gut feelings and treat them as a valid form of data.

Table 6 Do you prefer intuitive or analytical approaches to decision making?

Tick one box for how each statement (1–10) applies to you in general. Next write the score for each statement in the 'Analysis' or 'Intuition' column (e.g. 'Agree' for Statement 1 scores 3 points and goes in the 'Intuition' column); 'Neutral' means in between 'agree' and 'disagree'. Add up your totals for each.	Strongly agree	Agree	Neutral	Disagree	Strongly disagree	Analysis	Intuition
1. I'm good at noticing things about people or situations that others overlook.	☐ 4	☐ 3	☐ 2	☐ 1	☐ 0		
2. I find that my initial impressions about people or situations usually turn out to be right.	☐ 4	☐ 3	☐ 2	☐ 1	☐ 0		
3. I like to solve problems using structured techniques such as listing pros and cons, tables, flowcharts, etc.	☐ 4	☐ 3	☐ 2	☐ 1	☐ 0		
4. I prefer to 'go with my gut' rather than analyse all the eventualities.	☐ 4	☐ 3	☐ 2	☐ 1	☐ 0		

5. I like solving problems and making predictions by figuring out patterns and trends in data.	☐ 4	☐ 3	☐ 2	☐ 1	☐ 0
6. I often just know, without knowing how or why I know.	☐ 4	☐ 3	☐ 2	☐ 1	☐ 0
7. I usually mull things over for a considerable time before taking a decision.	☐ 4	☐ 3	☐ 2	☐ 1	☐ 0
8. Solving puzzles, brain teasers and riddles using logic and reasoning gives me little pleasure.	☐ 0	☐ 1	☐ 2	☐ 3	☐ 4
9. I prefer to solve problems and take decisions by gathering as much information as possible.	☐ 4	☐ 3	☐ 2	☐ 1	☐ 0
10. I don't believe it's possible to take a good decision by just 'going with your gut'.	☐ 0	☐ 1	☐ 2	☐ 3	☐ 4
Total score for Analysis					
Total score for Intuition					

Workout 3: Your Intuition Quotient (NQ)

Your 'Intuition Quotient' (NQ, to distinguish it from IQ) can be calculated using the scores from Workout 2 as follows:

$$NQ = (\text{Intuition score} / 20) - (\text{Analysis score} / 20)$$

The value of NQ can range from $+1.0$ (highly intuitive) to -1.0 (highly analytical). Positive and negative are purely arbitrary. Plot your position using a pointer on the NQ-ometer (Figure 8). Your NQ indicates whether you have a preference for intuition (positive score, right-hand side of the meter) or analysis (negative score, left-hand side of the meter) when solving problems and taking decisions. If you don't have any particularly strong preference for either intuition or analysis, your score will tend to be closer to zero. If you're in a team, you could plot members' scores on a 'team NQ-ometer'.

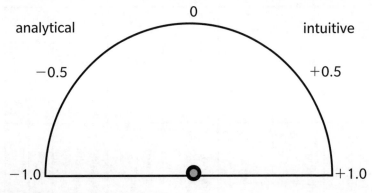

Figure 8 The 'NQ-ometer'

Workout 4: Start small

For people who are more analytically inclined and used to treading carefully when they take consequential decisions, the idea of going with their gut feelings can seem a little daunting. One way to build confidence in intuition is to practise with inconsequential decisions, for example to go with your gut on what to wear, or what to choose from a restaurant menu. Taking quick intuitive decisions in low-risk decisions will help you to step up to taking bigger decisions and gradually build up the skill of knowing if and when to trust your gut. The best advice is: don't jump in at the deep end.

Workout 5: Mindfulness meditation

Have you tried *asking* your intuition what it thinks? We normally think of intuition as an involuntary response that just presents itself, uninvited, to tell us what it thinks. The voice of our intuitive mind can sometimes be drowned out by the incessant chatter from our analytical mind. However, it's possible to create the mental space for intuition to have its say.

Mindfulness meditation is a well-established method for quieting the analytical mind and creating a space for the intuitive mind to have its say.

There are lots of resources available that will help you to practise mindfulness meditation if you feel that this is something that might help you to tune in to your intuitions.[27]

Notes

1 Winfrey, O. (no date) 'What Oprah knows for sure about trusting her intuition', Oprah.com. Available online at: https://www. oprah.com/spirit/oprah-on-trusting-her-intuition- oprahs-advice-on-trusting-your-gut (accessed May 2024).

2 Rowan, R. (1987) *The Intuitive Manager*. Aldershot: Gower, p. 8.

3 Sadler-Smith, E. (2016) '"What happens when you intuit?": Understanding human resource practitioners' subjective experience of intuition through a novel linguistic method', *Human Relations*, 69(5), 1069–93.

4 Lieberman, D. (2014) *The Story of the Human Body*. London: Penguin, p. 91

5 Soosalu, G., Henwood, S. and Deo, A. (2019) 'Head, heart, and gut in decision making: Development of a multiple brain preference questionnaire', *Sage Open*, 9(1), 2158244019837439; Gerrie, H. (no date) 'Our second brain: More than a gut feeling', The University of British Columbia: Faculty of Medicine. Available online at: https://neuroscience.ubc.ca/our-second-brain-more-than-a-gut-feeling/ (accessed May 2024).

6 PwC (2014) 'Big business decisions driven by gut instincts as well as gigabytes – PwC report'. Available online at: https://pwc.blogs.com/press_room/2014/09/big-business-decisions-driven-by-gut-instinct-as-well-as-gigabytes-pwc-report.html.

7 CNN (2002) 'A one-on-one interview with Bill Gates', CNN.com/Sci-Tech, 1 March. Available online at: http://edition.cnn.com/2002/TECH/industry/02/28/gates/.

8 Parekh, K. (2023) '"Sixth sense, gut feeling": How can power of intuition help you in day-to-day life?', *The Economic Times*, 29 July. Available at: https://economictimes.indiatimes.com/news/how-to/sixth-sense-gut-feeling-how-can-power-of-intuition-help-you-in-day-to-day-life/articleshow/102230476.cms?from=mdr.

9 Lagerberg, F. (2014) 'Asian leaders value creativity and intuition more than Europeans do', *Harvard Business Review*, 5 June. Available online at: https://hbr.org/2014/06/asian-leaders-value-creativity-and-intuition-more-than-europeans-do.

10 Isaacson, W. (2011) *Steve Jobs*. New York: Simon & Schuster, p. 35.

11 Kaplan, D. (2017) 'Meditation for intuition (or the third eye)', *Forbes*, 31 July 2017. Available at: https://www.forbes.com/sites/dinakaplan/2017/07/31/meditation-for-intuition-or-the-third-eye/.

12 Sadler-Smith, E. and Shefy, E. (2007) 'Developing intuitive awareness in management education', *Academy of Management Learning & Education*, 6(2), 186–205.

13 Moitoso, M. (2019) 'How to make better decisions: Integrating emotions and rationality', *Alongside You*. Available online at: https://www.alongsideyou.ca/how-to-make-better-decisions/.

14 Damasio, A. R. (1994) *Descartes' Error*. London: Quill, p. 188.

15 Damasio (1994), p. 173.

16 Baer, D. (2016) 'How only being able to use logic to make decisions destroyed a man's life', *The Cut*, 14 June. Available online at: https://www.thecut.com/2016/06/how-only-using-logic-destroyed-a-man.html; The Aspen Institute (2009) *This Time with Feeling: David Brooks and Antonio Damasio*. Available online at: https://www.youtube.com/watch?v=IifXMd26gWE.

17 Damasio (1994), p. 45.

18 System 1 (2017) *System 1: Unlocking Profitable Growth*. London: System 1 Group, p. 218.

19 Pearson, J. (2024) *The Intuition Toolkit*. Cammeray, NSW: Simon & Schuster, pp. 2–5; p. 37.

20 Damasio (1994), p. 189.

21 Damasio (1994), p. 175.

22 Damasio (1994), p. 174.

23 Sadler-Smith, E. (2023) *Intuition in Business*. Oxford: Oxford University Press, p. 150.

24 Kandasamy, N., Garfinkel, S. N., Page, L., Hardy, B., Critchley, H. D. and Coates, J. M. (2016) 'Interoceptive ability predicts survival on a London trading floor', *Nature: Scientific Reports*, 6(1), 32986, p. 5.

25 Kandasamy *et al*. (2016).

26 Winfrey, O. (no date) 'What Oprah knows for sure about trusting her intuition'.

27 For example, Kaplan (2017).

step 3

Know when, and when not, to trust it

The wisdom of intuition does not follow the rules of logic. It is a purveyor of possibilities.'

Frances E. Vaughan (author of *Awakening Intuition*)[1]

- -

This chapter will help you to distinguish between situations in which you can legitimately trust your gut feelings and those situations in which you cannot.

- -

How to take an important decision

Loyalty programmes are one of the best ways to boost a business's market share. They come in various guises, including points-based (for example supermarket loyalty cards), tiered (for example British Airways bronze, silver, gold and platinum levels) and paid. In the early 2000s, Amazon had been searching for a loyalty programme. Then, out-of-the-blue, Charlie Ward, a relatively junior software engineer, pitched the idea in an employee suggestion box of paid membership for fast, free shipping. At the time, Amazon offered customers free shipping on purchases of $25 or more, as long as they were willing to wait a few extra days for their order to arrive. Ward's idea was that some customers would be willing to buy membership and would be likely to spend more and shop more if they were part of a fast, free shipping loyalty scheme.[2]

When Amazon's finance team modelled fast, free shipping, the numbers, in Jeff Bezos's own words, were 'horrifying'. A red flag was that the 'big eaters' at the Amazon buffet were likely to buy lots of one-dollar items that required two-dollar shipping. This isn't a good way to make money. In fact, this was a sore point for Bezos: he'd been criticised in the media because Amazon retail wasn't making much in the way of profit. A mischievous financial journalist even asked Bezos: 'Mr Bezos, do you even know how to spell profit?' Bezos's reply was far-sighted: 'Yes,' he said, 'P R O P H E T'!

As far as the financials were concerned, fast, free shipping was a non-starter. Plus, the probability of whether the idea would fly or flop simply couldn't be known in advance. Fast, free shipping was a risky decision for which Amazon knew it couldn't compute an answer. But it also knew it was a decision that it had to take sooner or later. Fortunately, Bezos's familiarity with the territory of online retailing gave him an intuitive grasp of what might and might not work.

As a seasoned CEO, Bezos knew that data can only take you so far and that a radical idea in an uncertain situation ultimately can't be reduced to a set of odds for success or failure. His second-to-none familiarity with online retailing gave him the sense that fast, free shipping really could be a game changer. In the final analysis, he chose to go with his gut. Reflecting on this decision in 2018 in an interview at the Economic Club of Washington, he said: 'If you can make a decision with analysis, you should do so. But it turns out in life that your most important decisions are always made with instinct and intuition, taste and heart.'[3]

Amazon Prime has been a resounding success. Following its launch in the USA in 2005, it's proven to be one of the world's most successful subscription services with over 100 million members who spend on average $1,400 per year compared to $600 for non-Prime members. In choosing to go with his gut, Bezos put his credibility on the line. Had it not worked, the consequences could have been dire for the business and dented Bezos's reputation as a superstar CEO.

The big decision of whether or not to go with the Prime idea wasn't one that Bezos had met before; nobody had. It was a problem where uncertainty was centre stage and the probability of success couldn't be calculated. But having said that, the territory wasn't so unfamiliar as to be unfathomable; Bezos had enough about him in terms of his experience of online retailing to be able to take a punt and make the big judgement call. Intuitive intelligence is Bezos's inner GPS for navigating uncertainty and has helped to make him into one of the world's leading, and richest, business people.

Takeaway

Intuition comes into its own when experienced decision makers have to take uncertain decisions in familiar territory where the odds for success or failure can't be computed.

Good environments for going with your gut

Gary Klein, our Big thinker from Part 1 who discovered the recognition-primed decision (RPD) model, has documented numerous incidents of experienced firefighters, missile battery commanders on warships, neonatal nurses and others who used their intuitive muscle power in fast-moving, high-stakes situations, and whose actions saved both life and property. In a graphic example of the power of intuition, Klein described the case of neonatal nurse Linda who was looking after baby Melissa.

Melissa was a premature baby in a neonatal intensive care unit (ICU) in a hospital in the USA. Linda was new to the neonatal unit and was given primary responsibility for Melissa's care. Linda had noted Melissa's decreased temperature, a bleeding heel stick, general lethargy, some bloating and mottled skin. She noticed each symptom (Klein calls them 'cues') in isolation but as such didn't see them as particularly significant, *on their own*. What Linda hadn't realised was that, taken together, these cues are classic signs of sepsis. Linda didn't put the pieces together to create a bigger picture of Melissa's predicament. It was only when another nurse, Darlene, who had six years' experience in the unit, happened to walk past Melissa's cot at the end of her shift and noticed something about the baby that 'just looked funny'. Darlene pieced the cues together intuitively and deduced that Melissa most likely had sepsis. She contacted the duty physician immediately and requested antibiotics and a blood test. If Darlene had delayed the antibiotics until the blood test results came back, Melissa would probably not have survived.

What was the difference between Linda and Darlene that made such a difference to Melissa's life?

The difference was that Darlene was dealing with an uncertainty (why was Melissa's condition deteriorating?) but she was in familiar territory (six years' experience as a neonatal ICU nurse). Linda, on the other hand, was dealing with the same level of uncertainty but she was in unfamiliar territory (new to the neonatal ICU). As a result, Darlene, unlike Linda, had a much better awareness for the totality of Melissa's situation; she was able put together all of the separate cues into a bigger picture and decide intuitively that Melissa was a baby in big trouble.[4] Once the totality of Melissa's situation 'clicked', Darlene read between the lines, her anomaly detection system went into overdrive and sounded the sepsis siren. This is intuitive intelligence in action: something didn't look right, Darlene had a strong suspicion that it was serious, she acted decisively and, as a result, saved a baby's life.

Spotlight on intuition
A failure to disagree

The question of when, not if, you should go with your gut was the subject of a famous 'failure to disagree' between two of intuition's 'big thinkers': the decision researcher Gary Klein and the psychologist Daniel Kahneman, celebrated for his two minds model (see Part 1).

Kahneman made his research reputation in the 1970s in studies of when, how and why intuition gets it wrong. In a series of famous experiments with his colleague Amos Tversky, mostly using students as subjects in decision lab research he demonstrated that intuition can lead us badly astray if it's used as a mental shortcut (the technical term is a 'heuristic') to solve problems and take decisions that it's not suited to. When this happens, going with your gut can lead to significantly biased – and sometimes just plain wrong – judgements and decisions. It's like using the wrong tool for the job in hand. For example, using a spanner instead of a screwdriver to tighten a screw doesn't work particularly well. This work contributed to Kahneman being awarded the Nobel Prize in economics in 2002 (he didn't get the prize in psychology because there isn't one).

Klein, on the other hand, has focused his attention mainly on intuition's upside by studying how experienced people, such as

➤

firefighters, nurses and managers, take consequential decisions often in extreme situations in the real world. The remarkable people whom Klein was interested in studying were those who 'knew without knowing how or why they knew'.

Given that Kahneman and Klein had very different takes on intuition, when they came together to write about intuition for *American Psychologist*, the American Psychological Association's top journal, they, and everybody else, expected them to vehemently disagree about whether people should or shouldn't go with their gut: most people thought that Klein would be for it and Kahneman would be against it.[5]

However, to everybody's surprise, this didn't happen. They famously failed to disagree because they agreed that it's the situation (they refer to it as the 'environment') that decides whether going with your gut is the right thing to do or not.

Kahneman and Klein's short answer to the question of 'When should you go with your gut?' is, 'it depends' on *both* the person (whether they have enough knowledge and experience) *and* the situation (whether it lends itself to intuitive predictions).

Some situations are right for intuition: Kahneman and Klein call them 'high-validity environments'. A high-validity environment is where there are predictable relationships between cues (things that are observable in the situation) and outcomes (what might happen in that situation). In other words, in a high-validity environment, the presence of a set of cues can (for example Melissa's symptoms) be associated with a potential outcome (sepsis). In sports, an experienced football coach who has developed a deep understanding of the game would be able to read how a game was progressing in terms of the balance of play, assess how individual players were performing in terms of their body language, attitude and energy, and make adjustments to tactics and strategy accordingly by repositioning or substituting players. The cues in terms of the balance of play and how individual players were coping enables a seasoned coach to predict potential outcomes. Intuitive prediction is possible only where there are relationships between cues and outcomes in the situation itself. If such relationships exist, then the situation has high validity and prediction is possible. However, if there aren't any, then the situation has low validity and prediction is not possible.

But the thing is that not everyone even *sees* the same cues or, even when they do see them, they may not *sense* their significance in the same way. Intuitive decision makers see cues and sense their significance intuitively without necessarily being able to explain why, instead they 'just know.'

Medicine and firefighting aren't precise sciences where Cue A predicts Outcome B precisely. In Kahneman and Klein's words, they're environments of 'fairly high validity' which makes them legitimate situations to go with your gut so long as you have familiarity with the territory and the requisite knowledge and experience. It's the fact that there are relationships between cues (for example the sight, sound and smell of a blaze) and outcomes, which makes prediction possible (for example 'If I hit this blaze with a high-velocity jet of water, it'll come under control').

In the case of Melissa's suspected sepsis, Linda noticed all the relevant cues but she didn't put them together into a bigger picture and work out in the heat of the moment that Melissa was in big trouble. This was because Linda was in unfamiliar territory. But even though Darlene saw the *same* cues as Linda, to Darlene they took on an altogether different meaning because she was in familiar territory; collectively, they made sense and set off her intuitive alarm bell. Darlene's appreciation of the totality of the situation – her 'situation awareness' – made the difference. It told her that Melissa needed urgent help.

A finely tuned situation awareness gives experienced decision makers the ability to see the bigger picture, grasp its meaning and the implications, and project ahead to what's likely to happen in the near future. This is because there's a good likelihood of there being a relationship between what the experienced decision maker sees (the cues) and what's likely to happen (the outcome).[6] But, as noted above, the same cues can mean different things to different people depending on their level of experience and how prepared they are to receive them.

Trusting your gut is a good idea in situations where you're experienced enough to spot the right cues, know what they mean and use them make predictions about outcomes. Darlene's intuitive intelligence enabled her to 'read between the lines', whereas Linda was reading literally what was 'on the page'. Darlene's anomaly detection system had been 'trained' (analogous to the way in which AI systems are trained) over a number of years to distinguish between critical and non-critical situations. The fact that intuitive anomaly detection is a behind-the-scenes process (because it's non-conscious) makes it opaque to experienced decision makers themselves: they simply know without knowing how or why they know. Klein and his colleagues used a questioning technique called 'cognitive task analysis' (CTA; developed by Robert Hoffman and others) to understand how experienced decision makers 'know without knowing'.

Takeaway

A decision-making environment has high validity if there are reliable relationships between cues and outcomes. This makes intuitive prediction possible and is a good basis for going with your gut.

Bad environments for going with your gut

The financial pages of newspapers are full of advice about which shares to sell, hold or buy. But making intuitive predictions about the ups and downs of the value of an individual company's share price is notoriously difficult. If it were easy then this information would already be reflected in the price. Daniel Kahneman and Gary Klein call this a 'low-validity environment' for using intuition. The situation is simply too noisy and too random. Forecasting whether the price will rise or fall is riven with unpredictability.[7]

Even though it's always possible to find lone voices who've made a good gut call on a stock price, a realistic implication for budding investors is that it might not be such a good idea to trust your gut feeling about the value of an individual share price.* On the other hand, it would be much wiser to trust the intuitions of an experienced firefighter or neonatal nurse, football coach or manager for that matter, in their area of expertise because even though there's still uncertainty over outcomes, they're operating in familiar territory where the validity is higher than in stock picking.

To make things more complicated, as we discovered in Part 1, the intuitive mind is a consummate pattern-recognition system, so much so that it'll sometimes see a pattern where none exists. This adds to the chances of building bad intuitions in low-validity environments. It's analogous to seeing a relationship between a cue (for example, ice cream sales that are higher in summer) and outcome (for example deaths by drowning that also are higher in summer) that doesn't exist. A spurious connection can be made between the cue, ice cream sales, and an outcome, the number of deaths by drowning. Of course there's no causal link but they both go up in the summer and down in the winter. There's a pattern, for sure, but it's a product of warm weather; there is no link between ice cream sales and deaths by drowning. To make the link between ice creams sales and death by drowning could be an example of what Joel Pearson, the author of *The Intuition Toolkit* (2024) calls a 'mis-intuition'. It's also behind superstitious behaviour; for example Serena Williams tying her shoelaces in a specific way and bouncing the ball a certain number of times before serving. The technical name for seeing connections or meaning in unrelated events is 'apophenia'. In extreme situations, it may be related to loss of contact with reality ('psychosis') and belief in psychic phenomena, but also heightened levels of creativity.[8]

---

* As we discovered in Step 2, there's some evidence to suggest that at the very highest levels, as with chess grandmasters, the most experienced and high-performing traders do sometimes trust their intuitions. So, the picture isn't as black and white as portrayed by Kahneman and Klein, but their fundamental point stands: for most people, individual stock picking is a low-validity environment for intuition.

Spotlight on intuition

Intuitions, echo chambers and black swans

Our intuitions, because they involve feelings, can have a powerful hold over us. This amplifies the danger of making intuitive predictions in low-validity environments. Because intuitions so often *feel* right – and especially if our analytical mind is complicit in concocting a story for why we *think* they're right – they make us susceptible to looking for evidence that will verify the good or bad vibe that we have about an object, person or situation.

Imagine you intuitively believe in the power of a plant-based diet to improve general health and longevity. If you sought out media information that supported your idea, focused on and only remembered positive findings about a plant-based diet and health, and sought out opinions form other plant eaters that supported the hunch that you've had all along that plant-based was the way to go, you'd be demonstrating 'confirmation bias'. This is not a good way to build intuitive muscle power: it's simply looking for evidence to support what you'd like, or want, to believe is true.

Social media platforms make the situation much worse because they use algorithms that personalise content precisely to users' preferences and feed them information that is aligned with their beliefs and values. Used undiscerningly, social media can become an echo chamber for our intuitions, be they right or wrong. Not only that, by acting as an amplifier and an echo chamber for false information, they can actually help to build bad intuitions. The fact that people appear to be largely unaware that they're being manipulated by a machine makes what's going on all the more malevolent.

We'll return to confirmation bias, and how to de-bug it, in Step 6.

Human beings aren't natural 'falsificationists': in our minds, if it *feels* right it must *be* right. This idea calls to mind the famous example given by the philosopher of science Karl Popper about the understandable inference, based on common experience, that 'all swans are white'. How many people have seen a black swan? But to falsify this claim, we shouldn't be looking for more white swans; instead, if we really wanted to test the 'all swans are white' hypothesis, we should search high and low for the one black swan that could falsify the intuition that all swans are white.[9] This is how science works: hypotheses are formulated and then exposed in experiments to the possibility of being falsified.

Going back to social media as an example, to get round this source of bias, perhaps users of social media could tweak their 'feeds' to increase the likelihood, metaphorically speaking, of a black swan being spotted, for example by seeking information from outside the orbit of their immediate interests and preferences. One of the hazards of trusting your intuition unreservedly is that the intuitive mind, being a pattern recognition system par excellence, likes to have its preferences, and sometimes its prejudices, confirmed.

Going back to validity: in low-validity environments there aren't any clear and predictable relationships between cues and outcomes because the situation is simply too noisy and turbulent. In these situations, there simply won't be any strong regularities that can be used as a basis for intuitive judgements and few, if any, learnable rules that link cues and outcomes.

We know that experts' intuition works well in environments where there are clear and predictable relationships between cues and outcomes – these are the higher validity environments that Kahneman and Klein were referring to. This is one reason the chess experts can reconstruct the board from memory and why they trust their gut. Chess is a higher validity environment than stock picking.

We also know that intuition works less well in environments where the relationships between cues and outcomes are noisy and random; this makes it much harder for a decision maker to predict outcomes on the basis of the available cues.

Long-term forecasting of major geopolitical events, such as invasions, wars, coup d'états and revolutions, is an example of a notoriously low-validity environment. Several decades ago, the eminent political scientist Philip Tetlock compared the ability of highly educated and experienced political experts to predict the outcome of major geopolitical events (for example whether there'd be a non-violent end to apartheid in South Africa, whether the Soviet Union would break up, etc.) with the predictions of novices who simply read the newspapers. Surprisingly, the experts were no better than the novices at making long-term predictions about major geopolitical events.

Does this mean that we shouldn't trust experts?

No it doesn't. But more precisely, it depends on the environment in which the expert's intuition has been acquired and in which it's being used to make a prediction or take a decision. Of course we should trust experts, up to a point and in the right situations. But Tetlock's conclusion was that the problem wasn't the experts' knowledge and credentials, which were beyond reproach, the problem was the situation in which they were trying to make predictions.

The environment in which major geopolitical events take place is simply too noisy, turbulent and random to be able to be predicted accurately. Noisy situations are hard to make sense of, let alone make predictions in, because patterns may be obscured in a morass of data or they may be non-existent in the first place. There simply may not be any pattern to be comprehended. This makes accurate intuition impossible because intuition works by pattern matching.

Kahneman and Klein's 'failure to disagree' (see the Spotlight earlier) about whether intuitions should or shouldn't be trusted rests on two fundamental questions about when, and when not, to go with your gut. First, do the observable cues support the prediction of outcomes with any degree of confidence? The cues Darlene noticed supported her prediction of Melissa's sepsis. Without any link between cues and outcomes, a situation is going to be so noisy and turbulent that trusting your intuition is going to be little better than guesswork. Second, are the rules behind the predictability of the situation learnable with experience and feedback? Major geopolitical events are notoriously difficult to predict. The rules behind them, if indeed there are any, aren't learnable, even if as the US author Mark Twain is reputed to have said: 'History doesn't repeat itself but it often rhymes.'

The bottom line is that whether going with your gut is the right thing to do or not depends on two things: the decision maker themself *and* the situation in which the decision is being taken. An analogy is cutting paper with a pair of scissors; it's only possible to cut the paper with scissors if the two blades are working together. Likewise, to take a decision using intuition requires the right person (someone with the requisite knowledge and experience) and the right situation (a situation where it's reasonable to assume that intuitive prediction is possible). Without these two conditions – right person right situation – intuition cannot 'cut through'.[10]

Takeaway

If a situation is noisy, unstructured and turbulent, then it's likely to have low validity for making predictions. This isn't a sound basis for intuitive judgement and, if intuition gets it right in such situations, it's more likely to be down to luck rather than judgement.

Intuition, uncertainty and risk

Uncertainty is at the heart of decision making in professional and personal life. Most decisions that we take, whether it's to choose between a latte or a cappuccino or which of two job offers to take, involve uncertainty to a greater or lesser extent. The outcomes are uncertain (for example 'Will the latte be better than the cappuccino?' and 'Will job A turn out to be better than job B?') and each decision involves a level of risk. But, even though they're often bracketed together and used interchangeably, 'risk' and 'uncertainty' aren't the same thing. Here's why.

If I choose to bet a significant amount of money, say £100, on throwing a three with six-sided dice, I can assess the level of risk of losing my money by making a simple calculation. The question of 'what's the chance of winning £100 by betting on throwing a three?' is solvable either by the analytical mind doing the calculation itself (dividing one by six) or by outsourcing the calculation to a machine, such as calculator (the chances of success are one in six or 16.67 per cent). Risk is where there's a known probability regarding an outcome: my chances of winning £100 by throwing three on a six-sided dice are one in six (around 17 per cent), similarly, my chance of winning the lottery is quantifiable at around 1 in 45 million.

Probability can guide us as to the likelihood of success in situations that can be quantified; for example, I buy a lottery ticket in the full knowledge that my chances of winning are slim, to say the least, and the risk of losing my money is high. But at least I know the odds. If I buy a ticket, I'm making the judgement call that the £2 gamble is worth the risk. Uncertain outcomes, on the other hand, are much harder, and sometimes impossible, to quantify; for example, Jeff Bezos could not quantity the odds of fast, free shipping being the success that it turned out to be, but he was justified in going with his gut because he was confronted by an uncertain situation *and* he was in familiar territory.

Big thinker
Frank Knight

Frank Knight (1885–1972) was Professor of Economics at the University of Chicago. He's famous for being one of the first economists to make a proper distinction between risk and uncertainty. He said that a decision is risky when the possible outcomes and the probability of their occurrence are known; for example, my decision to buy a lottery ticket is risky. A decision is uncertain when the possible outcomes are not known and neither is their probability of occurrence; for example my decision to accept my current job when it was offered to me was taken under conditions of uncertainty because I didn't know what the outcome would be – of whether it is a good decision or a bad decision – or what its probability of occurrence was at the time. 'Knightian uncertainty' is when it's not possible to put a probability on a possible outcome. Here are three insights from Frank Knight on uncertainty and intuition:

- In commenting on the use of probability risk assessment in weather forecasting Knight said: 'The farmer or the old salt [sailor] who uses no such process of analysis and measurement may often predict the weather with as much reliability [as a weather forecaster]. His processes are largely unconscious, whether [or not they are] truly intuitive or only unconsciously rational [it amounts to the same thing].'[11]

- Knight also remarked that decision making under uncertainty involves 'not reasoned knowledge, but "judgement", "common sense", and "intuition"' because the future – which is by definition novel and unpredictable – 'depends on the behaviour of an indefinitely large number of objects and is influenced by so many factors' and in using our judgement, common sense or intuition we 'infer largely from our experiences of the past'.[12]

- One way of getting better at judging and predicting isn't by always analysing things into their elements and trying to measure them but by 'educating and training our intuitive powers'.[13]

We'll never be able to understand fully, and improve, how managers actually take decisions without admitting that intuition (Knight might call this 'unconscious rationality') is one way, and sometimes the only way, of dealing with uncertainty.[14] This applies to decision making in both personal and professional life.

Decision making under conditions of risk involve known levels of chance (for example, 1 in 45 million), decision making under conditions of uncertainty is a different matter: there's no measurable probability to go on. It goes without saying that it's impossible to assign odds to many of life's most important decisions, such as which course to study, which job to take, which person to marry, which house to buy, which product or service to launch, etc.; nonetheless, we have to act. Many of life's big decisions involve decision making under uncertainty. Odds couldn't be put on the likelihood of Amazon Prime being a success, nonetheless, it was a situation in which a decision had to be taken and going with gut instinct was, for an experienced business leader in familiar territory, a legitimate thing to do.

Bezos chose to act, but *not* choosing to take a decision, whether by analysis or intuition, also can have significant consequences. These are the 'opportunity costs' of the paths not taken. If Bezos had lacked the courage to follow his intuition, the added value of Prime to Amazon's bottom line and customers' experience wouldn't have been realised. Bezos gambled on his gut instinct being right. This was a reasonable thing to do. The American poet Robert Frost wrote about this in his poem *The Road Not Taken*: 'Two roads diverged in a wood, and I – I took the one less travelled by, And that has made all the difference.' At the end of the day, while computers excel at solving well-defined puzzles, humans excel at sensing solutions to open-ended problems, uncertain situations and unknown unknowns, which takes them down the road less travelled into uncharted territories and new opportunities and discoveries.

Spotlight on intuition
Gambling with your gut

A story on the BBC news website in December 2023 was headlined 'US man uses "intuition" to win lottery six times'. Vietnam war veteran Raymond Roberts had been playing the lottery for over 20 years. Then, one day 'out of the blue', his intuition told him 'don't just buy one ticket buy *six* and use the *exact* same numbers on each ticket.' He reportedly 'felt good' about the numbers because they were a carefully concocted combination of significant birthdays and anniversaries. It paid off: Mr Roberts won over $2 million.[15]

Even though the odds of winning the UK National Lottery are known (1 in 45 million), might I be justified in going with my gut if, for example, I happen to notice some interesting cues in going about my day-to-day business; for example if I keep coming across the number seven? Perhaps this could be a sign that I should choose numbers that are multiples of seven? Would this be a wise thing to do? Undoubtedly not: it's impossible for there to be any relationship between the cues (my seeing sevens) and the outcome (of potentially winning the lottery). So, in general, would it be a good idea to trust my intuition in lottery picking? In the absence of a magical sixth sense, probably not. The outcome is random, there are no patterns to be recognised, nor are there any relationships between cues (seeing sevens) and outcomes (winning) to be learned in the first place. There's no intuitive muscle power to be built in this situation. This doesn't mean to say that it isn't worth taking the risk, it's just that intuition will have nothing to do with the outcome.

In Mr Roberts's case, there was no relationship between significant birthdays and anniversaries and the winning numbers, they just happened to come up. He admitted that he'd been 'feeling good' about and playing those same numbers for the past 20 years.[16]

One of the conundrums of intuition, given that it's not a precognitive sixth sense, is that whether trusting going with your gut was a wise thing to do can't be known before the event. Whether it was a wise thing to do can only be known *after* the fact. In this respect, a gut call is a gamble of sorts, but it's also a fine judgement based on the decision maker's honest assessment of how familiar they are with the territory, their capabilities and track record and whether the situation lends itself to going with your gut.

The chances of making a successful gut call can be improved greatly by understanding if, how and when trusting intuition is likely to work. This minimises the chances of failure and maximises the chance of success.

Decisions that involve risk are quantifiable and are solvable. As Bezos recommends, if you're faced with a decision where the risks can be quantified, then it's wise to use analytics (human beings' System 2 is good at this, but machines are even better). However, decisions that involve uncertainty where the future is unknowable and surprises happen can't be quantified in the same way. The question of what's the best thing to do in such situations can't be solved in terms of probability but it can, by the right person, at the right time and under the right conditions, be judged intuitively based on a skilful reading of the situation.

This highlights the fundamental difference between the intuitive mind and the analytical mind: the intuitive mind *senses* while the analytical mind *solves*. Many of life's biggest decisions involve a mixture both of risk and uncertainty. This means that both calculation and analysis and fine judgement and intuition are likely to have a role to play.[17] At the end of the day, good decision making isn't a trade-off between *either* analysis *or* intuition, it's a blend of *both* analysis *and* intuition, and of sensing *and* solving. The art of good decision making is deciding if, when and how to use analytical solving and intuitive sensing.

Takeaway

The art of good decision making involves knowing if and when to trust your gut and how to combine intuition (sensing) with analysis (solving) to get the best results.

Dig deeper

In their book *Radical Uncertainty*, John Kay (an Oxford Economics Professor) and Mervyn King (Governor of the Bank of England from 2003 to 2013) argue that our habit of thinking in terms of probability is falling short, has given us a 'false understanding of our power to make predictions'. They believe that this way of thinking has led to many of our current economic, social and political problems. Kay and King argue that intuition is not an irrational response that we'd be well-advised to suppress, it's a behaviour that evolution has 'honed for us' and learning has 'reinforced in us' to enable us to cope in an uncertain world.[18]

In a nutshell, when should you trust your intuition?

Intuition is a trustworthy guide in familiar territory where the relationships between the cues and outcomes are reliable, stable and learnable; this makes intuitive prediction a reliable guide for experienced decision makers.

Workout : Using a cue assessment table

1 Choose a consequential decision with which you are currently faced.
2 What *cues* are available to you to help you take the decision? Use a cue assessment table to organise your analysis (see Table 7 for the example of an employee hiring decision).

Table 7 Cue assessment table for employee hiring decision

Consequential decision: Employee hiring decision		
Cues that are available to you	**Holistic evaluation of cues**	**Action**
1 Candidate's CV 2 Candidate's performance on psychometric tests 3 Candidate's PowerPoint presentation 4 Candidate's performance at interview	Candidate has relevant qualifications and experience. Psychometric test scores were satisfactory. Candidate's PowerPoint presentation was exemplary. Candidate's responses to questions about prior employments felt evasive and unconvincing. Significant doubts warrant further investigation	Seek further information about candidate's employment history and track record, then revisit overall assessment

Fill in the cues on the blank version of the table (Table 8). Add more rows to the table as necessary.

Table 8 Blank cue assessment table

Consequential decision:		
Cues that are available to you	**Holistic evaluation of cues**	**Action**

3 What does your *holistic evaluation* (i.e. both analysis and synthesis) of all the cues altogether tell you about the decision with which you are faced?

4 What *action* will you take on the basis of your overall assessment?

5 In the employee hiring decision discussed earlier in this chapter, the 'candidate's PowerPoint presentation' cue could overshadow the other cues because the panel felt good about the candidate's PowerPoint skills. However, the panel perhaps needs to ask themselves: is the ability to do an excellent PowerPoint presentation likely to be a valid indicator of how well they will perform in the job itself?

6 Could the panel be at risk of substituting the easier-to-answer PowerPoint question for the harder-to-answer question about potential job performance?

7 Are you wedded to any of the cues in your consequential decision because you feel good about them; are they likely to be useful in their own right irrespective of what you feel about them?

8 How does this affect your overall assessment?

Notes

1 Vaughan, F. E. (1979) *Awakening Intuition*. New York: Doubleday, p. 177.

2 Greene, J. (2015) '10 years later, Amazon celebrates Prime's triumph', *The Seattle Times*, 2 February. Available online at: https://www.seattletimes.com/business/amazon/10-years-later-amazon-celebrates-primes-triumph/.

3 CNBC (2018) 'Jeff Bezos at the Economic Club of Washington', 13 September. Available online at: https://www.youtube.com/watch?v=xv_vkA0jsyo.

4 Klein, G. A. (2003) *Intuition at Work*. New York: Doubleday, pp. 7–8.

5 Kahneman, D. and Klein, G. (2009) 'Conditions for intuitive expertise: A failure to disagree', *The American Psychologist*, 64(6), 515–26.

6 Endsley, M. R. (2015) 'Situation awareness misconceptions and misunderstandings', *Journal of Cognitive Engineering and Decision Making*, 9(1), 4–32.

7   Kahneman and Klein (2009).

8   Fyfe, S., Williams, C., Mason, O. J. and Pickup, G. J. (2008) 'Apophenia, theory of mind and schizotypy: Perceiving meaning and intentionality in randomness', *Cortex*, 44(10), 1316–25.

9   Menand, L. (2005) 'Everybody's an expert', *The New Yorker*, 27 November. Available online at: https://www.newyorker.com/magazine/2005/12/05/everybodys-an-expert.

10 This is based on Herbert Simon's famous scissors metaphor: 'Human rational behaviour is shaped by a scissors whose blades are the structure of task environments and the computational capabilities of the actor.' Simon, H. (1990) 'Invariants of human behaviour', *Annual Review of Psychology*, 41, 1–19.

11 Knight, F. H. (1935) *The Ethics of Competition*. New York: Harper Brothers, p. 109

12 Rindova, V. and Courtney, H. (2020) 'To shape or adapt: Knowledge problems, epistemologies, and strategic postures under Knightian uncertainty', *Academy of Management Review*, 45(4), 787–807.

13 Frantz, R. (2004) *Two Minds: Intuition and Analysis in the History of Economic Thought*. New York: Springer, p. 104.

14 Alvares, S., Afuah, A. and Gibson, C. (2018) 'Editors' comments: Should management theories take uncertainty seriously?' *Academy of Management Review*, 43(2), 169–72.

15 BBC News (2022) 'Man uses "intuition" to win lottery six times', *BBC News*, 23 December. Available online at: https://www.bbc.co.uk/news/world-us-canada-64042271.

16 Cosic, M. (2022) 'Man uses "intuition" to win lottery six times scooping nearly $2million', *Daily Mirror*, 23 December. Available online at: https://www.mirror.co.uk/news/us-news/man-uses-intuition-win-lottery-28801766.

17 Gigerenzer, G. (2022) *How to Stay Smart in a Smart World*. London: Allen Lane, p. 40.

18 Kay, J. and King, M. (2020) *Radical Uncertainty: Decision-making for an Unknowable Future*. London: Bridge Street Press, p. 172.

step 4

Think
without thinking

'Intuition is a form of wisdom, the gift of knowing without reasoning. When you're not forced to overthink things it's amazing the clarity that emerges. But we like to convince ourselves otherwise.'

Dame Angela Ahrendts (former CEO Burberry and Senior VP Retail at Apple)[1]

- -

This chapter will help you to understand how it is sometimes possible to think without thinking by letting your intuitive mind do some of the heavy lifting.

- -

Knowing more than we can tell

The nineteenth-century German philosopher Arthur Schopenhauer, a 'big thinker' if ever there was one, believed that 'half of our thinking takes place unconsciously'.[2] This may be something of an underestimate. In trying to understand what Schopenhauer was getting at, let's begin with a mundane example.

What's the best way to learn how to ride a bike? This isn't a trick question.

The best way to learn how to ride a bike is to ride a bike.

But, if you're a bike rider and had to *explain* to someone else how to ride a bike, what would you say? This might be a trick question.

A bike rider wouldn't, in all likelihood, be able to *tell* someone else how to ride a bike. It would be much easier to *show* them. As far as bike riding goes, many people can do it but can't explain how. An instructor can tell you how, for example, to use the brakes (this is called 'explicit knowledge' because it's out there and can be put into words). But it's only through experience that you get to learn how, for example, to brake effectively on the road. Plus, it's hard to explain how you do so in words because the knowledge is 'tacit' as opposed to explicit (more on this later).

The long and the short of it is that bike riders *know* more than they can *tell*. This principle extends to many other aspects of skilled performance: Klein's firefighters and neonatal nurses knew more about firefighting and sick infants than they could tell; experienced hedge-fund traders who go with their gut and return better-than-average P&L know more than they can tell; Jeff Bezos knew more than he could tell about whether or not Amazon Prime was likely to work as did Steve Jobs about the potential of the graphical user interface – they all 'just knew'.

Anyone who's reached the level of 'unconscious competence' knows more than they can tell. Anyone who's successfully used their intuition to solve a problem or take a decision also knows more than they can tell.

One thing that bike riders, firefighters, neonatal nurses, hedge-fund traders and CEOs have in common is that they rely on a kind of knowledge that's hard to put into words but that turns out to be not only highly effective but invaluable in practice. It's called 'tacit knowledge' (from the Latin *tacere*, meaning 'silent'). Tacit knowledge is the stuff that we know but we find hard, and sometimes impossible, to articulate. It can't be captured in a manual or a checklist.[3]

Big thinker

Michael Polanyi

Michael Polanyi (1891–1976), the Hungarian-British 'polymath' and all-round authority in chemistry, economics, philosophy and many other subjects besides, coined the phrase 'we know more than we can tell' in his most famous book *The Tacit Dimension* (1966).[4] It seems as though great minds do indeed think alike: Polanyi's idea fits nicely with Schopenhauer's claim that half our thinking takes place unconsciously. Here are three quotes from Polanyi on intuition:

- 'Intuition can't be written down, it can only be transmitted by doing'.[5]

- 'For genius-level scientists like Einstein, intuition is "a work-a-day skill for scientific guessing with a chance of guessing right"'[6] (more about this later in the discussion of the 'standard model of creativity').

- 'Intuition is "*the* fundamental power of the mind".'[7]

Polanyi's view was that a novice develops intuition by watching and working with an expert. This is how knowledge gets transferred from one mind to another. Some people think it's the only way. A good way to develop intuitive muscle power is to find a role model who's an intuitive expert whom you can emulate, and who can put you back on the right path if you go astray.

In the world of work, call-centre employees are trained to handle calls using checklists and protocols. After a while, the protocol becomes habituated to the extent that the employee doesn't need to refer to the checklist anymore; their call handling 'action script' or 'recipe' becomes second nature to them. In this respect, they have automated expertise. They could tell you what they do and how they do it, if asked the right questions.

But consider the following vignette in which an experienced call-centre agent receives a seemingly genuine call from an apparently disgruntled customer:

Emma (experienced call centre agent):	Good morning, Liam. My name is Emma. How can I help you today?
Liam (apparently disgruntled customer, clearing his throat):	Hello. I've just had the shock of my life. I've checked my credit card statement and I've been charged £1,500 by a high-end store in London's West End for, um, a purchase that I know nothing about it. Well I guess someone's stolen my card details and probably gone on a spending spree at my expense. I'd like you to cancel it immediately please.
Emma:	Thank you, Liam. I can understand how you must feel. I'm sure we can sort this out. Bear with me one moment and I'll bring up your account details and have a look at what's happened.
Liam (while waiting for account details to load):	I have to say, um, this is outrageous. As if I can afford to shop at these kinds of places on my wages. It's just not the kind of thing I do. Somebody's obviously got hold of my card details. I think you need to tighten up your security. I'm surprised you don't bother to double check when people are spending so much money. It all sounds way too lax.

At this point, the alarm bells start to sound for Emma. She's noticed not only Liam's belligerent and offended demeanour, but there's something else hard to pin down in his tone of voice. Armed with this hunch, she decides to dig deeper.

Emma:	If you don't mind waiting, Liam, I'll just go back over your account history. That might shed some light on the problem.
Liam:	Well, okay but, um, I haven't got all day.

Sure enough, Emma notices a small number of significant transactions at high-end retail stores in Paris and Milan. This contradicts Liam's claim of never making any significant purchases.

Emma (inquisitively):	Liam, I've just noticed some older transactions on your account for purchases for several hundred euros made at a couple of high-end stores in Paris and Milan, and you settled your account without any problems. I wonder, would you mind if I asked if you can remember these transactions?
Liam (defensively):	Ah, well … now you come to mention it, I might, um, have bought a few things, but it's so long ago. Really, I'd appreciate it if we got to the bottom of this as I have to get back to work.
Emma (knowingly):	Yes, of course, Liam. I'm sure it won't take a moment longer. Perhaps if I could ask you to cast your mind back and provide some more information about these older transactions before we get on to the most recent one, that might help?

At this point, Liam realises that he's been lumbered and starts to backtrack.

Liam: Well actually, I remember now. I did make those purchases when I was on a couple of business trips and, um, now you come to mention it I had another one recently for around £1,500 which slipped my mind completely. It was a present for my partner.

Emma: That's perfectly understandable Liam, it happens all the time. I hope your partner was happy with such an expensive gift! Anyway, now that we've got to the bottom of this one, I'll make a note of it on your account in case anything like this ever happens again.

Liam: Okay Emma, thank you.

Emma: Is there anything else, Liam, that I can help you with?

Liam: No, that's all for now. Thank you for all your help.

Emma: You're welcome, Liam. And remember if you have any more questions don't hesitate to give us a call. We aim to please. You have a great day!

This vignette illustrates how something else can happen as a result of learning from experience. In certain situations, for example dealing with out-of-the-ordinary situations that can't always be captured in a checklist, there are likely to be certain manoeuvres that an experienced call handler can perform but that are hard for them to put into words. They 'just know'. Their intuition helps them to build customer empathy and rapport, but it also helps them to deal with surprises, stops them being wrong-footed in difficult situations and, as in the Liam and Emma vignette, detect the whiff of a potential fraudster.

This story aligns with research in forensic psychology that indicates that lies can be detected more accurately when less-conscious intuitive mental processes (rather than more conscious deliberative mental processes) are used. It suggests that intuitive lie detection may be a fundamental capacity of the human mind that evolved for 'deception detection'.[8]

Reflecting on it afterwards, Emma sensed something in Liam's demeanour and tone that put her on high alert. When asked to pin it down, she said that she gave him the benefit of the doubt at first, but there was something else that convinced her that he was trying to con her. This is why she dug a little deeper. Experienced call handlers, like the fictitious Emma, know more about how to handle tricky situations than they can tell.

But if tacit knowledge can't be spoken or written down, how can it be passed on from expert to novice?

The best way for a novice call handler to learn from an intuitive call handler, and hence gain access to their tacit knowledge, would be by observing them, practising what they've witnessed themselves and getting feedback on their performance from someone who knows.

The best way to make the journey from novice to expert is by being in 'touching distance' of an expert, whether that's riding a bike, handling calls, fighting fires or saving sick babies. The learning process itself has four stages: having an experience; reflecting on the experience; drawing conclusions from the reflections; applying the reflections (the lessons learned) to similar experiences next time around.

This is called the 'experiential learning cycle'.[9] Wheeling around this cycle builds intuition. Over time, and with good coaching and timely and accurate feedback, the novice climbs to the expert level and eventually arrives at the stage of being unconsciously competent.

Experience, when properly managed, is the best way to build intuitive muscle power. But for it to work well, three things need to be in place:

1 *The experiences themselves need to be stretching.* It's no good just sticking to the things you can already do well; that would be like going to the gym and using the same piece of equipment for a whole workout – you'd have great biceps but weak quads.

2 *There needs to be support from an expert.* It's like being coached in tennis or golf or by a personal trainer in the gym – your mistakes get spotted and remedied much more quickly with a coach than learning by yourself through trial and error.

3 *The learner needs get feedback.* To be effective, feedback needs to be timely, the learner needs to be told what they're doing right and wrong, and what they need to do to improve.

Intuitive muscle power is built up as a result of the right kind of experiences, in the right circumstances and with the right type of support. The eminent social psychologist Seymour Epstein referred to System 1, or the intuitive mind, as the 'experiential system' because he saw one of its main purposes as to learn from experience[10] and build intuitive muscle power.

Spotlight on intuition
Practice is 'the name of the game'

The time that it takes to become an intuitive expert who can reliably and justifiably trust their gut depends on how complex the task is. For riding a bike, it can take a few hours to become reasonably competent; to become a concert pianist, as we discovered in Step 2, takes around 10,000 hours of intensive practice, plus it helps, in this case, to have big hands (the great Russian composer and pianist, Sergei Rachmaninov, could span 13 notes on the keyboard).

One of the founders of the Swedish pop group Abba, Björn Ulvaeus, recognised the contribution that intense learning had on developing his song-writing 'muscle power'. He spent a large part of his teenage years listening over and over again to The Beatles' records; he's convinced this was instrumental in his hit song-writing journey. In an interview with the *Financial Times*, Ulvaeus said: 'They've [Beatles' songs] been lingering in your subconscious in some form ever since you heard them for the first time. You could say that you've been "trained" by them.'[11] Abba is one of the most successful pop groups of all time with hits such as 'Mama Mia', 'Dancing Queen' and of course 'The Name of the Game'.

Skilled performance at the expert level is 'non-conscious'; it's hard to put into words and isn't available to those who haven't had the right amount of experience. One of intuition's Big thinkers, Daniel Kahneman, said that we all perform feats of intuitive expertise many times each day; it's how we 'get by' day in day out. With the right kind of experience, coaching, practice and feedback, complex skills – such as fighting a fire, saving a sick baby's life, writing pop songs, playing the piano, giving a lecture, call handling and hedge-fund trading – become 'programmed' into the unconscious to the extent that expert performers, who were once novices themselves, can't explain how they do what they do. Their learnings have become habituated into intuitions which gives them the ability to respond quickly and, most of the time accurately, without knowing how or why.

Spotlight on intuition
The intelligence of the unconscious

The term 'unconscious' refers to mental processes that are outside of awareness.* The American Psychological Association defines the unconscious as the region of the psyche that contains 'repressed impulses'. Even though they're not accessible, these impulses, which may sometimes come with unpleasant connotations, can have negative effects on thoughts and behaviour via various desires and drives, impulses and urges.[12]

In this dark, Freudian perspective, consciousness is the tip of a mental iceberg where primitive and animalistic irrational urges rage and fester beneath the surface. They manifest outwardly in dreams and slips of the tongue ('Freudian slips') and cause all sorts of issues in our emotional and social lives.

But the unconscious has a bright side as well. Our unconscious mind influences thoughts and behaviour positively in ways that are beneficial. This alternative view of the unconscious is sometimes referred to as the 'adaptive unconscious'. The technical term 'adaptive' in psychology means 'of benefit to the organism by helping it to survive and thrive in its environment'. A lot of what goes on in the human mind, as Schopenhauer claimed, occurs outside of conscious awareness; by so doing, it quite naturally improves decision making without any sinister connotations of repression.[13]

The mental processing that goes on in the adaptive (or intelligent) unconscious is an aspect of a system that's been

---

* According to Harvard Medical School, professional fields such as psychiatry, psychology and neuroscience tend to use the word 'unconscious' rather than 'subconscious'. Freud himself used both 'subconscious' and 'unconscious' 'interchangeably from the outset'. From here on, I'll use the term *unconscious* rather than *subconscious*, see: https://www.health.harvard.edu/blog/unconscious-or-subconscious-20100801255.

designed by nature to function with peak efficiency. It means we're able to carry out high-level complex mental work in two parallel modes: one that's conscious, verbal and analytical; and the other that's non-conscious, non-verbal and intuitive. The two modes complement each other. One 'senses' while the other 'solves'. This makes perfect sense.

The eminent German psychologist Gerd Gigerenzer said that the unconscious mind's efficiency and effectiveness is a result of three important things about the human brain and how it works:

1 Our attention can only focus on one thing at a time, that's why we find mental multitasking difficult, for example it's impossible to count backwards and say the alphabet at the same time.

2 Once a process becomes unconscious, it can't interfere with our attention; this is fortunate because it frees up scarce mental resources for higher priority tasks, such as compiling a spreadsheet, writing an email, having a difficult conversation, etc.

3 Our brain has evolved to perform as many tasks as possible unconsciously and intuitively – this is why we sometimes know without knowing how or why we know.

This is also why Gigerenzer refers to intuition as 'unconscious intelligence'[14] and is probably why Schopenhauer's claim that 'half of our thinking' is unconscious is an underestimate.[15]

One of the ideas behind the concept of unconscious intelligence is that certain types of complex, higher-level mental work (for example playing chess, taking strategic business decisions, saving sick babies, deciding whether or not to accept a job offer, choosing a partner, etc.) can be performed by the intuitive mind. This helps the human brain, to use the technical jargon, 'optimise the use of scarce mental resources'. Using a computer analogy: it frees up processing capacity so that the analytical mind doesn't have to do all the hard work, and it can get on with problems that require authentication, clarification, computation, explanation, justification, optimisation, rationalisation, reconciliation, resolution and validation since these are the things it excels at.

> ## Takeaway
>
> With the right kind of experience, coaching, practice and feedback, much of the knowledge that's used to take decisions on a daily basis becomes 'programmed' into the intuitive mind. This knowledge is tacit and unconscious and therefore can't interfere with attention and take up brain space.

Taking smarter decisions by thinking less

Imagine that you're faced with the decision of buying a complex video camera with lots of features costing around £500. Would it be better to deliberate long and hard or simply go with your gut?

Now imagine that you're faced with the decision of buying a bottle of shampoo costing around £2.50. Would it be better to simply go with your gut, or deliberate long and hard?

The answer, as we shall see, is not only surprising; it's contrary to common sense.

The question of whether it always pays to think long and hard when solving problems and taking decisions intrigued the Dutch psychologist Ap Dijksterhuis. He and his colleagues conducted a series of remarkable experiments that suggest it might be possible to take smarter decisions by thinking less.

Dijksterhuis's theory is based on an idea that's by now familiar to us, namely that there are two fundamental modes of thinking. He refers to them as 'conscious thought', which has limited capacity and works, to use a computer analogy, by 'serial' processing;

and 'unconscious thought' which has a broad 'bandwidth' and works by 'parallel' processing. Conscious thought isn't better than unconscious thought or vice versa. They're just different; they both can work well, it's just that they do so under different circumstances.

In one experiment, Dijksterhuis and his colleagues investigated levels of satisfaction among buyers of various consumer items depending on how much they deliberated, in other words depending on whether they'd used conscious or unconscious thought in their decisions. The researchers compared people's satisfaction in choosing a simple item (such as the £2.50 bottle of shampoo) versus a complex item (such as the £500 video camera) in terms of whether they deliberated long and hard (conscious thought) or simply went with their gut (unconscious thought). Contrary to expectations, people who didn't think long and hard about their choices were more satisfied with their selection of the complex item (for example the video camera) than the people who thought long and hard about it. For the simple items, the pattern was reversed: people who thought longer and harder about the choice of shampoo were more satisfied than those who didn't.

Similar results were found when people were asked to choose between two types of car: one that had four features and one that had twelve. The features included mileage, handling, boot size, colours, newness, leg room, sunroof, aftersales service, sound system, cupholders and environmental friendliness. As anyone who's ever purchased a car will testify, in this situation, there's a lot going on and a lot of information to process. While four features are manageable by conscious thought, twelve features will overload conscious thought because twelve exceeds the capacity of the working memory (it breaks the '7±2' items rule for working memory capacity). The results, which echoed those of shampoo/video camera experiment, are shown in Figure 9. The conscious thinkers made a better choice of car with four features; the unconscious thinkers made the better choice of car with twelve features.

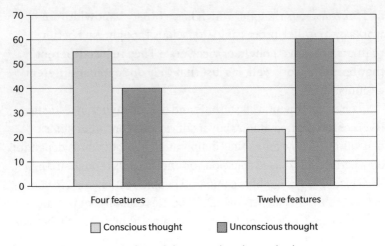

Figure 9 Percentage of participants who chose the best car as a function of complexity of decision (four versus twelve features) and mode of thinking (conscious versus unconscious)

Source: Dijksterhuis, A., Bos, M. W., Nordgren, L. F. and Van Baaren, R. B. (2006) 'On making the right choice: The deliberation-without-attention effect', *Science*, 311(5763), 1005–7.

Dijksterhuis came up with the unconscious thought theory (UTT) to explain what he thought might be going on:

- Unconscious thought has greater processing capacity than conscious thought: this makes it better suited to deal with complex problems and fits neatly with the idea of the intuitive mind (System 1) being a parallel processing system.

- Deliberately thinking about something requires the use of working memory: as we know, working memory is constrained by the information processing bottleneck of seven items plus or minus two; the intuitive mind, on the other hand, doesn't have the same limit and it can handle a heavier workload.

- Conscious processing concentrates on things that happen to be the focus of our attention: as a result, it overlooks or discounts things that are in our peripheral vision. It's analogous to looking for our lost keys under the nearest streetlamp because that's where the brightest light happens to be.[16] This is not a good way to find your lost keys or to take complex decisions or solve perplexing problems.

This could explain why, in another experiment, Dijksterhuis and his colleagues found that people who worked hard on generating novel solutions to problems (for example think of as many uses as you can for a paper clip, a brick, etc.) came up with ideas that were less creative than people who were distracted deliberately and forced into an unconscious thinking mode; for example by doing an anagram that fully occupied their working memory. Unconscious thought, by looking in places that weren't 'under the streetlight' so to speak, helped them to think outside the box.

The good news from all of this is that, by allowing the intuitive mind to do some of the heavy lifting, it may actually be possible to 'think without thinking' and hence become smarter by thinking less.[17]

Big thinkers

Ap Dijksterhuis and Madelijn Strick

Ap Dijksterhuis and Madelijn Strick are two Dutch psychologists who, in the early 2000s, (along with other colleagues) shed new light on the power of thinking without thinking. They called their theory 'unconscious thought theory' (UTT) and their hypothesis the 'deliberation without attention' hypothesis. They did lots of lab work with student participants and the results were published in prestigious scientific journals such as *Science* (the premier peer-reviewed journal of the American Association for the Advancement of Science). Here are some thoughts from Dijksterhuis and Strick on unconscious thought and intuition:

- 'The outcome of unconscious thought is intuition, the inner conviction, gut feeling, or hunch that something is the way it is without (yet) knowing exactly why.'[18]

- 'By appointing a goal to the unconscious, one can to some extent steer intuitive processes.'[19]
- 'Intuition excels under circumstances where lots of information has to be taken into account.'[20]

Dijksterhuis and Strick's hypothesis is significant, not least because it goes against the idea that the unconscious mind is dumb or stupid. Unconscious thought can be both efficient and effective even when – or perhaps especially when – making complex decisions (such as which car to buy) and dealing with high-level mental tasks (such as whether or not go with the untested idea of a loyalty programme based on fast, free shipping) in uncertain situations.

An important point that sometimes gets overlooked (the second in Dijksterhuis and Strick's list above) is that it's not simply distraction that kickstarts unconscious thought. Unconscious thought can be 'goal-directed'; in other words, the intuitive mind can be 'told' in advance that a choice needs to be made or a problem needs to be solved, for example the night before we intend working on the problem. Once it's been put on alert, the intuitive mind gets to work behind the scenes. When it's done its 'homework', it communicates what it thinks we ought to do as gut feeling, hunch or vibe and sometimes as an insight or 'eureka' moment.†

Takeaway

Intuition is an outcome of unconscious thought; how productive it is depends on the situation and the unconscious thinker's level of expertise.

---

† Not surprisingly, given its contentious nature, UTT has been subjected to a fair amount of critical scrutiny. For a comment on the contrary voices see: https://www.scientificamerican.com/article/unconscious-thought-not-so-smart-after-all1/.

Illuminating experiences

Why did a leading thinker of the German post-enlightenment, Artur Schopenhauer – who as a philosopher we might think of as the personification of the power of the intellect – believe that half of our thinking takes place unconsciously?

The experience that led him to this remarkable conclusion is likely to be familiar to many of us. In Schopenhauer's own words:

'I have familiarized myself with the factual data of a problem; I do not think about it again, yet often a few days later the answer to the problem will come into my mind entirely from its own accord; the operation which has produced it, however, remains as much a mystery to me as that of an adding-machine.'[21]

Schopenhauer referred to this process as 'unconscious rumination' – a chewing over of the problem by the unconscious mind while the conscious minds gets on with other things. It's a phenomenon that has fascinated people over the centuries. The first recorded, and undoubtedly most famous, episode is the 'eureka moment' of the third century BC Greek mathematician and scientist Archimedes.

Archimedes, who lived in the Greek colony of Syracuse in Sicily, is reputed to have been commanded by King Hiero II to work out the volume of an elaborate crown made of precious metals in order to be able to calculate its density.

The back story is that the king thought his metalsmith had adulterated what was supposed to be a crown of pure gold with cheaper silver in order to cheat him. Hiero, who had a reputation as a tyrant, needed to find out so that he could mete out the necessary punishment. Archimedes' challenge was to work out the crown's volume, and therefore its density, without pummelling it into a regular block which would have allowed its length and breadth to be measured easily but would have destroyed the beautiful crown.

The story goes that, having reached an impasse with the problem, Archimedes was taking a bath one day and happened to notice the level of the water rising slowly and then spilling over the lip of the bathtub as he immersed himself. The amount of water being displaced was equal to the volume of Archimedes' body that was under water. It's called the principle of displacement and is still used to this day in mathematics and engineering.

Out of the blue, the solution to the problem became immediately obvious to Archimedes: by immersing the crown in a vessel filled with water and measuring the amount of water it displaced he would know precisely what its volume was and therefore could calculate its density.‡ Archimedes is reputed to have leapt from his bath and run naked through the streets proclaiming 'Eureka!', meaning 'I have found it!'.

While Archimedes was distracted from his pressing problem, his unconscious mind was nevertheless on the alert and actively looking for a solution while his conscious mind was occupied with other things. It's a familiar phenomenon that most of us have experienced ourselves or at least heard of in other people. According to creativity researcher David Perkins, taking a mental time-out by walking the dog, going for a run, taking a bath, etc. not only restores mental energy it also creates a space for what he calls 'fertile forgetting' of assumptions that might have been roadblocks on the way to finding a solution.[22]

Another name for Archimedes' eureka, or 'light bulb', moment is an 'insight'. Insights are arrived at typically after we've reached an impasse and allowed our perplexing problem to incubate unconsciously. After a period of thinking without thinking, the solution often unexpectedly and miraculously pops into our heads.

The Archimedes story prompted the great English intellectual and social reformer of the late nineteenth and early twentieth century, Graham Wallas (who was also one of the founders of the prestigious London School of Economics) to study similar stories from mathematical and scientific discovery. He looked to the first-hand

‡Density is weight divided by volume (e.g. grams per cubic metre). The density of gold (19.32 g/cm³) is almost twice that of silver (10.49 g/cm³).

accounts of geniuses such as the French mathematician Henri Poincaré and the German physicist Hermann von Helmholtz. Wallas published his ideas in a book called *The Art of Thought* in 1926, which was as much about unconscious thought as it was about conscious thought.

Wallas was one of the first big thinkers to recognise how important unconscious thought is in high-level mental work. He recommended that, when we hit a mental roadblock, we should think about things other than our perplexing problem, or better still, that we 'rest from any form of conscious thought' whatsoever. Wallas's theory has become the standard four-stage model of creative problem solving in psychology:

1 *Preparation:* deep immersion into a problem, for example Natalie's team of software developers have been tasked with creating a new food delivery social media app. They brainstorm ideas, conduct market research, etc. but eventually hit a brick wall.

2 *Incubation:* having reached an impasse, Natalie suggests they put the problem to one side; team members take a break from actively thinking about the project by doing another task, taking a time-out, socialising, going to the gym, etc.

3 *Illumination:* the 'aha' or 'eureka' moment when insight happens; Natalie is out walking in the park with her partner when she suddenly comes up with an idea that will set their app apart from competitors. This is her eureka moment.

4 *Verification:* the more arduous task of working through the solution, for example the idea for the app is shared with the team, discussed, analysed, refined and implemented.

Preparation and verification are the 90 per cent that Thomas Edison was referring to when he said that, 'Genius is 10 per cent inspiration and 90 per cent perspiration.' Having arrived at the insight, the problem solver, like Archimedes, can literally see the solution to the problem that's been perplexing them (Figure 10).

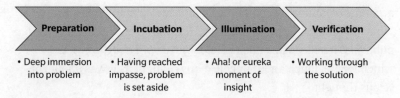

Preparation	Incubation	Illumination	Verification
• Deep immersion into problem	• Having reached impasse, problem is set aside	• Aha! or eureka moment of insight	• Working through the solution

Figure 10 The standard (four-stage) model of creativity

Even though the insight seems to come out of the blue, it's actually the product of intense, but unconscious, mental work. This often happens when the problem solver takes a step back, has a period of mental relaxation, either deliberately or by being distracted from the problem.

Wallas's model (Figure 10) fits with Dijksterhuis's unconscious thought theory: hard mental labour is sometimes best delegated to the unconscious mind, typically by switching attention to something else or 'sleeping on it'.

A helpful hint for problem solvers is that unconscious thought can be 'goal-directed'. For example, before he went to bed, the Pulitzer prize winning US author Norman Mailer used to tell his unconscious mind that he'd be at his desk writing the next day. By setting his unconscious mind some homework, Mailer was deliberately instructing it to do the necessary 'prep'. When the actor Dame Judi Dench works on learning a script, she needs to be distracted by busying herself ('play cards, go for a swim, anything') in order to 'leave it to my subconscious and trust that the internal engine is making adjustments and processing everything' and let it do the work.[23] To get the maximum benefit from sleeping on a problem, it's a good idea to deliberately set some homework for your unconscious mind while giving your conscious mind a reprieve.

In business, there are plenty of examples of eureka moments that have driven business innovation and success. 3M's ubiquitous Post-It Notes were the product of the serendipitous coming together of two things: the frustration of a 3M scientist, Art Fry, at his page markers constantly falling out of his hymn book at Sunday services; and a non-sticky glue invented by another 3M scientist, Spencer Silver, which was a solution wating for a problem to come along.

The problem and its solution came together in Fry's epiphany: one Sunday, he suddenly saw a practical use for Silver's purely speculative invention when he had a light bulb moment for using it to create the ubiquitous yellow stickies as bookmarks for his hymn book. The rest is history: Post-It Notes are now available in more than 150 countries and altogether there are thousands of Post-It products.

Spotlight on intuition
Insight and the brain

Researchers have discovered a 'hot spot' in the brain that 'lights up' whenever we have an Archimedes-type moment. In a series of groundbreaking experiments, they wired up their participants to an EEG (electroencephalograph) machine, gave them word puzzles where they had to come up with one word that connects together three seemingly unrelated words, and monitored brain activity to see what happened when the solution popped into participants' heads.

For example: what word connects 'fish', 'mine', and 'rush'?[§] The answer is in the footnote below.

What typically happens is that the answer isn't obvious immediately but, through a neurological process known as 'spreading activation', the connection is eventually made and the linking word is found suddenly. Spreading activation takes time: to get to the eureka moment can take seconds or minutes, depending on the difficulty of the puzzle. It's the familiar phenomenon of having a nagging problem and the solution just popping into your head when you're least expecting it.

When the connection is made, the problem solver experiences a 'light bulb' moment. Light bulb moments are insights, not intuitions.

➤

---

§ The connecting word is: 'gold'. These are called 'remote association tests' (RATs) because the words are related but the links between them are remote and hence not immediately obvious.

By monitoring the brain's electrical activity using EEG, and blood flow using fMRI scanners, the researchers located a sudden burst of high-frequency electrical activity, known as 'gamma waves', in the anterior superior temporal gyrus (aSTG) of the brain's right temporal lobe. The aSTG is just above the right ear (Figure 11).

The researchers concluded that the right hemisphere is good at coming up with far-removed associations, while the left hemisphere is good at coming up with near-neighbour associations. This could be one explanation for the idea that creativity is somehow linked to the right hemisphere. It's worth remembering, though, that insight and intuition are different: while insight might happen in the right hemisphere, intuition isn't confined to the right side of the brain.

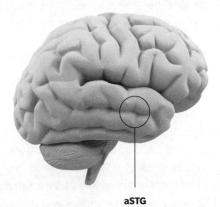

aSTG

Figure 11 Approximate location of the anterior superior temporal gyrus (aSTG)

Anna Tsekhmister/Shutterstock

There are clear links to innovation in business. Creativity involves making novel and remote connections – Steve Jobs called it 'joining the dots' – and thinking outside the box. Neuroscientists call it the 'neural signature' of the 'aha!' moment and 'almost literally the spark of insight', pinpointing not only the likely origin of our own creative ideas but also many of humanity's greatest achievements.[24] Jobs also said that to join the dots we need to have the dots in the first place. By this he meant that not only do we need to be immersed deeply in our field, but we also need to be open to new ideas as well.

There may also be links to a recently discovered network in the brain called the 'default mode network' (DMN). The DMN is most active when the brain's executive network (EN), which is the system that's hard at work when we're consciously focused on a mental task, is at rest. In the words of one of the leading experts on the DMN, Marcus Raichle of the Washington University School of Medicine, it's associated with 'relaxed states of quiet repose' such as 'daydreaming' and 'mind wandering'.[25] The DMN may be the brain's 'visionary network' that evolved to link seemingly unrelated ideas together in order to come up with creative solutions to problems.[26] Researchers have also found that mindfulness meditation training (MMT, which involves consciously engaging in a 'state of present moment, non-judgemental attendance') increases interconnectivity in the DMN which might help to explain the beneficial effects of MMT on creativity.[27]

It's well-known that Steve Jobs was a meditator. In his biography he's quoted as saying that, 'If you just sit and observe, you will see how restless your mind is. If you try to calm it, it only makes it worse, but over time it does calm, and when it does, there's room to hear more subtle things.' Jobs was convinced that this is when 'your intuition starts to blossom and you start to see things more clearly and be in the present more. Your mind just slows down, and you see a tremendous expanse in the moment. You see so much more than you could see before.'[28]

Creativity comes from both depth and breadth of knowledge and experience. Creative geniuses often have a range of interests that have been overshadowed by their main achievements: Einstein was an accomplished violinist; Leonardo da Vinci was highly skilled in painting as well as in astronomy, physics and biology; Nikola Tesla was a poet as well and being famous as an engineer and scientist; the Nobel Prize-winning physicist Richard Feynman was a proficient percussionist; and Jobs was into calligraphy, Japanese culture, Buddhism and above all simplicity.[29]

Intuition and insight are related in that they both involve unconscious mental work (thinking without thinking) but their outcomes are different. Here's why:

- Insight involves certainty because the solution is visible and obvious and you get to know more or less right away if it'll work or not.

- Intuitions, on the other hand, are more intangible, more of a sense that something might work, and are much harder to pin down; they give a sense of direction towards a solution.

- Intuition is essentially a judgement because the outcome of going with your gut can't be known at the time.

- Whether or not going with your gut was a wise decision only becomes known after the fact.

Graham Wallas, whose work we met earlier and who came up with the four-stage standard model of creativity, also wrote about the relationship between insight and intuition. He found that before the illuminative moment sparks into life something quite curious sometimes happens: problem solvers often have an inkling that something is *about* to happen. It's as though their unconscious mind is putting them on notice that the solution was 'in the mail'. Wallas quoted one thinker as saying: 'I often know that the solution is coming, though I don't know what the solution will be.' Wallas called these experiences 'intimations':** 'dim feelings' and 'vague impressions' that come through as 'queer, strange, funny or disconcerting' sensations.[30] This is like Oprah Winfrey's 'still, small voice' that she uses to help confirm her direction of travel.

A number of notable scientists have reported experiencing these 'faint signals' that they take as pointers for the right direction. They're faint in that they're hard to pick up on, but they can be a strong sign that the problem solver is on the right track to a major breakthrough. For example, one Nobel Prize-winning scientist in medicine (Michael S. Brown, 1985) felt that he and his team seemed

---

** From the Lain word *intimare* meaning 'to announce'.

to be guided spookily by an 'invisible hand' that pointed them in the right direction:

'As we did our work, I think, we almost felt at times that there was almost a hand guiding us. Because we would go from one step to the next, and somehow we would know which was the right way to go. And I really can't tell how we knew that.'

Another famous Nobel Prize winner, this time in economics, said: 'I consider that I have good intuition and good judgment on what problems are worth pursuing and what lines of work are worth doing ... [and these] come through maybe 80 per cent of the time.'[31]

Intimations are a vague feeling of a mind seething and simmering over a perplexing problem. They're fragile and faint; as such they're worth listening out for and listening to. But, in being coaxed from the twilight of subconsciousness into the full daylight of consciousness, intuitive insights need to be shielded from unwelcome interruptions.

A classic example of the power of intimations and the perils of unwelcome interruptions is the eighteenth-century poet Samuel Taylor Coleridge's unwelcome visitor, the 'person from Porlock': The story goes that while composing his famous poem *Kubla Khan*, Coleridge awoke from three hours of 'profound sleep' with 'a distinct recollection of the whole [poem]' but at that very moment was unfortunately disturbed by a 'person on business from Porlock'.[††] After having been detained for over an hour, he found, to his 'mortification, that though he still retained some vague and dim recollection' of the vision, most of it had 'passed away like the images on the surface of a stream onto which a stone has been cast'.[32] Coleridge's lesson to us all is that in moments of intense mental work privacy is well worth protecting, and light bulb moments should be captured before they disappear or get displaced by the unwelcome 'visitor from Porlock'.

---

†† Coleridge was recuperating in a lonely farmhouse in between the villages of Linton and Porlock in southwest England.

Takeaway

Intuitions aren't insights; insight 'sees' the solution to a problem, whereas intuition 'senses' the solution. Intimations come before insights and may signal the right direction of travel; intimations are creative intuitions.

Dig deeper

John Kounios and Mark Beeman's *The Eureka Factor* (2015) 'unlocks the mechanisms behind intuitive flashes and inspiration'. Gary Klein's *Seeing What Others Don't* (2013) explains when, why and how insights are formed.

In a nutshell, let your intuitive mind do the thinking

Intuition and insight are both products of unconscious thought. However, intuitions aren't insights; insight 'sees' the solution to a problem, whereas intuition 'senses' the solution. Intimations come before insights and may signal a direction of travel towards a breakthrough.

Workout 1: Doing without doing

1 How do you deal with those perplexing problems that often lead to a mental roadblock? Do you hammer away at them in the hope that they'll relent? An alternative might be to just let go of the problem, at least for a little while.
2 Here are some tried-and-tested tips and techniques to declutter your mind and mental relaxation (Table 9).

Table 9 Tools for thinking without thinking[33]

Declutter	Switch to a completely different and perhaps more mundane work task, such as filing an expense claim or filling out a timesheet; switch to a non-work task by doing an anagram or sudoku puzzle, playing a computer game, doodling or switch off completely by daydreaming, reading a newspaper and chatting with a colleague, friend or family member
Relax	Give your whole self a timeout by taking a walk, getting a change of scenery, listening to music, doing breathing exercises, mindfulness mediation or simply sleeping on the problem
Sleep	Never underestimate the importance of sleep; it helps with 'fixation forgetting' by flushing out stale ideas that might have become roadblocks to out-of-the-box thinking. Sleep is for dreaming; the zone in between waking and sleep has proven to be a place where novel connections can be made
Capture	It's also a good idea to keep a notepad or phone by your bedside or with you when you're taking a timeout so that when an idea does come you have some way to capture it
Detach	Beware of 'persons from Porlock'; when you're doing important work, create the conditions so that you're more isolated and less likely to be disturbed. The James Bond writer Ian Fleming is famous for writing his books in a fortnight; the secret of success was the rule of 'forced boredom'; Fleming would isolate himself in a mundane room, in a place that offered no distractions, which forced him to focus only on his writing (this is an example of shaping your environment to bring about a desired outcome)

3 Giving your brain a 'bypass' using these and the other techniques will help you in creating the space for intuition to have its say and for creative connections and insights to emerge from your unconscious.

Notes

1 Ahrendts, A. (2013) 'The power of human energy', TEDx Hollywood. Available online at: https://www.youtube.com/watch?v=mZNlN31hS78.

2 Schopenhauer, A. (1970) *Essays and Aphorisms* (R. J. Hollingdale, trans.). London: Penguin. (Original work published 1851) cited in Dijksterhuis, A. and Nordgren, L. F. (2006) 'A theory of unconscious thought', *Perspectives on Psychological Science*, 1(2), 95–109.

3 The difference between *tacit* knowledge and *implicit* knowledge is beyond the scope of this chapter, but essentially tacit tends to be more personal (like possessing bike-riding skills) and implicit tends to be more contextual (for example having an intuitive knowledge of what is culturally acceptable in a situation).

4 Polanyi, M. (1966) *The Tacit Dimension*. New York: Doubleday.

5 Tartaro, A. (2021) 'The roots of tacit knowledge: Intuitive and personal judgment in Polanyi's early writings (1939–1946)', *Tradition and Discovery: The Polanyi Society Periodical*, 47(2), 23–33.

6 Polanyi, M. (1966) 'The logic of tacit inference', *Philosophy*, 41(155), 1–18, p. 6.

7 Polanyi, M. (1966) *The Tacit Dimension*. New York: Doubleday, p. 18, emphasis added.

8 Albrechtsen, J. S., Meissner, C. A. and Susa, K. J. (2009) 'Can intuition improve deception detection performance?', *Journal of Experimental Social Psychology*, 45(4), 1052–5; Ten Brinke, L., Stimson, D. and Carney, D. R. (2014) 'Some evidence for unconscious lie detection', *Psychological Science*, 25(5), 1098–105.

9 Kolb, D. A. (2014) *Experiential Learning: Experience as the Source of Learning and Development*. Upper Saddle River, NJ: Pearson Education.

10 Epstein, S. (2010) 'Demystifying intuition: What it is, what it does, and how it does it', *Psychological Inquiry*, 21(4), 295–312.

11 Ulvaeus, B. (2023) 'Take a chance on AI – but protect the musicians', *Financial Times*, 4 November. Available online at: https://www. ft.com/content/e4c43938-43d7-462b-bcff-70404fe44e5a.

12 APA Dictionary of Psychology: 'unconscious'. Available online at: https://dictionary.apa.org/unconscious (accessed May 2024).

13 Wilson, T. D. (2002) *Strangers to Ourselves*. Cambridge, MA: Belknap Press, p. 8.

14 Gigerenzer, G. (2023) *The Intelligence of Intuition*. Cambridge: Cambridge University Press, p. 3.

15 Gigerenzer (2023), p. 3.

16 Klein, G. A. (2011). *Streetlights and Shadows: Searching for the Keys to Adaptive Decision-Making*. Cambridge, MA: MIT Press.

17 Dijksterhuis, A. and Strick, M. (2016) 'A case for thinking without consciousness', *Perspectives on Psychological Science*, 11(1), 117–32.

18 Strick, M. and Dijksterhuis, A. (2011) 'Intuition and unconscious thought', in Sinclair, M. (ed.) *Handbook of Intuition Research*. Edward Elgar Publishing, p. 29.

19 Strick and Dijksterhuis (2011), p. 30.

20 Strick and Dijksterhuis (2011), p. 35.

21 Schopenhauer (1851) in Dijksterhuis and Nordgren (2006), p. 95.

22 Perkins, D. (2000) *Archimedes' Bathtub: The Art and Logic of Breakthrough Thinking*. New York: W. W. Norton, p. 191.

23 Evans, J. (2024) 'The amazing associative machine', *Janet Evans*. 6 March. Available online at: https://www.janet-evans. co.uk/6-the-amazing-associative-machine/.

24 Kounios, J. and Beeman, M. (2015) *The Eureka Factor*. London: William Heinemann, p. 71.

25 Raichle, M. E. (2015) 'The brain's default mode network', *Annual Review of Neuroscience*, 38, 433–47.

26 Evans (2024); Shofty, B., Gonen, T., Bergmann, E., Mayseless, N., Korn, A. and Ram, Z. (2022) 'The default network is causally linked to creative thinking', *Molecular Psychiatry*, 27(3), 1848–54.

27 Bremer, B., Wu, Q., Mora Álvarez, M. G., Hölzel, B. K., Wilhelm, M. and Koch, K. (2022) 'Mindfulness meditation increases default mode, salience, and central executive network connectivity', *Scientific Reports*, 12(1), 13219.

28 Isaacson, W. (2021) *Jobs*. New York: Simon and Schuster, p. 49.

29 Anon. (2018) 'Steve Jobs had a surprising passion that drove every decision he made', *Inc*. 5 February. Available online at: https://www.inc.com/quora/steve-jobs-had-a-surprising-passion-that-drove-every-decision-he-made-and-we-can-all-learn-from-it.html.

30 This is Wallas quoting, among others, the great US pragmatist philosopher John Dewey, see Wallas, G. (1926) *The Art of Thought*. London: Jonathan Cape, pp. 97–8.

31 Sadler-Smith, E. (2008) *Inside Intuition*. Abingdon: Routledge, p. 67.

32 Anonymous (July 2000) Kubla Khan; Or, a vision in a dream. A fragment. *The Victorian Web*. Available online at: https://victorianweb.org/previctorian/stc/kktext.html.

33 Hobson, N. (2023) 'Genius creator Ian Fleming wrote each of the James Bond books in less than 2 weeks by using the rule of forced boredom: A tool for hyper-productivity and success', *Inc*., 23 November. Available online at: https://www.inc.com/nick-hobson/genius-creator-ian-fleming-wrote-each-of-james-bond-books-in-less-than-2-weeks-by-using-rule-of-forced-boredom.html.

step 5

Tune in and translate

'You must train your intuition; you must trust the small voice inside you which tells you exactly what to say, what to decide.'

Ingrid Bergman (1915–82, three-time Oscar-winning actor)

This chapter will help you to develop techniques to tune in to your intuitive mind and translate what it might be trying to tell you.

If something doesn't look right, go and find out why

In the course of their duties, police officers must carry out a wide variety of challenging and demanding tasks: everything from saving someone's life, to vehicle stops, to drug busts to distinguishing between truth and lies. Getting these decisions right, or wrong, can have significant consequences not only for public safety but also for society's attitudes towards policing. In many such situations – which often are time-poor and/or rich in ambiguity and uncertainty – police officers have little option but to go with their gut if they're to take decisive action to resolve serious situations. The most accomplished officers have learned how to tune in to their gut feelings, interpret what their intuitive mind is telling them and use this information intelligently to protect life and property.

A good illustration of this was the seemingly innocuous incident that my colleague Cinla Akinci and I studied as part of a project on intuition in police work. As it turned out, there was much more to this seemingly straightforward situation than met the eye.[1]

An experienced officer, 'Officer A', was dispatched to a superficially routine complaint about 'someone banging on someone else's door' and causing a commotion. Not surprisingly, this had upset the neighbours, but on a Saturday night these kinds of calls aren't uncommon. By the time Officer A had got there, the troublemaker had fled the scene. On first glance, there wasn't much for Officer A to do except reassure the residents, log it and move on to the next job.

But something just didn't seem right about the whole situation. In Officer A's own words: 'It just felt as though something was ... there was *more* going on than they'd said.' And, if it weren't for the 'feeling that something wasn't right', he would have moved on. But because his gut was telling him that something didn't stack up, he decided to probe and ask a few more questions; sure enough, the answers he got 'seemed a little bit odd'. This piqued his curiosity even further.

The trouble was that there was nothing in the information Officer A had been given – and police officers have to act on information –

that could've led him to think that something else had gone on. Again, in his own words: 'It was just something wasn't right, and that's *all* I could think of.' The people inside the property didn't say anything to make him think, 'Oh, there's more to this, or there's something else that's gone on.' Instead, they were quite calm about it and didn't want to take it any further.

But, again, it just didn't seem right to him: something at the 'back of his head' told him that 'there's *something else* here, and I don't know what it is *yet*'. He couldn't move on from the 'fact' (his word not ours) 'that there was something else' and he needed 'to *do* something more with this'.

Like many of the experienced officers we interviewed, Officer A was like a 'dog with a bone': he couldn't let go and, as it turned out, in this incident his intuition was right. Behind it all was an allegation that a serious sexual assault had taken place. This came to light only because of his persistent questioning and further investigation. Officer A was tuned in to his intuition. He used it as a form of 'data' and translated his gut feelings into action by digging deeper. Without his intuitive intelligence and alertness the incident could have been bypassed, and who knows where it might have led?

How does this stack up in terms of the differences between automated expertise and holistic hunch that we met in Part 1? Officer A's intuition wasn't automated expertise because no action script (for example 'call for assistance') was activated; however, his intuition was a holistic hunch in that it told him things didn't 'stack up'. He had enough experience to know that he needed to interrogate the situation and resolve it by further investigations.

There was plenty going on behind the scenes of this seemingly innocuous incident; but there was also frenetic psychological activity going on back stage. Officer A's intuitive mind was trying to tell him something in the only language it knows – gut feelings – which needed to be noticed and translated. His analytical mind on the other hand didn't have anything hard and fast to go on; without his intuitive mind yelling at him he probably would have walked away.

Fortunately, Officer A had enough nous to realise this and tune in to his gut feelings, trust them, and the wherewithal to give his hunch the necessary airtime and find out what was behind it. We found this multiple times in the research. Another highly accomplished officer summed it up as 'if something doesn't look right, go and find out why'.

This incident illustrates a crucial difference between intuitive thinking and analytical thinking: they communicate to us on different 'wavelengths'. This is because:

- The intuitive mind is a complex, unconscious information processing and pattern recognition system that operates on a non-verbal communication 'wavelength'.

- The analytical mind is a complex, conscious information processing system that operates on a verbal communication wavelength.

The intuitive mind has its own unique non-verbal channel (we experience it as gut feelings, hunches and vibes) to tell us what it thinks.* To receive information from our intuitive mind and make sense of what it's telling us, it's necessary to do two things: tune in to it, and then translate gut feelings into a language that the analytical mind can work with and also that we can share, given that most decisions involve other people.

There are a number of tried-and-tested techniques that can help you to tune in so as to 'hear' what your gut might be trying to tell you. We'll look at two in this chapter: the metaphor method and the imagery method.

It's also worth bearing in mind that tuning in and translating are important not only for the person experiencing the intuition but also for other people who might be affected by a decision to 'go with your gut'. If you're not able to translate your intuitions into compelling arguments that you can communicate to others, then you're likely to have trouble in convincing *them* to go with *your* gut. Not only that, but other people can also be an invaluable sounding board for stress testing our intuitions – more on this in the next chapter.

---

* The 'it' is the intuitive mind which, as explained below, is just a metaphor.

> ## Takeaway
>
> The intuitive mind communicates what it 'thinks' via a non-verbal channel; the analytical mind communicates what it thinks via a verbal channel.

Metaphors and intuition

A common response to the 'what happens when you intuit?' question (see Step 2) is: 'When I intuit I get a *funny feeling* that things don't stack up.'

I tried to tune in to other people's gut feelings in my research by asking people, 'What happens when you intuit?' However, gut feelings are beyond words. For this reason, they have to be translated into a metaphor or image to make them intelligible to another person. Ray Kroc's feeling about whether to buy out the McDonald brothers was, metaphorically speaking, in his 'funny bone'.

A metaphor is a figure of speech in which one thing is described in terms of another thing that has similar characteristics. For example, the term 'gene mapping' uses a cartographic metaphor; gene mapping does not literally produce a spatial representation of the genome.[2] Similarly, the person who is the 'black sheep of my family' isn't a sheep of any colour.

In a metaphor, one thing *is* another thing for the sake of comparison and communication, for example 'work *is* a nightmare', 'time *is* money', 'Juliet *is* the sun': work, time and Juliet are not disturbing dreams, financial instruments or solar objects, respectively.[†]

Metaphors connect (the technical term is 'cross-map') a 'target' (in the examples above they are work, time and Juliet, these are the things you're interested in communicating your feelings about) with a 'source' (in the examples nightmare, money and sun – the things

---

[†] Metaphors are direct comparisons using 'is'; similes are indirect comparisons using 'like' or 'as': 'as cool as a cucumber'.

you're comparing the target to get your point across). The point of connecting a target with a source is to communicate an intrinsic feature of the target that's hard to get across by any other means; for example there's something about Juliet that makes Romeo feel quite good. It's a way of translating feelings and thoughts about someone or something into something that someone else, who can never have access to them, can grasp.

In the 'black sheep of my family' metaphor, the cross-mapping is from a particular person (the family member) to an animal that's unlike others of its class (the black sheep, when most sheep are white). The metaphor, with the black sheep as the source, is used to make the point that the target person is unlike anyone else in the family.[3]

We use metaphors instinctively and automatically in everyday speech without the need to think about them. For example, in 'he is on fire', the target is the 'he' in question, the source is 'fire' and the 'he' has a quality like the thing, 'fire', in the source; in this case, the person has intense heat and energy (Figure 12).[4]

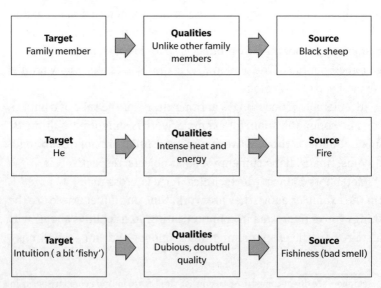

Figure 12 More targets and sources in metaphors

Spotlight on intuitive intelligence
The 'two minds' metaphor

The idea that the intuitive mind operates on a non-verbal communication 'frequency' is a metaphor. Not only that, as far as the two-minds model itself is concerned, there aren't literally two 'minds' inhabiting our heads, nor are there two distinct parts of the brain that can be labelled as System 1 (where intuition happens) and System 2 (where analysis 'happens'). It's a metaphor.

Many distinct parts of the brain are involved in intuitive and analytical thinking and, by the way, the idea that intuition is in the right brain is both a metaphor and a myth. Therefore, to say that we have 'two minds in one brain' is not literally true. The two-minds model is just a metaphor for comparing and contrasting two complementary types of thinking.

One of the architects of 'dual-process theory' (the two-minds model), Nobel laureate Daniel Kahneman, said that we should treat System 1 and System 2 as 'nicknames' for fast, intuitive and slow, analytical types of thinking. As nicknames, and metaphors, they make it easier, especially for non-specialists, to understand the complexities of the mind and brain.[5]

It's worth pointing out that some psychologists worry that talk of System 1 and System 2 and of an intuitive mind and an analytical mind as a way of explaining how humans think and decide might be becoming as stale and 'vacuous' as talk of right-brain and left-brain thinking.[6] This is something we need to keep an eye on.

Intuitions are often linked to bodily sensations, such as smell, for example: 'My intuition tells me that his story is a bit "fishy"', in the sense of fish that has gone off with a connotation that is definitely bad. The link to bodily sensations, such as smell, not only makes them potent, it also makes their meaning understandable by someone other than the one person having the intuition. This is because both parties have the shared experience of being in a body, albeit different ones that can smell, hear, see, touch and taste. Intuition can be embodied in various physical categories, for example in terms of:

- *Smell:* for example 'This situation *stinks*' or 'It smells a bit *fishy* to me'.
- *Temperature:* for example 'The fact that he was too *cool* about it all made me feel uneasy'.
- *Vision:* for example 'A *light came on* and I just knew what their agenda was'.
- *Position and orientation:* for example 'What she was saying just didn't *stack up*', etc.[‡]

The common answer of '… I get a funny feeling that things don't stack up' to the 'What happens when you intuit?' question is metaphorical because a connection is made from the target (what an intuition feels like) to a source, in this case, the 'position and orientation' of 'upness' (as opposed to 'downness').

This tells us something about the essence of the gut feeling because position involves an evaluation: for example 'up is good' and its opposite 'down' is 'bad'. The comparison helps to communicate the quality of the gut feeling to someone else. The metaphor 'When I intuit I get a funny feeling that things don't stack up' expresses the inexpressible feeling that the situation is not 'up' and therefore is not 'good'.[§]

To sum up, and aside from the linguistic technicalities, metaphors give someone else a sense of what an intuition that they're not privy to is like for the person who's actually experiencing the intuition. Metaphors are a good way to get our gut feelings across to someone else.

[‡] Embodied metaphors are technically known as 'primary metaphors' because they can't be reduced any further; this is why they're 'ultimately embodied'.

[§] Incidentally, there's another figure of speech at work here as well: 'funny' in the sense of funny-peculiar rather than funny-amusing. Also, bear in mind that the term 'gut feeling' itself may also be a metaphor for those people who don't literally experience intuitions as a sensation in their internal organs.

Big thinker
Marcia Emery

Dr Marcia Emery is a psychologist, consultant and college professor who has brought intuition into the corporate world and non-profit sector through her training seminars and publications. Emery has written about and used metaphors extensively with her clients. In her *Intuition Workbook*, Dr Emery defines intuition as 'Clear knowing without being able to explain how one knows' and 'knowledge gained without logical or rational thought'.[7] In *Powerhunch*, she argues that the key to success in our professional and personal lives is to use intuition daily and 'incorporate intuition as an equal partner with logic'.[8] One of the benefits of doing so is that information 'sent' by the intuitive mind 'provides shortcuts that will immensely expedite' problem solving and decision making. Several of the ideas in this section are based on Emery's work.[9]

You might be forgiven for thinking, based on what's been said so far, that metaphors for intuition are exclusively negative or bad and, as such, signal 'avoid'. But this isn't the case; they can also be positive and good, and therefore signal 'approach'. By way of example, here are some more responses that people gave when I asked them what happens when they intuit:

- 'An idea bubbles *up* in my awareness and it feels right' (no bubbles as such are involved but they are pleasant things – think of fizzy drinks – that always go up and the orientation of 'up' is good).

- 'Something *clicks* inside' (nothing literally clicks but a movement that ends in a 'click' signals a coming together, a sense of coherence, a completion or a realisation).

Psychologists use the technical term 'valence' (also known as 'hedonic tone') to describe the 'sign' associated with an intuition:

- A good vibe or gut feeling is 'positively (+) valenced' (+ve hedonic tone).
- A bad vibe or gut feeling is 'negatively (−) valenced' (−ve hedonic tone).

An intuition metaphor, whether it's positively or negatively valenced, captures the essence of how someone feels about an object, person or situation. Table 10 lists some common metaphors for intuition and provides a useful guide for the 'precise use of vague language' to convey the essence of a gut feeling, hunch or vibe.[10] One of my favourite metaphors from the list is 'radar' because it captures the idea of the intuitive mind as a sensing system for not only coping with threats, but also spotting opportunities.

Table 10 Some common intuition metaphors

Alarm	Alert	Beacon
Detector	Gauge	GPS
Gut feeling	Gut instinct	Hint
Hunch	Inkling	Inner compass
Inner sensor	Inner voice	Intimation
Murmur	Odour	Radar
Scent	Sensor	Siren
Smell	Spidey-sense	Trace
True north	Vibe	Voice
Warning bell	Whiff	Whisper

To sum up: a gut feeling is ultimately a private thing that can never be fully known by another person,[11] but metaphors provide one way to tune in to the intuitive mind and make the inexpressible more expressible.

Takeaway

Metaphors are a way of giving voice to an intuitive mind that lacks the capability to communicate through the verbal channel.

Imagery and intuition

As far as the intuitive mind is concerned, a picture really is worth a thousand words. This is because the intuitive mind evolved to deal with *real* things in a *real* context (for example reading someone else's motives and intentions in a close-knit social group). The analytical mind, on the other hand, which came on to the scene quite late in human evolution, excels with abstractions and intellectual tasks.

As far as images are concerned, human beings have much better visual acuity than most other animals.[12] Visual images are about as real as it gets for human beings; if I were a bat or a worm my world would 'look' very different. For humans, visual images have a fluency about them that makes them an effective and efficient way to get a message across to an intuitive mind that has evolved over hundreds of millennia to be highly attuned to imagery.[13]

A good example of the power of pictures to influence human behaviour are the changes that have been made in cigarette packaging over the years in attempts by governments to reduce smoking. Cigarette packages in the bad old days were replete with bright colours and aspirational names such as Embassy, Lucky Strike, Marlboro, Senior Service and Silk Cut printed in large fancy typefaces. Nowadays, cigarette packages in the UK are designed to reduce positive messaging by being in a non-shiny drab dark brown, brand names have to be in a set position, font and size, and all other trademarks, logos, colour schemes and promotional images are prohibited.[14] The idea is that an intuitive mind that's constantly on the lookout for attractive visual images that might signal opportunity for food or pleasure will be inclined to ignore them. At the same time, the packages are designed to increase negative messaging by using a much larger typeface for health warnings and gruesome images of the effects of smoking on the human body, including rotting teeth and lungs and a baby inhaling smoke. Again, a visually inclined intuitive mind that's attuned to spotting threats will tend to notice them and be repelled automatically. These measures (along with other measures including tax increases) have helped to reduce smoking rates in the UK from over 50 per cent in the 1970s to around 17 per cent today.[15]

Spotlight on intuitive intelligence
Pictures and purchasing

Advertisers have known about the power of the intuitive mind over buyers' behaviour for a long time. Research by the marketing consultancy System 1 (named after System 1 – the intuitive mind – in the two-minds model) has found that having pictures on packaging speeds up consumer decision making and reduces hesitation by between 10 and 20 per cent. Put the other way round: having text rather than pictures on packages is more likely to increase the time a consumer has to think things through and engage in analytical thinking; this is risky for sellers because it means consumers might change their mind. From a seller's point of view, this is to be avoided if at all possible.

Fluency through visual recognition by the intuitive mind is crucial when products are competing for attention on the supermarket shelves where there are a plethora of products and, for most people, a dearth of time. Having a familiar picture prompts an easy-to-answer question, 'Do I recognise this brand?'. The intuitive mind, because it works on the least effort and 'cognitive miser' principles, prefers easier-to-answer questions over harder-to answer questions. Moreover, changing a product's packaging that consumers' intuitive minds have become habituated and attuned to can be risky; this is one reason companies are reluctant to rebrand their products.

> System 1's (the company) recommendation to advertisers is to boost the power of imagery by minimising front-of-package messaging; maximising emotional appeal and maximising brand distinctiveness and design coherence.
>
> This gives a product a 'hot line' into the intuitive mind. The goal isn't to increase deliberation by allowing System 2 to get in on the act, but instead to reduce it by going direct to System 1.[16]

Daniel Kahneman reminded us that the intuitive mind enjoys creating and hearing coherent stories because they help it to make sense in of an incoherent world by 'stripping away some of the difficulty, some of that complexity, some of the internal contradiction'.[17] Two of the best ways to communicate with the intuitive mind are through stories (narratives) and pictures (visual images).** The intuitive mind finds them intrinsically more interesting, compelling and useful than sterile descriptions and abstract ideas. On the other hand, the best way to communicate with the analytical mind is through verbal information and abstract ideas because these are things that it prefers to work with and is adept at handling.

Takeaway

The intuitive mind is more receptive to information that's presented as visual images and stories.

** In psychology, mental imagery can refer to other modalities such as sound (an internal representation of a noise). Here we'll use 'imagery' to mean visual imagery.

Visualisation

As well as being more receptive to visual images, the intuitive mind is also capable of producing mental images of its own. Mental imagery is the process of accessing perceptual information (sight, sound, smell, touch and taste) from memory. The technique of visualisation can be used to create the illusion of sights, sounds, smells, touches and tastes in the mind's eye, mind's ear, etc.

Mental images can be representations of things that exist in the outside world (real things, such as a zebra) or representations of things that only exist in the inner world of the 'mind's eye' (imagined things, such as a unicorn). Even though images can occur in any of the five sensory modalities, the most common type of image and the easiest to conjure up in the mind's eye is a visual image.

Spotlight on intuition
Visualisation in health care

Visualisation is a powerful technique for accessing our thoughts and affecting the relationship between mind and body. According to the Johns Hopkins Hospital in Baltimore, visualisation has been used successfully in medicine for reducing pain and controlling a range of physical symptoms, including nausea.

Clinicians at Johns Hopkins use a technique known as 'palming'. It involves placing the palms of your hands over your eyes and closing them and then being invited to: visualise the colour that's associated with the pain, stress or anxiety, usually red; and then change the visualised colour to a more relaxing one such as green. This has been found to reduce levels of pain, stress and anxiety.

Clinicians at Johns Hopkins have also used 'guided imagery' as a relaxation technique to help patients cope with physical and mental health problems. Under the guidance of a qualified practitioner, imagery has been used to help patients manage anxiety, stress and depression, reduce pain, lower blood pressure, lessen nausea and give them a better overall sense of control and well-being. Resources on guided imagery are available widely on the web including freely available ones from health care providers such Johns Hopkins.[18]

As well as having therapeutic value, visualisation is a powerful tool for tuning in to the intuitive mind. Experienced and successful intuition practitioners such as Marcia Emery have used this technique successfully with their clients. She claims that imagery gives access to regions of the mind that aren't normally available to conscious awareness.

An intriguing visualisation exercise was developed by another well-known intuition practitioner, Frances Vaughan: she invites her clients to make a slow, deliberate, imaginary journey inside a house and describe what they 'see'. The client is guided to notice the entrance, go through the front door, enter each of the rooms one by one, notice the furniture and contents of the rooms, take note of the doors and windows and, for example, whether they're open or closed, descend into the basement and notice what's there, ascend into the attic and describe what they find there, etc. Clients are then invited to make sense of the images that have arisen.

These images, which are allowed to arise automatically, are a window into a person's intuitive feelings about an object, person or situation; for example, 'Is the colour of the door significant?', 'What might the fact that the windows are open mean?', etc.

Guided imagery is used also in emotional guidance, counselling and therapy. It can involve the use of the other senses, for example, by asking clients to report on the sounds, smells, tastes, etc. that arise in their inner world.

In Vaughan's guided imagery method, some people 'visit' a house they know, others create an imaginary house in their mind's eye. The point of the exercise is for the client to allow images to surface intuitively, accept and trust them non-judgementally, and explore their meanings. For example, one of Vaughan's clients had no trouble in identifying the metaphorical and symbolic aspects of her imagined house:

'The state of my house seems to reflect the state of my mind ... my head is cluttered with ideas, but I am reluctant to start the job of housecleaning ... I don't want to examine [the contents of the basement] but feel I must do ... I need to throw out a lot before I can be satisfied with myself ... I feel I am ready to begin the task of putting my house in order.'[19]

This method, according to Vaughan, not only gives clients access to the contents of their intuitive mind, but it also helps them to learn to trust the process of accessing their intuitive mind. Guided imagery is a tried-and-tested technique for tuning in to intuition and developing 'intuitive awareness'. When I've used it with MBA students, they report positive effects on their sense of perspective on issues, increased self-confidence, improved interpersonal sensitivity and a better understanding of their own thinking processes (the technical terms for this is 'meta-cognition').[20]

Visualisation can work in two ways: 'actively' or 'receptively'. In 'active visualisation', guided imagery is used deliberately to draw out intuitions, as in Vaughan's imaginary journey around a house. It doesn't have to be a house; it could be a walk in the woods, a meander along a riverbank, a stroll through a city park, etc. The important thing is to notice the things that arise in the mental journey; the house is simply the prompt.

On the other hand, in 'receptive visualisation', images are allowed to arise spontaneously without any prompting. In this respect, it's similar to musing and daydreaming. One of the most famous examples of receptive visualisation and the power of daydreaming is the case of the nineteenth-century German chemist Friedrich

Kekulé (1829–96) who discovered the ring structure of the benzene molecule (C_6H_6). His musings became a milestone discovery in the field of physical chemistry.

It all happened one evening in 1865 when Kekulé fell into a fireside reverie after a hard day's thinking about benzene; during his half-awake, half-asleep daydream, he 'watched' in amazement as the carbon and hydrogen atoms were: 'gambolling before my eyes ... in snakelike motion. But look! What was that? One of the snakes had seized hold of its own tail, and the form whirled mockingly before my eyes. As if by a flash of lightening I awoke.'

Why should the image of a snake swallowing its own tail be so important in solving Kekulé's perplexing problem of the structure of the benzene molecule?

Kekulé's big leap forward that came to him during this reverie was that the benzene molecule isn't a simple chain: this didn't tally with its chemical formula and just didn't make sense. The benzene molecule is in fact a chain that's folded back onto itself to make a ring structure, like a snake swallowing its own tail. As a ring, rather than a chain, the chemical formula of C_6H_6 now made perfect sense. Kekulé's insight was the product of a receptive visualisation. It transformed physical chemists' understanding of benzene, an important compound in many industrial processes including the manufacture of plastics, fibres, dyes, etc. As is so often the case, after the discovery was made, the solution seemed obvious (Figure 13).

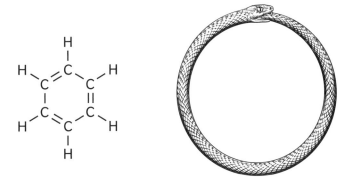

Figure 13 Ring structure of benzene and the uroboros

Christos Georghiou/Shutterstock

Some psychologists have suggested that Kekulé might have been in a 'hypnagogic state'. This is the place between wakefulness and sleep where visual images are often experienced spontaneously. But unlike in dreams, when images arise in a hypnagogic state, they're under some degree of conscious control. It's also a place where 'fertile forgetting' can liberate the mind and help it to get round mental roadblocks and impasses.

In terms of the neuroscience that's behind this, the brain's default mode network (DMN), which was discussed in Step 4, is active when the brain is in a relaxed state of quiet repose. It's been called the 'visionary network' because it's been associated with creative thinking; whether it was the DMN that was behind Kekulé's dream will never be known.

In the zone between sleep and full awakening, the dreamlike fluidity of the intuitive mind isn't under the rigid discipline of the analytical mind; yet there's just enough conscious awareness for intuitive insights to be captured and contained before they dissolve into thin air. This is why it's a good idea to have a notepad beside you for those occasions when the intuitive mind opens up. And, as someone once said: 'the mind is like a parachute, it works best when it's open'[††]; active and receptive visualisation are two ways of opening up the mind and creating the conditions for imaginative, and sometimes groundbreaking, connections to be made.

Big thinker
Frances Vaughan

Dr Frances Vaughan was a clinical psychologist, President of the Association for Transpersonal Psychology (which focuses on the spiritual and transcendental aspects of human experience) and a pioneer of intuition practice. Here are some thoughts

---

[††] This simile is from the 1936 movie *Charlie Chan at the Circus*, but its origins are uncertain.

from her inspiring book on intuition practice *Awakening Intuition*. The book's first chapter is called 'Tuning in to intuition' and involves three steps:

1 Quieting the incessant chatter of the analytical mind.

2 Learning to focus attention on the contents of the intuitive mind.

3 Cultivating a non-judgmental attitude to whatever comes into conscious awareness.[21]

Vaughan's conclusion is that you cannot *make* intuition happen but 'the more completely you identify with your inner experience the deeper you will be able to penetrate into the creative wellsprings of your intuition' and the more prepared you'll be to acknowledge and receive whatever it has to offer whenever it happens. A creative intuition is just the start: Kekulé himself cautioned that, 'We must take care, however, not to publish our dreams before submitting them to proof by the waking mind.'[22]

Dreams have long been thought of as a window into the intuitive mind. The Swiss psychoanalyst Carl Jung thought that the contents of dreams cannot be explained solely in terms of memory; he believed that they express primitive, archetypal material that arises from a 'collective unconscious'. The snake swallowing its own tail which Kekulé 'saw', the *uroboros*, is a circular alchemical symbol that has been found in ancient Greek manuscripts dating back more than two millennia. In Jungian psychology, the symbols that arise in dreams – such as the uroboros, the trickster, the sage, etc. – not only offer a glimpse into the unconscious mind but may also be part of a deep sedimentary deposit of 'ancestral experience'[23] that surfaces during intuitive episodes.

Whether the image that Kekulé tuned into accidentally in his torpor was Jungian archetype can never be known. But what is clear is that intuitions that have been communicated to the conscious mind as images and metaphors have played a key role in a number of momentous scientific discoveries. A famous example is the image the 16-year-old Einstein had of himself chasing after a beam of light in the vacuum of space in one of his famous thought experiments. This later led him 'intuitively' to the theory of special relativity.[24]

Following this 'Jungian' line of thinking, it's also been claimed that intuition operates at the level of 'supra-consciousness': a higher level of consciousness that transcends the analytical mind and the limited things that it can comprehend. There are tentative links to the paranormal, ESP and intuition as a 'sixth sense', as well as to spirituality and prophecy. Claims are also made for connections between intuition, supra-consciousness and quantum phenomena and the possibility of matter 'existing at the same time locally and non-locally' and the communication of knowledge across space and time through 'morphic resonance'.[25] This is the idea that memory is both inherent in nature and collective, and that there can be telepathy-like connections between organisms, such as dogs knowing when their owners are coming home. Readers who are interested in pursuing this line of thought, which is quite different to the muscular view of intuition, might like to start by reading the work of the quantum physicist David Bohm.[26]

Jung himself believed that certain images come into our psyche from a place that is 'more complete than consciousness' and contain a 'superior analysis' that consciousness hasn't been able to produce. He said: 'We have a suitable word for such occurrences – intuition.'[27] In Jung's psychology, 'sensing' perceives a situation as it appears through our sensory organs; 'intuiting', on the other hand, perceives unconsciously things that aren't immediately apparent.

Takeaway

The intuitive mind prefers to work with images as well as stories and metaphors. It's capable of producing mental images of its own volition in a process of 'creative intuition'.

Interpreting intuitions

The idea of intuition as a developable skill that's the product of pattern recognition process based on extensive prior learning and experience is called 'expert intuition'. As discussed in Step 3, this kind of intuition works best in high-validity environments (where the links between cues and outcomes make prediction possible) and in situations that are like those that have been encountered previously. However, there's another angle on this: while expert intuition is about learned patterns and prior associations and is past-oriented, creative intuition, on the other hand, is about sensing possibilities and novel connections and is future-oriented.[‡‡]

Creative intuition is 'an inexplicable sense of the possible and of what might be done'.[28] An example of a creative intuition was the sense that Steve Jobs had that consumers would want the iPad and iPhone *before* they knew it themselves. Similarly, Jeff Bezos had the sense that Prime would work without knowing beforehand that it would and went against the advice of his finance team. Reed Hastings, Netflix CEO, said that, even though the company invests heavily in analytics, 'The final call is always gut. It's informed intuition.' He even referred to one of his senior team as 'the man with the golden gut'.[29] Jobs, Bezos and Hastings had no way of knowing beforehand that the iPad, Prime and Netflix would work. They were in situations that were familiar to them but were working with uncertainty; this is where intuition, in the form of a holistic hunch, comes into its own. Nonetheless, each was prepared to take a gamble on their gut feelings; for all three of them it paid off but it goes without saying that this isn't always the case.

Because creative intuitions are products of an intuitive mind that communicates on a non-verbal wavelength via gut feelings, hunches and vibes to tell us whether something might or might not work, these holistic hunches are difficult to communicate to others. Nonetheless, they often have to be shared with others because

---

[‡‡] There are actually four types of intuition: creative, expert, moral, social. There might even be a fifth, 'spiritual'.

our decision making, be it in our personal or our professional lives, involves and affects other people. In business, holistic hunches have to be explained and 'sold' to colleagues, clients, customers and investors if they're going to stand any chance of being developed into a commercial innovation for a product or service. In other words, they have to be *interpreted*.

Metaphors and images are ways in which intuitive knowledge can be transferred from one brain to another. Both metaphors and images are a first step in the process of interpreting intuitions and making holistic hunches more explicit.

For the engineer and entrepreneur Sir James Dyson, inventor of the bagless vacuum cleaner, 'sketching is the first step in making your idea a reality'.[30] The idea for a bagless cleaner came to him suddenly after he saw a 30-foot high centrifuge in a sawmill for sucking up sawdust. He made the intuitive leap of shrinking the centrifuge down to make a vacuum cleaner that worked on the same principle. Numerous sketches and over 5,000 prototypes later, Dyson arrived at the machine that bears his name and revolutionised the world of domestic appliances. Dyson has gone on record as saying that he trusted his intuition over the market research that said, for example, that the clear bin on the Dyson wouldn't work because people didn't want to see the dirt. The marketeers' analysis was wrong and Dyson's intuition was right: see-through bins have become the new normal.[31]

Spotlight on intuitive intelligence
From intuiting to interpreting

Early on in the development of the Apple Macintosh, Steve Jobs had a really tough time articulating an idea that was so revolutionary that it didn't yet exist and was hard for others to imagine. This was a challenge: in the words of Joshua Michael Stern, the director of the movie, *Jobs*, 'He [Jobs] could see it, taste it, knew what it felt like, but he didn't have all the language because it didn't exist yet.'[32]

Language failed Jobs because the Apple Mac was a creative intuition communicated to him on a non-verbal frequency from his intuitive mind. He often became frustrated that people couldn't fathom the idea of the mass-produced, personal computer. In one scene in the movie Jobs says:

'This thing is for the everyman. That's our end user. It's the school teacher. It's the garbage man. It's the kid. It's some grandma in Nebraska. We need to make this thing simple. It's got to work [pause] like an *appliance*.'

Following up this analogy, Jobs visited the kitchen appliance section of Macy's in Palo Alto, studying the elegant simplicity of everyday things, especially the Cuisinart products, which make household chores cleaner, friendlier and more fun.

Jobs tuned in to the intuitive mind's predilection for images when he insisted that the Macintosh must look 'friendly': as a result, it evolved to resemble a human face, taller and narrower than other computers with a disk drive below the screen 'suggesting a head'.[33]

Jobs used the 'appliance' metaphor to communicate and shape his intuitive insights about the future of personal computing; Dyson used the analogy of a saw mill centrifuge to shape his vision for a bagless vacuum cleaner. Had Jobs used a different metaphor, for example a 'business assistant', it might have led to very different interpretations and the world of personal computing might have looked quite different.[34] Jobs and Dyson both knew that it's impossible to bring people with you unless you're able to interpret your intuitions and communicate their creative potential.

How we tune into and interpret the workings of the intuitive mind has a significant bearing on what they 'look' like when they emerge into the cold light of consciousness. Language is our main tool for interpreting intuitions. It's through words, typically in the form of metaphors, that things that were once private gut feelings, hunches and vibes get named and become public. It's only when one person's holistic hunches and creative intuitions become real to others that they can start to *believe* in them and then start to *do* things with them.

Takeaway

Creative intuitions (holistic hunches) are products of an intuitive mind that communicates on a non-verbal frequency; they have to be interpreted and shared with others before they can be put into practice.

Dig deeper

Read more about how to tune in to your intuitive mind in Frances Vaughan's classic *Awakening Intuition*; it's 'essential for anyone interested in developing his or her innate intuitive potential'.

In a nutshell, tuning in to your intuitive mind

The intuitive mind communicates what it 'thinks' via a non-verbal channel; metaphors and images are a way of giving intuition a voice which then has to be interpreted before it can be put into action.

Workout 1: The metaphor method

1 One way of tuning in is to focus on how an intuition makes us *feel* about an object, person or situation. This is called the 'affective content' or the 'affective charge' of the decision (where 'affect'

refers to feelings). The affect in question can be a good feeling or a bad feeling. This is called the 'valence'; positive valence is a good feeling and vice versa.

2 Expressing a gut feeling in terms of its 'embodied' features, such as smell, touch, sight, sound and taste, gives a window into what's most important about a gut feeling and how powerful the feeling is.

3 Think of an object, person or situation about which you currently have or have recently had an intuition, for example, something that someone said to you but didn't sound quite right, an opportunity that attracted you but felt a bit 'risky', etc.

4 Express your gut feelings about it in metaphorical terms in relation to the five senses, for example 'Their story just didn't smell right', 'I could see this working', etc.

5 It can be helpful to 'map' your metaphors in terms of the valence (whether it's positive or negative) and intensity (how strong it is) (see Table 11).

Table 11 The metaphor method

Sensory modality	Question	Valence	Intensity	Action
Smell	What does/did it smell like?			
Touch	What does/did it feel like?			
Sight	What does/did it look like?			
Sound	What does/did it sound like?			
Taste	What does/did it taste like?			

6 What does this tell you about you about how you feel about the object, person or situation? For example, if it's a 'bad smell' (negative valence), does that mean it's something to be avoided; if it's a 'clear view of a promising future' (positive valence) does that mean it's something to be approached?

7 What intensity is the valence (weak, moderate, strong)?

8 What does the metaphor, its valence and intensity tell you about how you should act in relation to the object, person or situation in the target domain, for example should you or did you 'approach' it or 'avoid' it? What were, or might be, its consequences?

Workout 2: The imagery method

1 An alternative way of tuning in and translating what our intuitive mind is trying to tell us is by generating images from familiar categories that capture its affective content. Dr Frances Vaughan, author of *Awakening Intuition*, innovated the imagery method and Dr Marcia Emery later adapted it in her *Intuition Workbook*. I've adapted it further here.

2 Think of something about which you currently have or have recently had an intuition, for example 'Which house to buy'.

3 Express your gut feelings about the object of your intuition as an image in relation to each of the categories in Table 12.

4 If the object of your intuition were an animal, what animal would it be; if it were a plant, what plant would it be; if it were a car, what car would it be; if it were a type of music, what type of music would it be? You don't have to use them all.

5 You can invent other categories to help you to tune in and translate.

6 What does the type of animal, plant, car or music tell you about how you feel about the object of your intuition?

7 If it was an image, how intense was it?

Table 12 The imagery method

Question	Intensity	Immediacy	Valence	Action
If it were an animal what animal would it be?				
If it were a plant what plant would it be?				
If it were a car what car would it be?				
If it were music what type of music would it be?				
What type of 'x' would it be?				

8 What does the intensity tell you about the object, person or situation?

9 Is the image positively or negatively valenced?

10 What does the image tell you about how you should act in relation to the object, person or situation, for example to 'approach' it or 'avoid' it?

Workout 3: The 'pull-up' technique

1 Marcia Emery also developed what she called the 'pull-up' technique as a way to gauge how you feel about an object, person or situation when framed as a question.

2 It's a bit like the coin-tossing method from Step 2. For example, if the question was 'Should I accept or decline a job I've been offered?', the pull-up technique works by actively generating an image to use to gauge your response to the question.

3   If the pull-up image is a traffic light, which light (red, amber or green) lights up after you've asked the question about the issue in question (for example, the decision of whether or not to accept a job offer)?

4   If the red light came on automatically, it might signal that your gut feeling is don't accept, if the green light came on, it might signal that you should accept the offer; if the amber light came on, it might signal uncertainty which could then be used as a prompt to get more information or mull it over for a little longer and then repeat the exercise.

5   Other pull-up images might include: doors (do they open or close in your mind's eye when you ask the question?); an elevator (does it go up signalling positive, or does it go down signalling negative?); two flags one with 'yes' on it and another with 'no' (which one is fluttering?).

6   Frances Vaughan noticed with her clients that they may try to push away the first image that arises spontaneously. The fact that they do so may be telling them something about how they feel.

Workout 4: Card decks and image banks

1   The imagery technique can also be used with decks of cards, or libraries of images (from the Internet or simply cut out of magazines randomly).

2   If you were helping someone to 'tune in and translate', you'd ask them to choose a card or an image from the image bank that resonates with a decision that they're faced with and invite them to say why they're drawn to the image (you could do this solo as well) as follows:

  • Turn off your thinking mind, and turn on your intuitive mind.

  • Call up the decision you're faced with.

  • Now allow yourself to be drawn to an image.

  • Why were you drawn to this image?

3 What does this tell you about the decision that you're faced with?[35]

4 The image is a direct prompt for the client to tune into their intuitive mind; the explanation of why they chose the card or image is their translation of their intuition into words.

Notes

1 Akinci, C. and Sadler-Smith, E. (2020) '"If something doesn't look right, go find out why": How intuitive decision making is accomplished in police first-response', *European Journal of Work and Organizational Psychology*, 29(1), 78–92.

2 Google dictionary: 'a figure of speech in which a word or phrase is applied to an object or action to which it is not literally applicable', i.e. when we speak of 'gene maps' and 'gene mapping', we use a cartographic metaphor.

3 Lakoff, G. and Johnson, M. (2008) *Metaphors We Live By*. Chicago: University of Chicago Press.

4 Wagener, A. E. (2017) 'Metaphor in professional counselling', *The Professional Counsellor* 7(2), 144–54. Available at: https://files.eric.ed.gov/fulltext/EJ1159711.pdf.

5 Kahneman, D. (2011) *Thinking, Fast and Slow*. London: Allen Lane, p. 30.

6 Bellini-Leite, S. C. (2018) 'Dual process theory: Systems, types, minds, modes, kinds or metaphors? A critical review', *Review of Philosophy and Psychology*, 9(2), 213–25, p. 223.

7 Emery, M. (1994). *Dr Marcia Emery's Intuition Workbook*. Englewood Cliffs, NJ: Prentice Hall, p. 9.

8 Emery, M. (2011). *Powerhunch*. Portland: Beyond Words Publishing, p. 222.

9 Emery (1994), p. xvii.

10 Battino, R. (2005) *Ericksonian Approaches: A Comprehensive Manual*. Carmarthen: Crown House Publishing, p. 2.

11 Lakoff and Johnson (2008), p. 224.

12 Caves, E. M., Brandley, N. C. and Johnsen, S. (2018) 'Visual acuity and the evolution of signals', *Trends in Ecology and Evolution*, 33(5), 358–72.

13 Epstein, S. (2014) *Cognitive Experiential Theory*. Oxford: Oxford University Press.

14 Department of Health and Social Care. (2021) 'Tobacco packaging guidance'. Available online at: https://assets. publishing.service.gov.uk/media/6079a6a88fa8f57356118bb2/ tobacco-packaging-guidance-great-britain-april-2021.pdf.

15 Best, A. (2017) 'This is the end of tobacco advertising', *Cancer News*. Available online at: https://news.cancerresearchuk. org/2017/05/19/this-is-the-end-of-tobacco-advertising/.

16 System 1. (2017) *System 1: Unlocking Profitable Growth*. London: System 1 Group, pp. 216–18.

17 Nesterak, E. (2021) 'A conversation with Daniel Kahneman about "Noise"', *Behavioural Scientist*, 24 May. Available online at: https://behavioralscientist.org/a-conversation-with-daniel-kahneman-about-noise/.

18 Johns Hopkins medicine (no date). *Imagery*. Available online at: https://www.hopkinsmedicine.org/health/wellness-and-prevention/imagery (accessed May 2024).

19 Vaughan, F. (1979) *Awakening Intuition*. New York: Anchor Books, pp. 91–2.

20 Sadler-Smith, E. and Shefy, E. (2007) 'Developing intuitive awareness in management education', *Academy of Management Learning & Education*, 6(2), 186–205.

21 Vaughan (1979), p. 34.

22 Anonymous (2015) 'Kekulé's dreams'. *The Net Advance of Physics*. Boston, MA: MIT. Available online at: https://web.mit.edu/ redingtn/www/netadv/SP20151130.html.

23 Anonymous (no date) 'The Uroboros'. *Compiler Press*. Available online at: http://www.compilerpress.ca/Competitiveness/Anno/ Anno%20Neumann3.htm (accessed May 2024).

24 Norton, J. D. (2005) 'Chasing a beam of light: Einstein's most famous thought experiment'. University of Pittsburgh. Available online at: https://sites.pitt.edu/~jdnorton/Goodies/Chasing_the_light/.

25 Sinclair, M. and Ashkanasy, N. M. (2005) 'Intuition: Myth or a decision-making tool?', *Management Learning*, 36(3), 353–70, p. 362.

26 Sheldrake, R. (no date) 'Morphic resonance and morphic fields – an introduction'. Shedrake.org. Available online at: https://www.sheldrake.org/research/morphic-resonance/introduction (accessed May 2024) and where a link can be found to: *Morphic fields and implicate order: A dialogue with David Bohm.*

27 Anonymous (no date) 'Carl Jung on intuition and intuitives'. *Carl Jung Depth Psychology.* Available online at: https://carljungdepthpsychologysite.blog/2020/05/07/intuitives/ (accessed May 2024).

28 Crossan, M. M., Lane, H. W. and White, R. E. (1999) 'An organizational learning framework: From intuition to institution', *Academy of Management Review*, 24(3), 522–37, p. 527.

29 Ferenstein, G. (2016) 'Netflix CEO explains why "gut" decisions still rule in the era of big data', *Forbes*, 22 January. Available at: https://www.forbes.com/sites/gregoryferenstein/2016/01/22/netflix-ceo-explains-why-gut-decisions-still-rule-in-the-era-of-big-data/.

30 Anonymous (no date) *Ideas.* James Dyson Foundation. Available online at: https://media.dyson.com/downloads/JDF/JDF_Prim_poster05.pdf (accessed May 2024)

31 Cadwalladr, C. (2014) 'James Dyson interview: "Vacuums are already smarter than people"', *The Guardian*, 9 May. Available online at: https://www.theguardian.com/technology/2014/may/09/james-dyson-interview-engineering-education.

32 Gallo, C. (2013) '"Jobs" film director reveals Steve's early struggle to communicate simply', *Forbes*, 13 August. Available at: https://www.forbes.com/sites/carminegallo/2013/08/13/jobs-film-director-reveals-steves-early-struggle-to-communicate-simply/.

33 Isaacson, W. (2012) 'How Steve Jobs' love of simplicity fuelled a design revolution', *The Smithsonian Magazine*, September 2012. Available online at: https://www.smithsonianmag.com/arts-culture/how-steve-jobs-love-of-simplicity-fueled-a-design-revolution-23868877/.

34 Crossan *et al.* (1999), p. 527.

35 Nelson-Garrison, N. (2021) 'Aha! Moments – Exercise 1 – Working with imagery to access intuition & go deeper with clients', *The Coaching Tools Company*, 06 October. Available online at: https://www.thecoachingtoolscompany.com/aha-moments-exercise-1-working-with-imagery-to-go-deeper-with-a-client-by-marcy-nelson-garrison/.

step 6

De-bias your intuitive mind

'I think unconscious bias is one of the hardest things to get at.'

Ruth Bader Ginsburg (1933–2020, Associate Justice of the Supreme Court of the United States)

This chapter will show you how to prevent your intuitive mind from taking control and jumping to wrong conclusions when it might be better for it to take a backseat.

Marvellous and flawed

Intuition is a puzzle and a paradox; it's been described as simultaneously 'marvellous' and 'flawed'.[1] Depending on how we use it,
intuition can be our friend or our foe and either help or hinder our
decision making. People who are intuitively intelligent make the
most of its powers while at the same time avoiding its perils. This is a
delicate balancing act.

So far, this book has mostly been about the upside of going with
gut feelings which are based on learning, practice and feedback –
the so-called 'expert intuitions'. But not all intuitions are the products of experience and expertise; some of them are the products of
mental shortcuts that can lead us up the garden path.

The aim should be to avoid being sabotaged by intuition's weaknesses while, at the same time, taking advantages of its strengths.
This chapter explains three ways in which you can de-bug your intuitive mind of its inherent tendency to be biased or just plain wrong in
certain types of decisions: beware of being a 'cognitive miser'; don't
let stereotypes hijack your decisions; avoid the 'confirmation bias'.

Beware of being a 'cognitive miser'

Daniel Kahneman, whose work we've already met, focused on intuition's failings. In a series of ingenious experiments, conducted with
his friend and colleague Amos Tversky, they demonstrated how
gut feelings can get it badly wrong. Unique amongst psychologists,
Kahneman and Tversky themselves were almost as interesting as
their pioneering discoveries. They were described in Michael Lewis's
book *The Undoing Project* as the 'Lennon and McCartney of psychology': each 'saw in the other something they lacked and understood
each other better than they understood themselves'.[2]

Kahneman and Tversky set in motion a whole programme of
research (it's called 'heuristics and biases') which demonstrated how
our intuitions can lead us badly astray when they're used for things

for which they're not well-suited. Kahneman, along with another colleague Shane Frederick, developed the well-known 'bat-and-ball problem' as a quick-and-easy exposé of how intuition can run our reasoning off the rails:

> **'A bat and a ball cost $1.10 in total. The bat costs a dollar more than the ball. How much does the ball cost?'**

What's your answer?

Around 80 per cent of people get the answer to this simple question wrong. They do so because they give the first answer that comes to mind without giving it much thought: 'The ball costs 10 cents.'

This is wrong. Here's why: $1.10 splits naturally – and intuitively – into $1 and 10 cents, and 10 cents 'looks' and 'feels' about right. Therefore, 10 cents is a plausible answer that comes quickly and effortlessly to mind: it's an intuitive, but in this case mathematically incorrect, response.

The answer '10 cents' is wrong because the difference between the price of the bat ($1) and the price of the ball (10 cents) would be 90 cents, and not a dollar. For the difference to be one dollar, as asked for in the question, the ball must cost 5 cents and the bat must cost $1.05. Getting the right answer requires the analytical mind to step in and do the simple math.

The ball-and-ball problem is an example of how the intuitive mind will take a shortcut when it seizes on an answer that seems right. However, in numerical problems where a precise answer is required, an answer that *feels* right won't suffice; it has to *be* right. This is an example of the 'quick-out-of-the-blocks' intuitive mind being too eager to answer a question that'd be better left to the analytical mind.

The shortcut to the wrong answer goes as follows: the intuitive mind makes its best guess; the answer seems plausible; the analytical mind doesn't intervene to correct the intuitive mind's impulsive response (even though it could've done so with only a small investment of effort); the end result is a wrong answer.

Kahneman described the people who say 10 cents as 'ardent followers of the principle of least effort'[3] which, at one time or another, includes most if not all of us. The situation can be easily remedied, but the bat-and-ball problem also shows the light touch with which the analytical mind monitors what the intuitive mind is up to.[4] This is because human beings tend to be 'cognitive misers'; in other words, for much of the time, we choose, unconsciously and automatically, to operate on a least mental effort principle.

Two eminent psychologists, Susan Fiske and Shelley Taylor, coined the term 'cognitive miser' back in the 1980s. It's based on the idea that because there are so many demands placed on a brain which is limited in its capacity to process information consciously, it'll take a shortcut whenever it seems reasonable to do so: hence the term cognitive miser. In technical jargon, 'the brain defaults to processing mechanisms of low computational expense' or more prosaically by 'being as stupid as [it] can get away with'.[5]

Big thinkers
Susan Fiske and Shelly Taylor

Susan Fiske and Shelly Taylor teamed up at Harvard University in the 1970s. As social psychologists they were interested in how mental shortcuts affect how we judge other people and social situations.

Their theory is that people process information about social situations at two different speeds: a slower and deliberate pace that involves analysing the available data; a faster and more impulsive pace that involves taking mental shortcuts to simplify complex decisions.[6]

Because the quick-and-easy approach is the default, people can sometimes be categorised intuitively based on things like race, gender and age. Going beyond such categories, to learn more about the individual person, requires motivation, analytical thinking and cognitive effort.

Susan Fiske herself commented that 'the social world is intrinsically complicated and our minds are limited, so we take shortcuts. You couldn't walk down the street if you were individuating [carefully analysing] everyone you pass.'[7] The upside of this is that it enables us to get through the day without analysing everybody and everything; the downside is that a result can lead to discriminatory behaviours. Fiske's career has been devoted to studying how to overcome harmful stereotypes in judging other people.[8]

In practice, this means that because our brains are hardwired to find solutions that take minimal cognitive effort, if we can come up with a credible, minimal effort, intuitive answer that feels right, then most of the time we will. One eminent psychologist remarked that the rule humans seem to follow is 'engage the brain only when all else fails'.[9] This is one reason so many of us automatically take mental shortcuts much of the time.

The realisation that we can be, through no fault of our own, cognitive misers wakes us up to the fact that, in the hurly burly of everyday life, many people will, at one time or another, adopt a least effort principle. When this happens our analytical mind takes a light-touch approach and decisions get delegated by default to the intuitive mind.

Daniel Kahneman described analytical mind as a 'lazy policeman' who fails to rein in the intuitive mind when it's about to go off the rails. This is important because, as we shall see, the intuitive mind can be a wayward partner and sometimes it needs to be controlled. If it's not reined in all sorts of problems can ensue, including bias, wishful thinking, prejudice and discrimination.

Being a cognitive miser has nothing to do with intelligence. We can all be guilty of it at one time or another. The students who were foxed by the original bat-and-ball problem were undergraduates at one of the USA's top universities.

A feeling for an answer can get us into the right ball park, if we're only spending a dollar and ten cents then five cents is loose change. If the price tag were $1,100,000; the difference between the right and the wrong answer – $50,000 – is significant and costly. Going with your gut in this situation could be an expensive mistake. This type of problem shouldn't be entrusted to intuition because it involves calculation.

Many of life's decisions contain an element of calculated risk, whether that's choosing the lottery numbers or deciding to set up a new business venture. However, the intuitive mind isn't good at calculating probability and risk. If intuition is left in the driving seat where computations are required, the decision is more likely to be swayed by how the intuitive mind feels rather than by whether the numbers are accurate or not.

Imagine you're a budding entrepreneur with an idea for a new product or service that you 'just know' will make a great start-up business venture. Irrespective of how you feel about the idea, what do you think the chances are on a 1–10 scale that if you go with your gut you'll still be in business in five years' time?

Clue: if you're thinking of setting up a small business from scratch with no experience, the data aren't encouraging.

Less than 40 per cent of small businesses set up in the UK in 2016 were still trading five years later. Framed the other way round: six out of ten, or three out of every five, fail after five years. This proportion is called a 'base rate';* in this case, it's the base rate of business start-up failures. Base rates are important in assessing the chances of success in all sorts of decisions, everything from getting married (the base rate of marriage break-ups is around 40 per cent in the UK) to gambling on the stock market (it's estimated that between 70 and 90 per cent of DIY retail investors lose money).

These statistics don't seem to put people off from taking the plunge in business or in nuptials. Spurred on both by passion for their idea and swayed by well-publicised stories of small business founders whose gamble paid off, novice entrepreneurs tend to

---

* Also referred to as the 'prior probability'.

significantly overestimate their chances of success. Likewise in DIY investing, gut instinct and ego combine to get in the way of proper strategy. Retail investors overestimate their knowledge, chances of success and ability to control the situation; consequently, most of them end up losing money.[10] Gut feelings can sometimes be an effective way to deceive yourself.

As well as neglecting the base rate of business failures, a budding entrepreneur or DIY investor who's emotionally attached to their idea or investment decision is exposed to another peril: when they have a positive gut feeling about a business idea or an investment opportunity, they're more likely to conclude that the risks of failing are outweighed by the benefits of it being a success. This is called the 'affect heuristic' where 'affect' refers to feelings. The psychologist and decision researcher Paul Slovic discovered the affect heuristic in the 1990s.

It's a mental shortcut based on how we feel about an object, person or situation. Slovic found an inverse relationship between risk and benefit based simply on whether we happen to like something or not:

- When we find we like something we tend to *overestimate* the associated benefits and *underestimate* the associated risks.
- When we dislike something we tend to *underestimate* the benefits and *overestimate* the risks.

The classic example of this is nuclear power: if we have an aversion to nuclear power (for example fear based on vivid memories or stories we've been fed about accidents, such as Five Mile Island and Fukushima), its benefits get played down and its risks get played up in our minds, and vice versa.

Being aware of the relevant data (such as business failure rates or the real risks of nuclear power) could be one way to counter the overconfidence or the illogical aversion that comes with neglecting base rates or being controlled by the affect heuristic.

That said, would knowing about the base rate of marriage breakups put people off from tying the knot? Probably not, as we're talking here about a primary emotion, love, which like other primary emotions, for example, anger, disgust, happiness, etc., has the power to trump gut feelings. Intuition isn't an emotion as such, let alone a primary emotion. It's a different category of feeling (see Step 2).

The fact of the matter is that the intuitive mind's combined lack of sensitivity to base rates and its propensity to be influenced unduly by how it feels about something is one of the downsides of going with your gut. Although, as we know from Step 2, without feelings we'd be frozen by analysis paralysis. Gut feelings energise our decisions. But when and how we allow them to sway our choices is a matter of intuitive intelligence.

Spotlight on intuition

The power of stories and the perils of small numbers

The popular business press is full of rags-to-riches stories of successful entrepreneurs whose business empires started out in their garage or living room and ended up as an IPO on Wall Street. In the early days, Jeff Bezos hosted Amazon in his garage. Salesforce began life in a one-bedroomed apartment in San Francisco. Google founders Larry Page and Sergey Brin began building their first search engine in their dormitory at Stanford University.[11] These stories can lure the novice entrepreneur's intuitive mind into taking risky decisions because they play on its tendency not only to believe plausible business propositions but also to confirm what it's been led to believe is true.

Well-publicised 'hits' are by definition small samples; they're the striking success stories that happen to get lauded in the media. On the other hand, there are countless unsuccessful entrepreneurs who ended up losing a shed load of money and failed to make the headlines. Amazon, Salesforce and Google are unrepresentative of the population of business start-ups. As such, they're flimsy evidence for the chances of a start-up being a success because, as we know, in the shadow of every two

> successful ventures are three that failed to make it past their fifth birthday.[12]
>
> The picture that these success stories conjure up isn't representative. In fact, it's highly unrepresentative. Taken at face value it can lead to overestimating the chances of success and underestimating the chances of failure. This can lead to nasty surprises in professional and personal life. For example, a start-up that receives positive feedback for its new product from the first ten customers who purchase it and concludes that the product will be a rip-roaring success is guilty of overestimating the chances of success and underestimating the chances of failure based on a small number of responses.

Being beguiled by small numbers can lead to errors in judgement and decision making because the human brain didn't evolve to solve probability problems, it evolved to take decisions on the basis of memorable stories that *look* and *feel* convincing. Among our distant ancestors these stories would have been passed around at the camp fire and in gossip.

In the bigger picture, the intuitive mind evolved to work with images, scripts, stories, metaphors and myths, rather than with abstractions and generalisations. The good news is that we have a parallel system – the analytical mind – that works well with numbers, abstractions and generalisations. We're fortunate that evolution has bestowed on us a brain that gives us the best of both worlds. The challenge is to combine them so that neither intuition nor analysis gets ahead of itself and tries to do things it wasn't designed for.

When our intuitive mind takes a shortcut to a plausible conclusion that feels right, for example 'the ball costs five cents' or 'this business venture feels like it will work', it can lead to overconfidence. The moral is:

- Don't put too much trust in your intuition for computational problems (like the bat-and-ball problem) because there's always the chance that it'll get the answer wrong.

- Don't put too much trust in your intuition for probability judgements (like small business success rates) because there's always the chance that it could sway you towards overly risky behaviours because of its disposition towards alluring stories.

- In situations of probability, statistics and risk it's better to use analysis rather than intuition because the chances are that the analytical mind will come to a more accurate judgement or decision.

But how is the example of the budding entrepreneur who fails to engage their analytical mind and overestimates their chances of success different from the example of Jeff Bezos's decision to trust his gut in setting up Amazon Prime?

The answer is in the difference between risk and uncertainty (see Step 3).

In deciding whether or not to set up a small business the chances of success can be quantified because the data are out there: only four out of ten will still be trading five years after starting up. The risks of success and failure are known. This is decision making under risk. A rational entrepreneur would be well-advised to take these data into account in deciding whether or not start a small business. At least they know what their chances are.

For Bezos and Amazon, Prime was uncharted territory. While other companies had used loyalty schemes, the probability of success or failure of this particular idea in Amazon couldn't be quantified. How many other Amazon Primes had been set up and could be judged successful or unsuccessful? This is decision making under uncertainty. Experienced CEOs often take their gut feelings into account, treating them as a reasonable 'data point' when deciding on whether or not to gamble on a big strategic decision.

Business angels do the same thing when deciding whether or not to invest in a start-up venture. They combine hard business viability data (BVD) such as market growth potential with softer person perception data (PPD) such as, in the words of one angel, 'noticing right away, sometimes within five seconds … of how you feel about them' as an entrepreneur. Successful angel investors use their good judgement and nous to prevent intuitive person perception overwhelming analytical BVD and vice versa.[13] They don't see it as a decision of *either* BVD *or* PPD holding sway, instead they take *both* BVD *and* PPD into account.

Takeaway

The intuitive mind is good at sensing but some decisions, especially those involving probability and statistics, are better tackled by solving and should be delegated to the analytical mind (or to a machine).

Beware of stereotypes hijacking your decisions

As well as being beguiled by small numbers, the intuitive mind can also be beguiled by stereotypes. The word 'stereotype' itself comes from the Greek words *stereos* meaning 'solid' and *tupos* meaning 'image' or 'impression': hence a stereotype is a solid image that is difficult to change.[14] This makes stereotypes 'sticky'.

One of the most famous problems in psychology is 'The Linda Problem'. It was an ingenious decision lab experimental task devised by Kahneman and Tversky in the 1980s to show how stereotypes can influence human judgement and decision making. It goes like this.

> **'Linda is 31 years old, single, outspoken and very bright. She majored in philosophy. As a student, she was deeply concerned with issues of discrimination and social justice, and also participated in anti-nuclear demonstrations.'**

Do you think it's more likely that Linda is a bank teller (Option 1) or that she's a bank teller who's active in the feminist movement (Option 2)?

Most people go for Linda is more likely to be a bank teller who's active in the feminist movement (Option 2) rather than Linda is merely a bank teller (Option 1).

If you chose Option 2 you're in good company; around 90 per cent of undergraduates at elite US universities who Kahneman and Tversky gave this task to also chose Option 2 but unfortunately you're also wrong.[15]

The fictitious Linda's description has been concocted deliberately to make her sound like someone who's likely to be active in the feminist movement (anti-discrimination, anti-nuclear, etc.) and unrepresentative of a typical bank teller who doesn't get involved in these sorts of issues.

The reason Option 2 is wrong is because 'bank tellers who are active in the feminist movement' is a subset of bank tellers therefore, numerically speaking, there must be fewer of them. When I use this exercise in class there's always a fair few people who find it hard to believe and have trouble accepting the right answer even when it's spelled out. But if you're still not convinced think of it – or draw it – as the overlap between active feminists and bank tellers as a Venn diagram: there have to be fewer of them.[†] In terms of sheer numbers and simple probability, Option 1 is more likely than Option 2.

If you, like the elite US undergraduates, got it wrong it's because your intuitive mind, and not your analytical mind, was in the driving seat.

Your low effort, cognitive miser of an intuitive mind likes to work on the basis of stereotypes, not statistics. It comes to a quick, low-effort evaluation of whether or not Linda fits with an image of 'bank tellers who are active in the feminist movement' or whether she sounds more like an ordinary 'bank teller'. Linda's description conjures up a solid, hard-to-shift image of what a stereotypical active feminist might look like. Judgement of Linda then proceeds on this basis: 'she *must* be one, what else could she be?'

[†] It violates logical principle known as the 'conjunction rule': a conjunction (A and B) cannot be more probable than one of its constituents (A or B).

Taking a decision on the basis of a stereotype is called the 'representativeness heuristic'. It's where a decision is made not using logic or probability but on how similar, or representative, an object, person or situation is to the stereotype that we hold in our heads.

Big thinker

Daniel Kahneman

Daniel Kahneman (1934–2024) was Professor of Psychology at the Princeton University and a fellow of the Center for the Study of Rationality at the Hebrew University in Jerusalem. Over six decades of seminal work by this Nobel Prize-winning scientist deepened our understanding of how people take decisions in uncertain situations. Towards the end of his long life Kahneman was described by another world-leading scientist as 'the world's most influential living psychologist'.[16]

Here are three essential insights about intuition from Kahneman's best-selling 2011 book, *Thinking, Fast and Slow*:

- 'We now understand the marvels as well as the flaws of intuitive thought.'[17]
- 'Expert intuition strikes us as magical, but it is not … each of us performs feats of intuitive expertise many times each day.'[18]
- Intuitive thinking 'is the origin of much that we do wrong, but it is also the origin of most of what we do right – which is most of what we do'.[19]

As well as being awarded the Nobel Prize in 2002, he was also the recipient of a Lifetime Contribution Award of the American Psychological Association (2007) and the Presidential Medal of Freedom (2013) awarded by President Barack Obama.

The Linda Problem is another example of where a heuristic, or mental shortcut, can lead to biased judgements of objects, people and situations. Our intuitive mind is adept in sensing similarities rather than solving probabilities. If it has to judge similarity then it needs something to compare the object with: this is where stereotypes come in. It's good at this because, as a consummate recogniser of patterns (even if they don't exist), that's what it evolved to do. It's also quicker out of the blocks than the analytical mind, so its first impression cements into place easily and can be hard to dislodge. There's a lot of scientific truth to the old adage that first impressions count: one reason for this is because they're automatic and intuitive.

If you're still not convinced that Option 2 is wrong, try this logical equivalent of the problem: is it more likely that, while I'm walking home this evening, I'll meet a grey-haired man (Option 1) or a grey-haired man with a black dog (Option 2)?

Spotlight on intuition
Answering the easy-to-answer question

One of the psychological processes that's at work when people judge Linda as more likely to be a bank teller who's active in the feminist movement rather than simply a bank teller is called 'attribute substitution'. It involves going for the easier-to-answer question rather than the harder-to-answer question. Attribute substitution fits neatly with the least effort and cognitive miser principles.

In the case of Linda it's quicker and easier to come to the view that she's a bank teller who's active in the feminist movement because she suits the stereotype, rather than thinking through 'what are the chances of Linda being one or the other?'.

In a recruitment and selection situation the easy-to-answer question is, 'Do I like the candidate's Power Point presentation?'; the harder-to-answer question is, 'Does this candidate have the requisite skills, capabilities and track record to do this job effectively?'. In a 'Dragons' Den'[‡] type situation the easy-to-answer question is, 'Did I like the entrepreneur's pitch?'; the harder-to-answer question is, 'What is the most up-to-date evidence for the proportion of businesses that have failed in this sector in the past 12 months and what is this entrepreneur's chances of bucking this trend?' Experienced 'dragons' are rarely beguiled by person perception, which isn't to say they *never* go with their gut; they do, sometimes.

In the US version of the show, 'Shark Tank', investor Daymond John had a gut feeling about a pitch for funding for the 'Scholly' app designed to help less-privileged students find scholarships based on their personal profiles. Despite the scepticism of some of the other Sharks, John offered Scholly $40,000 for a 15 per cent stake in the business jointly with Lori Greiner who was persuaded to come on board. Scholly's social purpose of 'scholarships made easy' aligned intuitively with Daymond John's ethics, values and beliefs. Scholly's inventor, Christopher Gray, subsequently landed on the *Forbes* Under 30 list of social entrepreneurs. Scholly has 3.5 million active users and has connected students with $100 million in scholarships.[20]

The stereotype of entrepreneurs as 'gung-ho' go-with-your-gut types who wield gut feelings as their secret weapon is something of a myth. Research by Kevin Groves and colleagues, which compared the extent to which three highly contrasting job types, accountants, actors and entrepreneurs, used intuition versus analysis, found that actors were high on intuition and low on analysis while accountants were the reverse; entrepreneurs, however, were much more balanced, having comparable levels of intuition and analysis (Figure 14).[21] The Oscar-winning actor Cillian Murphy, who played J. Robert Oppenheimer in the film of the same name, said that as far as acting is concerned: 'Instinct is the thing I rely on most. Everyone

---

[‡] 'Dragon's Den' is a reality TV show where budding entrepreneurs pitch their ideas to a panel of venture capitalists with the hope of securing an investment.

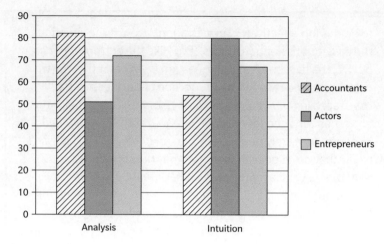

Figure 14 Preference for intuition and analysis for three different types of job (accountants, actors, entrepreneurs)

is obsessed with process ... but what I do in the rehearsal room just *happens*.'[22]

Another side to this is that letting the intuitive mind take control, especially where judging other people is concerned and particularly when they're people who aren't 'like us' (whoever 'we' might be), can open the door to prejudice, bias and discrimination. De-biasing the intuitive mind of its shortcuts is made harder because its workings are unconscious. This is one of the reasons why many organisations have invested in anti-unconscious bias training and it's why the top US judge Ruth Bader Ginsberg said, 'unconscious bias is one of the hardest things to get at' to which might be added 'and one of the hardest things to fix'.

It's a fact that gut feelings are potent and hard to ignore. But in many social judgement situations (for example entrepreneurial pitches, employee hiring, etc.) we need to have the self-awareness and nous to be able to press pause and step back and ask ourselves the question: 'Is there really something of substance that attracts me to or repels me from this person and their pitch or job application over and above simply liking or not liking them?'

Takeaway

The intuitive mind prefers easier-to-answer rather than harder-to-answer questions. When this leads to judging people, objects and situations in terms of stereotypes it can result in erroneous, biased, prejudiced and potentially costly and unethical judgements.

Beware of the confirmation bias

One of intuition's biggest flaws is that it can convince us easily that, 'If I *feel* good about a judgement, I must be *right* about it.'[23] Intuition's feel-good factor is important and useful because it impels us to action, helps us to avoid analysis paralysis, and also going with our gut can be more pleasurable than going against it. Intuition has this power over us because of the potency of gut feelings. Combined with its speed this can sometimes put the intuitive mind in a commanding position.

As we know, unlike the analytical mind, the intuitive mind avoids abstractions and generalisations; instead, it prefers real contexts and works best with images, stories, metaphors and myths. Creating stories helps us to make sense of events, but the inferences that follow from stories can be wrong sometimes.

The intuitive mind's liking for stories can cloud its, and our, judgement if we let it.

Imagine Hannah, a new appointee to the team that Jim is part of. Early on in her employment Hannah turns up late for a meeting a couple of days on the run. Jim, who had some misgivings about Hannah when she was first appointed, noted that Hannah is late. He then starts to create and then climb his own personalised 'ladder of inference' about Hannah: 'Hannah has been late for a couple of meetings recently', becomes 'Hannah is always late for meetings', becomes 'I've no doubt that she'll be late again', becomes 'Hannah is unreliable', becomes 'I knew my gut feelings about Hannah were right all along', becomes 'we should never have employed Hannah in the first place', becomes 'if they'd have listened to me we wouldn't be in this mess', becomes 'how are we going to get rid of her?'.

Jim's intuition has put two and two together and made five. More on this story anon. Ladders of inference create problems for us because we create and climb them without realising we're doing so.

The ladder of inference is a powerful thinking tool developed by the late Chris Argyris, Professor at Harvard. He used it to explain how people create and maintain assumptions, how these assumptions can affect how people think and behave and how they can be avoided. The practical value of analysing our ladders of inference is that by exposing the assumptions and intuitions that we hold about objects, people and situations it can help us de-bias our thinking.

Going back to Jim, what he doesn't know or need to know about Hannah, but her line manager does, is that she's been having some family issues at the moment, which mean that she's been detained at home on a few occasions. This sheds a different light on Hannah's turning up late which, if known about, could lead Jim to a totally different set of inferences and conclusions about Hannah.

Nonetheless, the story that Jim's intuitive mind has created about Hannah has taken on a life of its own. It now surreptitiously and subconsciously influences how he thinks and interacts with Hannah, in spite of the fact that it's based on an untested and false intuition about her. He even uses his intuitions about Hannah to predict how she's likely to behave in the future and how she should be treated.

The author of bestseller *Black Swan: The Impact of the Highly Improbable* (2008), Nassim Nicholas Taleb, calls this the 'narrative fallacy'. It's where the intuitive mind spins fanciful explanations for situations that could be explained just as easily in some other way. Narratives become fallacies when they're used to make sense of a situation based on insufficient or incorrect information; for example, as far as Hannah goes, Jim didn't know the half of it.

The intuitive mind is especially susceptible to these kinds of bias because of its preference for stories. It's very good at seeing links between things. This is why it sometimes sees patterns even if they don't exist. It has a tendency to force relationships onto data that can sometimes bind unrelated facts together. The intuitive tendency to see patterns and relationships where none exist can lead people to come up with unnecessary causal explanations for things that are better understood as a result of random variation, and can help to explain superstitious behaviour such as using lucky charms. It can even be linked to believing in ghosts and evil spirits.[24]

The flip side of the intuitive mind's prodigious power to make connections and perceive patterns is that this strength, when it's taken too far, can become a weakness for seeing patterns all over the place. This is the 'strengths into weaknesses' paradox: when it's overexercised a once-productive strength can turn into a destructive weakness. For example, perseverance is a good thing but when taken too far can become stubbornness. Other examples include confidence becoming irrational exuberance; attention to detail becoming obsessive preoccupation; independent mindedness becoming arrogance and assertiveness becoming belligerence.

This highlights one of the paradoxes of intuition: one of its strengths is its ability to perceive patterns and create connections, but this strength becomes a weakness when it forces unjustifiable connections on data or perceives patterns that don't actually exist. When it does so it can lead us up the garden path to biased judgements and faulty decision making. Knowing where to draw the line is a matter of fine judgement, nous and, ultimately, intuitive intelligence.

By weaving fancy narratives – whether they're accurate or not – the world makes more sense to the intuitive mind even though the logic of the story itself might be wrong. This is where Jim's intuitive mind led him astray. When we inadvertently create a false narrative we can end up distorting the facts and arrive at conclusions that are biased.[25] It's another example of where mental shortcuts can lead us up the garden path.

Narratives, which may or may not be accurate, make us feel confident enough, like Jim, to judge people and predict how they'll behave. Perhaps subconsciously he was, all along, looking for evidence to support the misgivings he already had about Hannah. His interpretation of the facts (she was late, after all) was spun into a causal relationship ('Hannah is an unreliable person, that's why she's always late') which he used to confirm his already-formed opinion about Hannah ('I knew all along that Hannah would turn out to be unreliable'). Jim looked for facts that would support his intuition while he was oblivious to any disconfirmation that might challenge because he *felt* that he was *right* about her. This was his mental model of Hannah; it was unjustified, but hard to dislodge. This is the 'confirmation bias'; when we *feel* we tend to *confirm* and what we confirm we tend to *do*.

One of the problems with making inferences from readily available evidence is that they can lead to wrong conclusions because different hypotheses may be compatible with the same data. For example, both the imagined (she's unreliable) and real (she has some family issues) explanations for Hannah's behaviour were compatible with the 'facts', depending on a person's knowledge and point of view. Facts can be selected to confirm our intuitions, but my facts may not be your facts, my mental model of the world might not be your mental model and, even worse, my facts can be selected to confirm my prejudices and reinforce my biased and inaccurate mental models about objects, people and situations. Social media amplifies this tendency.

Spotlight on intuition
Seeking disconfirming evidence

One of the twentieth century's most influential philosophers of science was Sir Karl Popper. It was he who came up with the celebrated parable of the black swan which we met in Step 3. Suppose a naturalist has a theory that all swans are white and sets out to prove this by collecting evidence of the existence of white swans. There would be no shortage of data: every swan I've ever seen has been white. Does this prove that his theory is true? Of course not. No matter how many white swans our 'all swans are white' naturalist finds he can never be sure that there isn't somewhere in the world a black swan lurking which will kill his theory stone dead.

To test the theory that 'all swans are white' it would be better to seek out non-white swans: this is Popper's principle of falsification which he proposed as a principle for scientific progress. Seeking more white swans would simply confirm what we already think we know about swans; it wouldn't allow any space for the mental model of 'all swans are white' to be disconfirmed and dislodged.

As far as intuitions are concerned, Popper's principle would suggest that we should treat them as 'provisional' and be prepared for and open to evidence that might prove them to be wrong. There is of course a practical problem with searching for disconfirming evidence: it could go on indefinitely, freezing decision makers into inaction and analysis paralysis when time might be of the essence. Sometimes we need to employ simple rules that are good enough approximations which will help us to take action (called 'fast-and-frugal heuristics'). Nonetheless, we should bear in mind the logical fact that they might be falsifiable.

Confirmation bias is the tendency to notice, focus on and give greater credence to evidence that fits with our pre-existing beliefs. The more white swans we see, the deeper our belief that all swans are white becomes entrenched. This is not unreasonable, however, there's always the possibility that a black swan might exist somewhere.

The confirmation bias can be rife in both personal and professional life: imagine a manager who intuitively believes that working in the office is more productive than working at home. To confirm this the manager might focus on office-based employees who've delivered outstanding results and simultaneously overlook, or choose to ignore, examples of office working leading to missed deadlines, burnout, etc.

To overcome confirmation bias, as well as seeking confirmatory behaviour for these beliefs, the manager ought to seek out evidence to disconfirm the idea that office working is more productive; for example by seeking input from employees who've had different experiences of office-versus-remote working, gathering instances of successful and unsuccessful office-versus-home working and listening to contrarian opinions that office working is better than working at home.

But why don't we actively seek disconfirmations for our hypotheses and intuitions?

One reason is that confirmations are about seeking connections between things and, as we know, the intuitive mind is a consummate connector and perceiver of patterns. This is one of intuition's upsides and a reason intuitive experts are able to see connections and notice patterns that novices are blind to. But the eminent psychologist Robin Hogarth saw this as one reason we don't tend to disconfirm readily: our intuitive mind is primed to learn from things that happen to occur together; it isn't primed to learn from things that don't occur together. This is how Klein's firefighters whom we met in the earlier chapters were able to respond intuitively; they did so by linking cues (such as colour, sound and heat) and with what they expected to happen next.

Intuitions are learned by confirmation of cue–outcome relationships (see Step 3) and experience. But it's a double-edged sword: on the one hand it's an efficient way to learn associations between cues and outcomes (like Pavlov's dogs) and to build intuitive muscle power; but on the other hand it can lead us into traps by becoming fixated on a single explanation or course of action.

Another reason Hogarth suggested we don't tend to disconfirm readily is that we prefer to be proved right rather than wrong. This is because most of us like to find that our ideas are right because we're emotionally attached to them and, for the same reason, don't like finding out they're wrong. Also, he noted, if we're proved wrong we then have to generate a new hypothesis to explain what might be going on, and this is likely to be effortful and not something that a cognitive miser is predisposed to.

Warren Buffet, one of the world's most successful investors, reputedly said, 'What the human being is best at doing is interpreting all new information so that their prior conclusions remain intact.'[26]

When this happens we end up concocting stories and creating connections that don't really exist.

Confirmation is an inherent and instinctive tendency of the human mind. Social media technologies amplify confirmation bias, reinforce prior attitudes and beliefs and build echo chambers in which people can hear their own voice or that of groups they identify with.[27] The algorithms that decide what we see on our smartphones select the most attention-grabbing content and tailor it to what they think our needs are. Our 'filter bubble' is our individual online universe of information which is customised for us by the algorithms that power the Internet.[28] They create for each of us an echo chamber of preconceived ideas and exclude information that might refute them. They show us more and more of what they think we want to see, which, in an attention-depleted world, also means less of what we might *need* to see. This can be a good way to build bad intuitions.

Social media addiction is common and is thought to have dire consequences for mental and physical health, including increased risk of depression, anxiety, loneliness, self-harm and even suicidal thoughts.[29] It confirms the user's beliefs and values in everything from product selection to political preferences. It can make people vulnerable to misinformation and manipulation and amplify not only our intuitions but also our prejudices.[30] It's antithetical to intuitive intelligence.

The last word on confirmation bias goes to Gary Klein. He actually challenges the received wisdom that people don't disconfirm. He gives the example of an experienced firefighter who initially thought he was dealing with a fire in a laundry chute on the lower floors that was about to spread up to the rest of the building. But this firefighter had the nous to check whether or not he was *wrong*. He circled the building and noticed fire coming out from under the eaves. This blew his laundry chute theory out of the water. The fire had already spread to the top of the building. He switched his strategy from trying to extinguish the fire to a search-and-rescue operation. All the inhabitants were saved.

Klein uses this as an example of an expert using their intuition to come up with a hypothesis but then also having the nous to test whether the hypothesis is correct. In this example, intuition and analysis worked together seamlessly. Klein's view is that the confirmation bias has been overplayed by psychologists based on results from clever laboratory experiments using undergraduates, and used to overclaim that people have a tendency to stick with their hypotheses. He thinks we might be better looking at how ordinary people and experts behave in the real world outside of the psychology lab and focus on problems of 'fixation' rather than confirmation bias.[31]

A position that acknowledges both the lab and the real-world views is that we should use our intuition to form initial hypotheses, trust these where our experience warrants it and where it seems reasonable to do so, but also, like the firefighter and the laundry chute fire, use doubt to correct the inevitable errors that can creep in to our 'gut calls' every now and then, even when we're in familiar territory. In other words, we shouldn't become unreasonably *fixated* on them. Klein's laundry chute firefighter used his curiosity and openness as a way to avoid being hypnotised by a hunch. Actively searching for facts that support our intuitions can lead us to falling foul of confirmation bias. On the other hand, being open to alterative interpretations can help us to hone our hunches and build intuitive intelligence. This is the subject of the next chapter.

Takeaway

The narrative fallacy and confirmation bias can seduce us into being overconfident in our intuitions. To counter this tendency we should seek alternative accounts for observed events and look for disconfirming evidence before we become too fixated on our intuitions.

Dig deeper

Daniel Kahneman's *Thinking, Fast and Slow* explains the two-minds model, explores the marvels and limitations of the human mind and gives practical tips for how to improve our decision making.

In a nutshell, de-biasing your intuitive mind

The intuitive mind is good at sensing, but decisions involving probability/statistics are better tackled by solving and should be delegated to the analytical mind (or to a machine). It's also adept at answering an easy-to-answer question and seeing patterns where they may not exist; this can lead to erroneous, biased and prejudiced judgements.

Workout 1: The ladder of inference

1 Do you create and climb ladders of inference?

2 By analysing our personal ladders of inference we can identify if and how we're intuitively jumping to conclusions and how we might reframe things to obtain more accurate and unbiased perceptions.

3 Consolidate your knowledge of the ladder of inference by mapping Jim's ladder of inference or one of your own (Figure 15). Start at the bottom and work through to the top.

4 One way to avoid jumping to conclusions is to pause on each step to do a reality check.

5 Now go back and insert a reality check for each step on the ladder.

Rungs	Inference	Reality check
6 Decide how to act		
5 Explain the situation		
4 Give your interpretation a label		
3 Interpret the data		
2 Data you select to attend to		
1 Available data to you		

Figure 15 A ladder of inference[32]

6 Be wary of climbing the ladder of inference; subject your intuitions to reality checks along the way to test their robustness and to avoid jumping to conclusions.

Workout 2: Jumping to conclusions

1 Focus on a belief about an object, person or situation that you hold strongly; for example, for Jim this was 'Hannah is an unreliable colleague.'

2 Write down your evidence for this belief.

3 Write down the evidence against this belief.

4 Does your belief stand up to scrutiny in the light of the for and against evidence?

Workout 3: Allow yourself to be wrong

1 Focus on a belief about an object, person or situation that you hold strongly; for example, for Jim this was 'Hannah is an unreliable colleague.'

2 What Jim might like to ask himself is: 'What if I was wrong in my belief about Hannah?' How would being wrong change Jim's relationship with Hannah?

3 Ask yourself the same question about your deeply held belief about an object, person or situation.

Workout 4: Beware of patterns of thinking

1 Focus on a belief that you're strongly attached to; for Jim this was 'Hannah is an unreliable colleague.'

2 Do you hold any similar beliefs about other objects, people or situations?

3 If you do, does this say anything about stereotypes that you might hold about objects, people or situations?

4 How do these stereotypes or patterns of thinking affect your relationship with said object, person or situation?

Workout 5: Open it up to the other side

1 Expose yourself to contrary views.

2 For example, if you typically tune in to left-leaning media, try switching now and then to right-leaning media and vice versa. Get your news from feeds other than TikTok or X, etc.

3 Does opening up to the other side affect your views and, if so, how? How does opening up make you feel? Warning: it might be uncomfortable at first.

Notes

1 Kahneman, D. (2011) *Thinking, Fast and Slow*. London: Allen Lane, p. 235.

2 Adams, T. (2016) 'The Undoing Project review – "psychology's Lennon and McCartney"', *The Guardian*, 11 December. Available online at: https://www.theguardian.com/books/2016/dec/11/undoing-project-michael-lewis-review-amos-tversky-daniel-kahneman-behavioural-psychology.

3 Kahneman (2011), p. 45.

4 Kahneman, D. and Frederick, S. (2002) 'Representativeness revisited: Attribute substitution in intuitive judgement', in Gilovich, T., Dale, G. and Kahneman, D. (eds) *Heuristics and Biases*. Cambridge: Cambridge University Press, pp. 49–81, p. 58.

5 Stanovich, K. E. (2020) 'Why humans are cognitive misers and what it means for the great rationality debate', in Viale, R. (ed.)

Routledge Handbook of Bounded Rationality. Abingdon: Routledge, pp. 196–206.

6 Anonymous (2020) 'Susan Fiske and Shelley Taylor recognized with a Frontiers of Knowledge Award for revealing the role of cognitive bias in social relations', BBVA, 16 April. Available online at: https://www.bbva.com/en/susan-fiske-and-shelley-taylor-recognized-with-a-frontiers-of-knowledge-award-for-revealing-the-role-of-cognitive-bias-in-social-relations/.

7 Ibid.

8 Fiske, S. T. (2004) 'Intent and ordinary bias: Unintended thought and social motivation create casual prejudice', *Social Justice Research*, 17, 117–27.

9 Stanovich (2020), p. 196.

10 Anonymous (2020) 'New research: Success is limited until DIY investors break bad habits', *Financial Times/Capital.com*. Available online at: https://www.ft.com/partnercontent/capital-com/new-research-success-is-limited-until-diy-investors-break-bad-habits.html.

11 Batchelor, M. (2022) 'Successful entrepreneurs whose ventures began in living rooms and garages', *CEO Magazine*, 27 June. Available online at: https://www.theceomagazine.com/business/start-ups-entrepreneurs/entrepreneur-success-stories/.

12 Statista (2024) 'Survival rate of new enterprises in the United Kingdom from 2007 to 2021, by years survived', *Statista.com*. Available online at: https://www.statista.com/statistics/285305/new-enterprise-survival-rate-in-the-uk/.

13 Huang, L. and Pearce, J. L. (2015) 'Managing the unknowable: The effectiveness of early-stage investor gut feel in entrepreneurial investment decisions', *Administrative Science Quarterly*, 60(4), 634–70.

14 Jones, E. E. and Colman, A. M. (1996) 'Stereotypes', in Kuper, A. and Kuper, J. (eds) *The Social Science Encyclopaedia* (2nd edition). London: Routledge (pp. 843–4). Available online at: https://figshare.le.ac.uk/articles/chapter/Stereotypes/10081154.

15 Kahneman (2011), p. 158.

16 Anon. (2024) 'Daniel Kahneman, renowned psychologist and Nobel prize winner, dies at 90', *The Guardian*, 28 March. Available online at: https://www.theguardian.com/science/2024/mar/28/daniel-kahneman-death-age-90-psychologist-nobel-prize-winner-bio.

17 Kahneman (2011), p. 10.

18 Kahneman (2011), p. 11.

19 Kahneman (2011), p. 416.

20 Field, A. (2024) '9 years after his shark tank splash, Christopher Gray updates Scholly's progress', *Forbes*, 19 May 2024. Available online at: https://www.forbes.com/sites/annefield/2024/03/19/9-years-after-his-shark-tank-splash-christopher-gray-updates-schollys-progress.

21 Groves, K. S., Vance, C. M., Choi, D. Y. and Mendez, J. L. (2008) 'An examination of the nonlinear thinking style profile stereotype of successful entrepreneurs', *Journal of Enterprising Culture*, 16(2), 133–59.

22 Ellison, J. (2024) 'The mesmerising normality of Cillian Murphy', *Financial Times HTSI Magazine*, p. 44.

23 Dane, E. and Pratt, M. G. (2007) 'Exploring intuition and its role in managerial decision making', *Academy of Management Review*, 32(1), 33–54, p. 39.

24 Risen, J. L. (2016) 'Believing what we do not believe: Acquiescence to superstitious beliefs and other powerful intuitions', *Psychological Review*, 123(2), 182–207; Sadler-Smith, E. (2011) 'The intuitive style: Relationships with local/global and verbal/visual styles, gender, and superstitious reasoning', *Learning and Individual Differences*, 21(3), 263–70.

25 Menashe, D. and Shamash, M. E. (2006) 'The narrative fallacy', *International Commentary on Evidence*, 3(1).

26 Chamorro-Premuzic, T. (2014) 'How the web distorts reality and impairs our judgement skills', *The Guardian*, 13 May. Available

online at: https://www.theguardian.com/media-network/media-network-blog/2014/may/13/internet-confirmation-bias.

27 Modgil, S., Singh, R. K., Gupta, S. and Dennehy, D. (2021) 'A confirmation bias view on social media induced polarisation during Covid-19', *Information Systems Frontiers*, 1–25.

28 Popova, M. (no date) 'The filter bubble: Algorithm vs. curator & the value of serendipity', *The Marginalian*, https://www.themarginalian.org/2011/05/12/the-filter-bubble/ (accessed May 2024).

29 Robinson, L. and Smith, M. (no date) 'Social media and mental health', *HelpGuide.com*. Available online at: https://www.helpguide.org/articles/mental-health/social-media-and-mental-health.htm (accessed May 2024).

30 Ciampaglia, G. L., Menczer, F. and The Conversation US (2018) 'Biases make people vulnerable to misinformation spread by social media', *Scientific American*, 21 June. Available online at: https://www.scientificamerican.com/article/biases-make-people-vulnerable-to-misinformation-spread-by-social-media/.

31 Klein, G. (2019) 'The curious case of confirmation bias', *Psychology Today*, 5 May. Available online at: https://www.psychologytoday.com/gb/blog/seeing-what-others-dont/201905/the-curious-case-confirmation-bias.

32 The Systems Thinker (no date) 'The ladder of inference'. Available online at: https://thesystemsthinker.com/the-ladder-of-inference/ (accessed May 2024).

step 7

Hone your hunches

'Trusting our intuition often saves us from disaster.'

Anne Wilson Schaef (US clinical psychologist and author)

- -

The previous step was about how to avoid using intuition in situations that it's not suited to. This chapter is about how to hone your hunches; think of it as a quality assurance system for intuition.

- -

A quality assurance system for gut feelings

Customer service staff and salespeople have a key role in generating revenue and maintaining high-quality service interactions with customers. In customer service interactions an analytical assessment of customers' behaviour isn't always feasible. Instead, customer service staff often have to rely on gut feelings about customers' needs, wants and behaviours based on thin slices of customers' behaviour. The ability to do so requires accurate 'person perception' based on cues, such as what customers say and non-verbal information such as facial expressions, hand gestures, jewellery, clothing, etc. An inaccurate intuitive person perception about customers' needs, wants and behaviours could have negative consequences not only for a service encounter but also for a firm's market position and financial performance.[1]

The pioneering intuition researcher Robin Hogarth used the example of a server in a Chicago restaurant, Anna, who thinks she has great intuition about which customers will leave higher tips. Anna's experience has led her to the intuitive inference that well-dressed customers leave higher tips. Her explanation is that well-heeled people have more money to lavish on tipping restaurant staff.

Naturally, Anna wants to maximise her earnings but is hard pressed for which customers to give her best attention to. Armed with this intuition, what's the obvious thing for Anna to do?

Of course, based on her intuitive inference, Anna should give her best attention to the better-dressed customers. Lo and behold because they get Anna's undivided attention they do indeed leave higher tips. The less well-dressed customers, on the other hand, rarely tip Anna because she always passes over them in favour of the better-dressed clientele.

Anna just goes with her gut; she hasn't tested her intuition but could do so if she wanted to.

For a start she could randomly assign her attention to customers irrespective of how well dressed they were to see what happened to their tipping behaviours. If she were feeling bold she might also have a go at asking the less well-dressed customers why they don't leave any tips.

Had she tested her intuition about well-dressed customers being the best tippers her gut feeling might have proven false. As it turns out, Anna's intuition has no basis in reality; it's a self-fulfilling prophecy. Had Anna stress tested her intuition she might have de-bunked her own intuition and worked out a different method of person perception to identify potentially high-tipping customers. Even though Anna's story is a fiction, researchers have found that when salespeople used both intuition and analysis in their interactions with customers their performance improved by more than 130 per cent.[2]

Intuitions are learned by making associations between cues and outcomes. The general point from Anna's story is that simply making an association between a cue and an outcome doesn't guarantee that the association that's being made is valid: the cue (well-dressed customers) and the outcome (generous tips) weren't linked even though they appeared to be.

This is called the 'illusion of validity'. It led to Anna seriously over-rating her ability to make accurate predictions; it also influenced how she did her job. Her intuitive person perceptions were nothing more than a mirage. This is a pity because the ability to make accurate person perceptions in a restaurant setting isn't something that can be outsourced to a machine. Consequently, this makes jobs like Anna's, and others that require accurate person perception, empathy and compassion, safer in an AI-dominated job market of the future.

To reinforce the point, consider the story of a student, let's call him Andrew, who was given a teddy bear, 'Lucky Ted', by his superstitious grandmother to take into exams. Andrew scored top marks with Lucky Ted beside him and now can't bear, no pun intended, to be without Lucky Ted whenever he takes an exam.

Illusions about fake connections are an effective way to build bad intuitions and superstitions. Andrew's initial success and his continued belief in Lucky Ted is an example of 'superstitious learning': a false connection is made between a behaviour (having Ted with him in exams) and a desirable outcome (good exam results), even though there's no connection between them.

Spotlight on intuition
Superstitious learning

One of the main ways in which humans and other animals learn is through association and reinforcement. For example, the dogs in Pavlov's pioneering psychology experiments in the early twentieth century learned to associate a neutral stimulus (a bell) with the presentation of food, as discussed in Step 1. After sufficient rounds of reinforcement learning the dogs salivated at the sound of a bell even though there wasn't any food.

Being hardwired for learning, the human brain is constantly on the lookout for associations between events. This is an efficient adaptation for learning in the real world, but it can lead to nonsensical behaviours as a result of accidental or illogical reinforcements. There's a famous story which may or may not be true of a man, let's call him Arthur, who accidentally put on a black shoe and a brown shoe for an interview; he got the job, and now wears a black shoe and brown shoe whenever he goes for a job interview, but keeps his feet well under the table.

Superstitious learning can become a hazard when the reinforcement operates subconsciously and an intuition becomes a superstition. It can fuel paranormal beliefs. Anna, Andrew and Arthur were the authors of their own superstitious learning. A number of famous people have been similarly afflicted. Charles Dickens is reputed to have carried a compass around with him so he could sleep facing north because he believed it would contribute to more productive writing. Bill Gates apparently is superstitious about his choice of notebook: it has to be a yellow legal pad.[3]

These kinds of errors are much less likely to occur if consequences can be linked to causes independent of the accidental reinforcement, for example if Anna was able to observe well-dressed customers tipping irrespective of the service they were given, or vice versa, or if Andrew did well in an exam on a day when he left Lucky Ted at home.[4] Had Dickens faced different directions in his sleep he might have come to a different conclusion about what made for a productive day's writing. Feedback can help to break nonsensical associations and guards against accidental reinforcements taking hold and becoming habituated into false intuitions.

Big thinker

Robin Hogarth

Robin Hogarth (1942–2024) was Professor of Behavioural Science at Universitat Pompeu Fabra in Barcelona. As well as making a major contribution to the study of decision making in general, Hogarth has made an enormous impact on the study of intuition. Here are three insights about intuition from Hogarth's 2002 book *Educating Intuition*:

- 'Processes of which we are not aware [i.e. intuitions] govern a huge proportion of mental life.'[5]
- 'Intuition is like expertise. It is acquired through experience and can be improved through practice.'[6]
- 'People have to learn why and when their intuitions are accurate or not.'[7]

One of Hogarth's main preoccupations was studying how the situation in which we learn our intuitions determine whether or not they should be trusted (more on this later).

Trustworthy intuitions are developed when we receive valid feedback on the results of our actions. By 'valid' we mean that the relationships between the cues in the situation and the outcomes that we're trying to predict are real, and not, as in the cases of Anna, Andrew and Arthur, imagined (see also Step 3).

One of Robin Hogarth's most powerful ideas was that a good way to build bad intuitions is to get zero or inaccurate feedback on the results of going with our gut. One of the best ways to build trustworthy intuitions is to get high-quality feedback. It's quality assurance (QA) system for intuition. To be 'high quality', feedback should be:

- accurate: it should tell you *if* your intuition was a hit or a miss
- diagnostic: in that it should tell *why* your intuition was a hit or a miss
- timely: it should be available to you in *good time* so that you can learn from it while things are fresh in your mind.

Imagine using your intuition to predict the outcome of a football match but never being told whether your gut feeling was right or wrong. If you never get to know if your football intuition is accurate or not, you can't calibrate and therefore can't build intuitive muscle power. If intuitions happen to work in the absence of feedback it's more likely to be down to pure luck rather than good judgement.

On the other hand feedback in chess checks all the boxes of being timely, accurate and diagnostic: a chess player gets to know immediately if and why going with their gut was a good idea (a hit) or not (a miss) depending on what happens in the game. This also builds their intuition about whether making a particular move in such a situation will be sensible next time they find themselves in similar circumstances.

Spotlight on intuition
Managers' 'stubborn' reliance on intuition

In spite of the widely held view among psychologists that analysis outperforms intuition in employee selection decisions, managers often place more reliance in their ability to read people and trust overall impressionistic judgements rather than objective methods using scientific tools and techniques. Managers have been described as 'stubborn' in their reliance on intuition in these situations.[8]

In research that I carried out with Andrew Miles on the use of intuition in recruitment and selection decisions, we found that managers used their intuitions in situations where there was an absence of hard data or the hard data itself was felt to be inadequate. They used it as an approximate indicator of a general 'overall impression' (person perception) of a candidate. One manager described it as forming an opinion of somebody 'pretty quick', another described it as 'like a tripwire in my head' based on experience that gave another manager the ability to think 'hmm, I've seen your type before'.

Even if it were possible to dislodge managers' stubborn reliance on intuition in hiring decisions, it seems unlikely that managers are likely to abandon this approach any time soon. This might be because they believe, perhaps with good reason and like the business angels who combined person perception data (PPD) with business viability data (BVD), that in these situations intuition can be a useful data point. The most effective way that we found in the HR research was to combine intuitive person perception with hard data and a sceptical, but not dismissive, attitude to the intuition. They opened it up to scrutiny; as one manager remarked: 'If ever I get a gut feel, I just try to knock that gut feel out somehow by asking questions that are going to disprove.'[9] I will return to this topic in the section on social intuition in the final chapter.

In the absence of high-quality feedback we can never get to know if going with our gut was the right thing to do. In the presence of high-quality feedback we'll hopefully get to find out. One of the most efficient and effective ways of getting helpful feedback is by being around an expert whom you can not only observe and absorb their tacit knowledge by osmosis, but who also can be asked, 'why did this work?', 'why didn't this work?' and 'how can I improve?'. This is how good coaching works in sports and in professional life. Another way is to co-opt a friend or a colleague to play the role of a sceptic. Coaches and sceptics are essential players in a constructive environment for honing your hunches.

Takeaway

Learning good intuitions requires feedback that is accurate, diagnostic and timely.

'Kind' versus 'wicked' learning structures

Experience is a paradox: as well as being the best teacher it can also be a great deceiver. How good a teacher experience is depends on the situation in which the learning takes place. Not only can we end up learning nothing from experience because the situation is simply too noisy but used badly, experience can be counterproductive by teaching us the wrong lessons, as it did with Anna. Her experience misguided her into believing that she had great intuition for spotting high-tipping customers. As a result she developed bad customer-tipping intuition.

Why are some situations bad teachers, while others are good?

The answer lies in the difference between what our 'Big thinker' Robin Hogarth referred to as 'kind learning structures' and 'wicked learning structures':*

- Kind learning structures: these are conducive to developing intuitions that can be trusted, for example learning to drive a car (see below).

---

* 'Structure' simply means the situation in which the learning takes place. The word 'structure' is preferred to 'environment' to avoid any confusion with high- and low-validity learning environments (see Step 3), although these two ideas are related.

- Wicked learning structures: these are conducive to developing intuitions that can't be trusted, for example the server Anna's hunch about well-dressed customers' tipping behaviours.

In terms of the differences between them, *quality of feedback* is the key. In a kind learning structure there's ample accurate, diagnostic and timely feedback. Chess is a prime example of a kind learning structure where feedback is quick and unequivocal: you find out at the latest by the end of the game whether going with your gut was the right thing to do. It's not surprising therefore that chess is a game where it's possible, with enough learning and experience, to develop excellent intuition.

Learning to drive a car is another example of a kind learning structure. The relationships between things that are under the driver's control, such as steering, acceleration, changing gears and braking, are stable across different cars and different driving contexts. Not only that, but there's also immediate and unambiguous feedback between operating the various controls and the behaviour of the vehicle. The skill of driving can be improved through repetition and practice and there are clear criteria for success against which the correctness of one's driving can be assessed. Driving has a kind structure in which to learn intuitive driving skills.

In wicked learning structures, feedback is absent or misleading. Anna's well-dressed customers gave her generous tips but not because they were well dressed. Perhaps Anna could have got to the bottom of why some people tipped well and others didn't if she'd have asked herself the two questions suggested by Robin Hogarth and his colleague Emre Soyer in their book *The Myth of Experience* (2020):[10]

- Am I *missing* something? Is there something here that's unobvious and I need to uncover to understand what's going on? For example, in the case of Anna she might have wondered, 'is dress really what's behind tipping behaviours or is there something else at work?'

- Am I getting *confused* by something? Is there something in the situation that's attracting my attention and confusing me? For example, a more reflective Anna might have speculated, 'is how a customer is dressed a distraction in understanding their tipping behaviours, and therefore should I focus on something else?'

Asking these questions can break the cycle of superstitious learning that builds bad intuitions. In honing our hunches we need to ask, 'what's really going on here?' and 'are the any distractions and diversions that might be stopping me from getting to what's really going on?' This of course involves co-opting the analytical mind to counterbalance the intuitive mind's tendency to weave a narrative that seems, on the face of it, to make sense.

Takeaway

Kind learning structures build good intuitions; wicked learning structures build bad intuitions.

Improving intuitions by feeding forward

So far, the focus has been on feedback as a way to hone your hunches. The opposite of feedback is 'feedforward'. Feedforward and feedback have the same aim: to improve outcomes, but they work in opposite directions.

Feedback is the traditional way of improving performance, for example in the workplace, employees are given feedback on their performance in an annual performance review or appraisal. In everyday life, feedback is ubiquitous, for example in online product reviews, 'likes' in social media, restaurant reviews, etc. It involves looking back. Feedforward, on the other hand, as the name suggests, involves looking forward.

In improving decision making, feedforward can be just as useful as feedback. The differences between feedback and feedforward are time, focus and outcome.

- *Time:* feedback focuses on past events whereas feedforward focuses on future events. In feedback, we rewind what Gary Klein has referred to as the 'DVD in our heads' of our actions and review how well or badly things went;[11] in feedforward, we fastforward the DVD of our plans and anticipate how well or badly things might go.

- *Focus:* feedback and feedforward focus on different aspects of the decision-making process. Feedback focuses on what happened as a result of a previous decision with the aim of improving similar decisions in the future by applying lessons learned, for example 'That intuition didn't work because … '; feedforward focuses on what might happen before a decision has been implemented by asking, for example 'My intuition is unlikely to work in this situation because … '.

- *Outcomes:* feedforward and feedback have different outcomes. The outcome of feedback is an 'autopsy' metaphorically speaking. It tells us what we should do next time, for example 'Next time I meet that scenario I probably need to … '; the outcome of feedforward is a hypothesis. It shapes plans to achieve a desired outcome, for example, 'To stop x from happening we should do y … ', 'To make a happen we should do b … '.

- *Feedback and feedforward are linked:* feedback feeds into feedforward because it uncovers what happened in similar situations in the past. This information can then be used to adjust plans beforehand in feedforward next time around. Feedback and feedforward are two sides of the same coin: they're both ways of learning what *went wrong*, or what might *go wrong*, and how to improve.

- *They're relevant to intuition in two ways:* first, feedback tells us when going with our gut was the right judgement call (these are 'intuitive hits') and when going with our gut was a bad judgement call (these are 'intuitive misses'), but to get the benefit of feedback we have to be open to recognising and acknowledging our intuitive misses as well as our hits. Second, feedforward is a way to stress test gut feelings before they're put into action so that we get to forestall any failures as much as is humanly possible before any mis-intuitions get the chance to kick in and cause any problems.

Two feedforward techniques for building intuitive muscle power are 'devil's advocacy' and 'pre-morteming'.

Takeaway

Feedback focuses on what has happened with a view to learning lessons from the past; feedforward focuses on what might happen so as to prevent failure. Both of them help to build intuitive intelligence.

Devil's advocacy

Becoming a saint in the Roman Catholic Church is a tough assignment. You have to have been dead for at least five years, then your track record as a servant of God gets dissected forensically by the Congregation of the Causes of Saints. If they think you've lived a life of heroic virtue, your case gets passed to the Pope himself for his scrutiny and ratification.[12]

In the Middle Ages, Pope Sixtus V established the use of a formalised dissenting voice – the Devil's Advocate (*advocatus diaboli*) – to deliberately oppose a candidate's case for canonisation. The aim was to expose any fatal flaws that might have been overlooked or downplayed in the candidate's conduct in their life on Earth.

A famous modern example of devil's advocacy is the Cuban missile crisis of October 1962, a 13-day brink-of-nuclear war confrontation between the USA and the Soviet Union over the presence of Soviet ballistic missiles in Cuba. The US president at the time, John F. Kennedy, asked his brother, Attorney General Robert Kennedy, to role play the Devil's Advocate by deliberately taking up a contrary position to hard-line proposals for a military strike. His role was to raise concerns about the situation escalating into an all-out nuclear war, even though he was actually in favour of tough action against the Soviets. Instead, the USA implemented a naval blockade, the

Soviets stepped back, and the world was saved from a potential nuclear Armageddon.

As in the Kennedy case, the Devil's Advocate does not necessarily have to believe in the counter-arguments they're making. Their dissent can be authentic or inauthentic and they put their counter-argument forward for the sake of debate. It's a good system in general, and especially as a way to guard against 'groupthink' where the views of a strong, powerful and vocal minority can drown out or intimidate naysayers to the extent that everyone ends up singing from the same hymn sheet. A famous example of where groupthink quashed dissent with catastrophic consequences was at NASA in the launch failure of the Space Shuttle Challenger on 28 January 1986. Managers at NASA weren't open to the opinions of expert naysaying engineers at Morton Thiokol who manufactured the Shuttle's booster rockets and advised against the launch because of the freezing temperatures. Groupthink won out and the launch went ahead against the advice of the Morton Thiokol engineers. The solid rocket boosters blew apart 73 seconds into the flight and all 7 astronauts perished.[13]

Devil's advocacy has been used to make decision-making processes more robust in high-stakes situations, for example in software security, the strategy of 'red teaming', which comes from war gaming, is used to test how well an organisation would respond to a genuine cyber attack. The Devil's Advocate red team role plays an external offensive security actor while the blue team role plays the organisation's own defensive cyber security squad.[14] It's also been used by the CIA to develop strategies for countering terror threats.[15] In military and security circles, red teamers are 'fearless sceptics' who 'assume the role of saboteurs'. Their job is to poke holes in plans long before boots are on the ground.[16] Devil's advocacy and red teaming are effective ways to challenge a gut feeling about a consequential decision before it's committed to and put into action.

One of the pitfalls of trying to be your own Devil's Advocate is that it's difficult, or well-nigh impossible, to be objective; it's especially hard as far as biases and prejudices are concerned because, as we know, much of the time they're unconscious. If you don't think you have any unconscious (implicit) biases, try the online Harvard Implicit Association Test.[17] People are often taken aback by their results.

It's much better to have someone else play the Devil's Advocate than try to be it yourself. They needn't be an authentic sceptic; they could role pay an inauthentic dissenting voice. The main thing is that they dissent and that they challenge the intuition itself, not the person whose intuition is being scrutinised.[†]

Spotlight on intuition
Authentic versus inauthentic dissent

There are mixed views about whether Devil's Advocates themselves should be emotionally or intellectually detached from the decision. In her book *In Defense of Troublemakers: The Power of Dissent in Life and Business* (2018), the US social psychologist Charlan Nemeth has shown that lack of dissent can sometimes lead to disaster, as in the case of the Jonestown massacre in Guyana in 1978 where dissenters were shot dead in the lead-up to a mass suicide in which over 900 followers of the Reverend Jim Jones drank Kool-Aid laced with a cocktail of sedatives and cyanide.

Nemeth argues for the power of 'authentic dissent' because it can bring groups closer to the truth. Nemeth believes that there's a difference between role playing in the sense of 'pretending to be'the Devil's Advocate and actually believing that a proposed decision is wrong. She thinks it's hard to have a real argument with a person who's pretending. She recommends that the Devil's Advocate is an authentic dissenter and that there's also a genuine diversity of perspectives in the room.

[†] Good devil's advocacy doesn't involve any dislike of the person (*ad hominem*), it must be an objective critique of the intuition itself.

In politics cabinet government can create the illusion of dissent but, even if a cabinet has diversity in terms of gender, race and age, it will, by its very nature, be politically and ideologically more-or-less aligned. For dissent to work in this situation, it would require authentic dissenters to be brought into the room.[18] For devil's advocacy to work, there needs to be a genuine diversity of views, whether that's in the cabinet room of a government or the board room of a business. Without this, leader's hunches can go unharnessed and hubris can take hold. A case in point was George W. Bush's decision to invade Iraq in 2003, which is considered to be one of the worst foreign policy decisions taken by a US president. Bush, who was a self-confessed intuitive decision maker, packed his top team with acolytes creating an echo chamber for his own preformed intuitions about whether Saddam Hussein's regime possessed weapons of mass destruction (WMDs), which it didn't.[19] The potentially dissenting voice of the Secretary of State General Colin Powell got drowned out.

In challenging any proposals, including intuitions, a good Devil's Advocate or an effective cabinet or executive board does three things: asks probing and provocative questions about the intuition; casts doubts on the intuition for the purposes of stress testing; puts the case for an alternative to the intuition.

Imagine you're on a hiring panel and your gut feeling gives you a bad vibe about candidate A. Before going with your gut it might be worth inviting some serious provocations from a Devil's Advocate, for example: 'You've taken against this person because they didn't go to the "right" university', 'You've taken against this person because of their ethnic background', or 'You've taken against this person because of their gender'.

The challenge for the 'intuitor' is to come up with credible and convincing responses that refute each of these statements. Intuitions that don't cave in under the pressure of a tough Devil's Advocate are more likely to be trustworthy than those that go unchallenged. As one of the participants in the research Andrew Miles and I conducted with HR managers commented (which was discussed in Step 2): 'Intuition is more of a valid response if it is shared' and therefore open to scrutiny. In high-stakes situations, the opportunity costs of not having a Devil's Advocate could be expensive, as they've proven to be in politics and in business time and time again.

> ## Takeaway
>
> Devil's advocacy is a feedforward technique that can be used to stress test a gut feeling prior to going with it.

Pre-morteming

The Nobel Prize-winning Danish physicist Niels Bohr is reputed to have said, 'Prediction is very difficult, especially about the future.' If we could predict the future it would make planning our personal and professional lives a whole lot easier. However, predicting something that doesn't yet exist is impossible, therefore a more realistic approach is to plan for those eventualities that *are* foreseeable. These are the 'known unknowns' which we can anticipate the existence of but don't have complete knowledge of because they haven't yet happened.

It's a sad but inevitable fact of life that many projects fall by the wayside, for example, in the UK, 6 out of 10 business start-ups fail and 42 per cent of marriages end in divorce.[20] Given that prevention is better than cure, it's better to forestall failures before they happen.

One way of doing so is by taking the idea of a post-mortem and turning it on its head and making it into a 'pre-mortem'. A pre-mortem is mental time travel: its main assumption is that a decision has been taken and it's led to a disastrous outcome. Its aim is to produce a plan that's resilient to any shocks that can be envisaged.

The pre-mortem technique was developed by our Part 1 Big thinker, Gary Klein. It's about 'being smart at the start'[21] and is the closest we'll ever get to a crystal ball that actually works. Klein's pre-mortem method has five steps: set the scene; imagine a fiasco; generate reasons for failure; consolidate the reasons under some main headings; re-plan the project; execute the project.

A pre-mortem is conducted *after* the decision has been made but *before* it's been taken, where decision making (deciding what to do) precedes decision taking (doing what's been decided). It can be used, for example, by imagining that a project has run off the rails, a product launch has failed, or a big event has flopped. Pre-morteming works by asking team members to come up with reasons for the fictitious failure before it's happened. They're asked to 'think backwards'.

Spotlight on intuition
Pre-morteming in action

Here's a not-so-fictitious example of pre-morteming in action.

- *Scene:* imagine you're leading a massive national infrastructure project for a high-speed electric rail link to connect the northern half and the southern half of a relatively small but quite densely populated island country. The aim is to cut commuter time, take the pressure off an already impossibly overcrowded road network, level up north-south divides and help you to achieve net zero emissions.

- *Fiasco:* now fast-forward the DVD and imagine that it's all gone badly wrong: the project is already over budget by 50 per cent, there's a potential seven-year delay, the plug has had to be pulled on half of the project between the Midlands and the North and losses to taxpayers amount to tens of billions of pounds.

- *Generate:* this is the main step, it's where every member of the project team thinks backwards, puts on their 'hindsight hats' and writes down as many reasons as they can come up with for why the plan de-railed so badly, even though it hasn't yet done so. In the session, each person in the group reads out their reasons for why the project has failed, one at a time until all the concerns have been aired. Doing it this way does three things: it gets all the ideas on to the table; it prevents

---

extroverts from dominating the discussion; and it means that project leaders can't sweep issues under the carpet.[22]

In the high-speed rail example, the reasons for failure might include: delays in local planning consent; engineering problems with dodgy ground conditions requiring more substantial reinforcements; land being more expensive to buy than anticipated; an uptick in inflation causing construction costs to escalate substantially; demolition costs around the main city in the south being higher than expected; bigger than anticipated costs of diverting underground gas, water and electricity pipelines as a result of deeper excavations and local protestors slowing the project with a concerted campaign of court cases and appeals.[23]

- *Consolidate:* the next stage in the pre-mortem is to identify the project's main vulnerabilities and consolidate them under main headings: for example, in the example, these might be 'engineering' and 'financial'.

- *Re-plan:* the last step is to work through how the main, in this case financial and engineering, stumbling blocks could be mitigated, for example how could the extra money be found if costs spiral, and what alternative engineering solutions will be available?

In this not-so-hypothetical example, the deliverable from a pre-mortem might have been a much more robust plan that would have been able to better withstand any engineering or financial curve balls.

In 2023, the plan for the UK's high-speed rail link, HS2, to connect the North with London via the Midlands was curtailed at Birmingham. As it happens, the project was criticised in a government report for a 'failure of governance and oversight on spiralling costs following years of warnings'.[24] It's not clear whether the HS2 project was pre-mortemed or stress-tested sufficiently.[25]

Pre-morteming's two biggest selling points are that it can sniff out problems before they happen and it can turn groupthink on its head. A particularly invidious feature of groupthink is that there's pressure to show loyalty to a group or a project just for the sake of it and not speak out for fear of rocking the boat. In a pre-mortem it's the other way round: speaking out actually shows loyalty to the group's wider and longer term interests over and above simply fitting in and singing from the same hymn sheet.

Doubts, even if they're only based on an intuition, are put out in the open rather than kept in the closet and allowed to fester, and issues get aired before they become critical. While no one hopes that a catastrophe will happen, the principle of pre-morteming is that it's better to give voice to bad vibes rather than be later proved right in a costly mistake that could have been avoided. The principle is that 'a gram of prevention is worth a kilogram of cure.'[26]

Ultimately, pre-morteming aims to produce a more robust plan that like any plan, isn't perfect and can never be immune from 'black swan' events. But at the very least – whether it's improved or abandoned – a pre-mortemed plan is likely to be more robust than one that hasn't been through the process.

Spotlight on intuition
Intuiting faint signals

A pre-mortem is a forum where people can flag up any 'faint signals' (sometimes called 'weak signals') that they've picked up and that might foretell a failure. Faint signals are quiet, subtle, indirect signs that may indicate the initial stages of a notable change or disruption in a future business environment. Because they're often ambiguous, incomplete or not widely recognised, faint signals are often things that only certain people (such as experts) are intuitively able to notice.

As well as foretelling failures, faint signals can help decision makers foresee successes as part of a 'scenario planning' process.

For example, some years ago there was a small but growing trend for people living in urban areas to opt for bike-sharing schemes, electric scooters and electric bikes. The seemingly-insignificant-at-first-glance trend (a faint signal) heralded a more systematic shift among urban dwellers for a decline in car ownership and a preference for more cost-effective and environmentally friendly modes of transportation.[27] This faint signal was part of a bigger shift to sustainability and a portent of a major transition in personal transportation.[28] The faint signal eventually became a strong sign and a significant trend.

Intuition in pre-morteming can work in two ways: it's a way to stress test an intuition (by asking, for example, 'Okay so you've gone with your gut and it's a fiasco, what are the possible reasons for its failure?'); and intuitions can be used in the 'generate reasons for failure' stage (by asking, for example, 'Are there any faint signals anyone can sense that might foretell a failure?').

When it's well run, the pre-mortem group is a safe space where people can feel comfortable in being a naysayer and not come across as pessimistic and disloyal without fear of being pilloried. Paradoxically, like the athlete who asks her coach, 'Where can I improve?', being open to the possibility of weaknesses in an intuition will help you to hone your hunches, pump up intuitive muscle power and build intuitive intelligence in the longer term.

Takeaway

Pre-morteming creates a safe space where people can voice any intuitive misgivings they may have about a consequential decision and for stress testing an intuition.

Dig deeper

Emre Soyer and Robin Hogarth's *The Myth of Experience: Why We Learn the Wrong Lessons, and Ways to Correct Them* (2020) takes a fresh look at experience and how it can deceive and mislead us.

In a nutshell, feedback and feedforward

Building intuitive intelligence requires feedback that is accurate, diagnostic and timely. Good intuitions get built in kind learning structures, bad intuitions in wicked learning structures, and hunches can be honed by feedback (for example devil's advocacy) and feedforward (for example pre-morteming).

Workout 1: Play Devil's Advocate

1 Consider a consequential decision that you are currently facing.
2 What does your intuition tell you about what to do?
3 Ask probing and provocative questions about the intuition or, better still, ask someone else to: casts doubts on the intuition; put the case for an alternative to the intuition.
4 Where does the devil's advocacy leave your intuition: is it intact or in doubt?
5 Has it stood up to scrutiny or has the devil's advocacy caused you to rethink?

Workout 2: Practising a pre-mortem

1 A pre-mortem is an 'autopsy' that's conducted before a decision has gone wrong. It's a planning technique developed by Gary

Klein that can be applied to stress test consequential decisions before they become set in stone.

2 Choose a consequential decision that you're currently facing. Pre-mortem it using the framework used in the example below (Table 13).

3 Your aim should be to produce a more robust plan.

4 Give your intuition free rein in the 'generate' stage to imagine as many reasons for failure as possible.

Table 13 Practising a pre-mortem

Stage	Example
Set the scene	A family is thinking about moving from a city centre apartment to a more expensive home in the countryside.
Imagine a fiasco	Fastforward events: they've moved and it's a disaster.
Generate reasons for failure	The wife's hunch is that they might not be able to pay the mortgage in a couple of years. The husband's gut feeling is that the house needs more renovations than first appears. The kids' have a bad vibe that they won't like the local school.
Consolidate the reasons under main headings	Finance; property maintenance; education
Re-plan the project	Get a five-year fixed-rate mortgage or take out insurance (finance) Have a detailed structural survey carried out (maintenance) Look at other schools that are commutable (education)

Workout 3: Recording hits and misses

Record and learn lessons from your intuitive hits and misses by: capturing what the decision was, where the gut feeling was in your body, whether it was positive or negative, how intense it was (high, medium or low), whether you followed it (yes or no), what the outcome was (was it a hit or a miss) and what you learned from the intuitive episode (Table 14). Collating these episodes would be a good way to build an intuition diary or journal. Journalling fosters intuitive awareness and builds intuitive intelligence by encouraging reflections on your gut feelings, hunches and vibes and how you used them, and whether they worked or not. By collating and comparing hits and misses patterns of success and failure may start to emerge.

Table 14 Recording an intuitive episode

What was the decision?	
Where was the 'gut feeling' (e.g. gut, head, etc.)?	
Was it positive ('for' the decision) or negative ('against' the decision)?	
How intense was it (high, medium or low)?	
Did you follow it (yes or no)?	
Was your intuition right (an intuitive hit) or wrong (an intuitive miss)?	
What did you learn from this intuitive episode?	

Notes

1 Hall, Z. R., Ahearne, M. and Sujan, H. (2015) 'The importance of starting right: the influence of accurate intuition on performance in salesperson–customer interactions', *Journal of Marketing*, 79(3), 91–109.

2 Hall *et al.* (2015).

3 Robson, D. (2022) 'Superstitious learning: Can "lucky" rituals bring success?', *BBC Worklife*, 12 July. Available online at: https://www.bbc.com/worklife/article/20220708-superstitious-learning-can-lucky-rituals-bring-success.

4 Scherer, K. R. and Tran, V. (2001) 'The effects of emotion on the process of organizational learning', in Dierkes, M. *et al.* (eds) *The Oxford Handbook of Organizational Learning and Knowledge.* Oxford: Oxford University Press, pp. 367–92, p. 378.

5 Hogarth, R. (2002) *Educating Intuition.* Chicago: University of Chicago Press, p. 14.

6 Hogarth (2002), p. 23.

7 Hogarth (2002), p. 24.

8 Highhouse, S. (2008) 'Stubborn reliance on intuition and subjectivity in employee selection', *Industrial and Organizational Psychology*, 1(3), 333–42.

9 Miles, A. and Sadler-Smith, E. (2014) '"With recruitment I always feel I need to listen to my gut": The role of intuition in employee selection', *Personnel Review*, 43(4), 606–27.

10 Soyer, E. and Hogarth, R. (2020) *The Myth of Experience: Why We Learn the Wrong Lessons, and Ways to Correct Them.* New York: Doubleday.

11 The metaphor of the 'DVD in the head' is from Klein's RPD work, see: Klein, G. A. (2003) *Intuition at Work.* New York: Currency Doubleday.

12 Anonymous (2014) 'How does someone become a saint?' *BBC News*, 27 April. Available online at: https://www.bbc.co.uk/news/world-europe-27140646.

13 Esser, J. K. and Lindoerfer, J. S. (1989) 'Groupthink and the space shuttle Challenger accident: Toward a quantitative case analysis', *Journal of Behavioral Decision Making*, 2(3), 167–77.

14 PwC (no date) 'Red teaming 101: An introduction to red teaming and how it improves your cyber security'. Available online at: https://www.pwc.co.uk/issues/cyber-security-services/insights/what-is-red-teaming.html (accessed May 2024).

15 Zenko, M. (no date) 'Inside the CIA red cell', *Foreign Policy*. Available online at: https://foreignpolicy.com/2015/10/30/ inside-the-cia-red-cell-micah-zenko-red-team-intelligence/ (accessed May 2024).

16 McCrystal Group (no date) 'Red team: Unleash divergent thinking, adapt to risk, prepare for the future'. Available online at: https://www.mcchrystalgroup.com/capabilities/decision-making/red-teaming (accessed May 2024).

17 The Harvard Implicit Association Test, available online at: https://implicit.harvard.edu/implicit/takeatest.html (accessed May 2024).

18 Schlitz, I. (2018) 'Stop playing Devil's Advocate, and other advice for better decision making', *Behavioural Scientist*, 10 July. Available online at: https://behavioralscientist.org/stop-playing-devils-advocate-and-other-advice-for-better-decision-making/.

19 Smith, J. E. (2017) *Bush*. New York: Simon and Schuster; Claxton, G., Owen, D. and Sadler-Smith, E. (2015) 'Hubris in leadership: A peril of unbridled intuition?', *Leadership*, 11(1), 57–78.

20 Dowling, S. (2023) 'What are the odds of a successful space launch?' *BBC Future*, 19 May. Available online at: https://www. bbc.com/future/article/20230518-what-are-the-odds-of-a-successful-space-launch.

21 Klein, G. A., Koller, T. and Lavallo, D. (2019) 'Bias busters: Premortems: Being smart at the start', *McKinsey Quarterly*, 3 April. Available online at: https://www.mckinsey.com/ capabilities/strategy-and-corporate-finance/our-insights/ bias-busters-premortems-being-smart-at-the-start.

22 Anonymous (2018) 'Is intuition in our work important? The value of pre-mortem analysis'. *42T*, August 2018. Available online at: https://blog.42t.com/news/the-pre-mortem.

23 Topham, G. (2020) 'Where did it all go wrong for HS2?'. *The Guardian*, 24 January. Available online at: https://www.

theguardian.com/uk-news/2020/jan/24/hs2-high-speed-rail-europe-infrastructure-project.

24 House of Commons Committee of Public Accounts (2024) *HS2 and Euston*, 24 January. Available online at: https://committees.parliament.uk/committee/127/public-accounts-committee/news/199769/hs2-verdict-scheme-now-very-poor-value-for-money-after-northern-leg-cancellation/.

25 For a discussion of whether or not red teaming was used in HS2 planning, see: https://assets.publishing.service.gov.uk/media/5a8203f640f0b62305b92065/exploration-of-behavioural-biases.pdf.

26 This is a paraphrase of Benjamin Franklin's famous aphorism: 'An ounce of prevention is worth a pound of cure.'

27 Mouratidis, K. (2022) 'Bike-sharing, car-sharing, e-scooters, and Uber: Who are the shared mobility users and where do they live?', *Sustainable Cities and Society*, 86, 104161.

28 European Environment Agency (2018) 'Perspectives on transitions to sustainability', EEA Report 25/2017. Copenhagen: EEA; Gilmore, N., Koskinen, I., Burr, P., Obbard, E., Sproul, A., Konstantinou, G. and Bruce, A. (2023) 'Identifying weak signals to prepare for uncertainty in the energy sector', *Heliyon*, 9(11), e21295.

part 3

Adding value with human intuition in the age of AI

'Some people call this "artificial intelligence", but the reality is this technology will enhance *us*. So instead of artificial intelligence, I think we'll augment *our* intelligence.'

Ginni Rometty (previously Chair, President and CEO of IBM)[1]

- -

This chapter will help you to appreciate the role that human intuition plays and will continue to play in judgement and decision making in personal and professional life in in a world in which AI is becoming increasingly important.

- -

Humans and algorithms have a 'history'

Human beings and mental labour-saving devices go back a long way. The abacus is believed to have started life in ancient Babylon over 3,000 years ago as a flat stone covered with sand or dust. Abacuses have been found in various incarnations all over the ancient world from China to North America.

A big leap forward occurred when William Oughtred invented the slide rule in England in the 1600s; it represented a shift from simple counting machines, such as the abacus, to an actual calculating machine. Since then, calculating machines have come on in leaps and bounds, through the pocket calculator of the 1960s to the world's most powerful 'exascale' computer at the Oak Ridge National Laboratory in Tennessee, which is capable of a mind-blowing quintillion, or 10^{18}, calculations per second[2] (for comparison, the age of the universe is estimated to be of the order of 10^{17} seconds).[3]

As well as creating counting and calculating machines, human beings have also been adept at inventing other types of mental labour-saving devices. Algorithms are one of these. At the most elementary level, an algorithm is a set of rules to be followed in a precise sequence to solve a problem, take a decision or complete a task. They range from the simple rules for making a cake (measure ingredients; mix ingredients; bake ingredients, in that order) to the algorithms used in complex deep learning and neural networks.

The development of complex algorithms has been accompanied by debates about whether or not they can outperform humans in complex mental tasks. This debate goes back a long way.

One of the first scientific studies of humans 'versus' algorithms was by the psychologist Paul Meehl in the 1950s. In his short but highly influential book *Clinical Versus Statistical Prediction* (1954), Meehl reviewed the evidence across 20 research studies which compared the clinical judgements of psychologists and psychiatrists with statistical predictions made according to a few simple rules.

For example, in a study of predicting first-year university students' grades: fourteen counsellors made their predictions based on 45-minute interviews, aptitude tests, high-school grades and personal statements; an algorithm made its prediction based on high-school grades and one aptitude test.

The algorithm's predictions beat 11 out of the 14 counsellors. The results provoked consternation and disbelief among professionals who'd always assumed that human judgement was indispensable (which it is for some tasks, especially where it's not possible to specify probabilities). Across the board in all 20 studies in Meehl's short book, the algorithmic method either gave a more accurate prediction or the humans' and the algorithm's predictions tied.

In a number of other studies, algorithms were found to outperform humans across the piece, including in predicting academic success, business bankruptcies, cancer patients' longevity and military training success. Meehl and his colleagues concluded that there's no reason *not* to use algorithms where they've been shown to be superior to human clinical judgement.[4] The power of algorithms has developed enormously since Meehl's time. For example, in 2024, BBC News reported that an AI tool developed by an NHS hospital in the UK successfully identified faint signs of breast cancer in patients that had been missed by human experts.[5] That said, it seems highly unlikely that an algorithm could have helped Jeff Bezos to take his decision for whether or not to go with the Amazon Prime idea given that this decision was a classic case of managing uncertainty rather than risk assessment.

Big thinker

Paul Meehl

Paul Meehl (1920–2003) was a clinical psychologist at the University of Minnesota and served as the president of the American Psychological Association. He set the statistical 'cat'

➤

among the clinical judgement 'pigeons' with his book *Clinical Versus Statistical Prediction* (1954) in which he demonstrated that algorithms outperform humans across a wide range of predictive tasks involving numbers and calculations.

Meehl's 'personal hunch' was that too much clinical time is wasted in doing 'jobs that could be done more efficiently, in a small fraction of the time' using 'complex statistical [algorithmic] methods'. For Meehl, moving to an algorithm-based approach in many of these tasks would represent progress because it would 'free the skilled clinician for therapy and research, for both of which skilled time is so sorely needed'.

In the situations studied by Meehl, it was possible to build algorithms in the first place because hard data were available that could be used to predict the relationship between inputs and outcomes. Inputs are those things judged by humans to be relevant. For example, in predicting reoffending behaviours, these would include offence type, number of previous offences and prior violations of prison rules. Outcomes are the things that can be captured numerically, for example reoffend or not reoffend, number of ex-prisoners reoffending, etc.

The technology of algorithms has moved on massively in the 70 years since Meehl's original work. Meehl foresaw the debates that are currently taking place about human intuition versus artificial intelligence; for example a recent article in *Forbes* was entitled 'AI won't replace human intuition'[6] while a web article from the world-leading INSEAD business school claimed that we should 'Leave intuition to the machines'.[7] The debate is set to continue.

Problem solving that involves pattern recognition can already be left to the machines, for example, artificial intelligence has been used successfully in detecting financial fraud, so much so that some vendors claim to have developed 'intuitive AI'. Unlike the traditional armed bank robbers with their guns and masks, modern-day bank robbers now sit in front of computer screens and commit their crimes across continents at the click of a mouse rather than the pull of a trigger. All it takes is for a criminal to steal a few dollars from hundreds of thousands of different accounts all around the world and the sums soon add up to millions. This money can then be used for all sorts of nefarious activities, including drug trafficking and financing international terrorism.[8]

Traditional rule-based AI detects patterns of unusual activity quickly and accurately across millions of financial transactions in ways that human beings or conventional IT systems could never hope to emulate. However, the newer AI systems, based on 'deep learning', are now able to pick up on patterns that traditional rule-based AI was blind to.

Traditional systems search for 'known unknowns', for example 'is this transaction fraudulent or not?', by detecting things that human beings know could be out there, can anticipate and are able to program the machine to look out for.* The newer more 'intuitive systems' are on the lookout for 'unknown unknowns', for example weird transactions the likes of which have never been seen before. By learning of their own accord, these systems are able to pick up on new and unfamiliar types of suspicious and counterfeit activities.[9]

The detection of tiny anomalies – which may show up as faint signals that no human could ever hope to spot – could indicate something untoward is going on. If the vendors of these systems are justified in their claims to have invented 'artificial expert intuition', where does that leave human intuition?

In certain predictive tasks, human beings can be outperformed by algorithms that can recognise complex patterns unerringly and

---

* This is one quadrant in the so-called Johari window of: 'known knowns': things we're certain of; 'known unknowns': things we know are there but we can't predict; 'unknown knowns': things others know but you don't; 'unknown unknowns': things we don't know that we don't know about because we haven't envisaged them (like black swans). It was made famous by the US Secretary of Defence, Donald Rumsfeld, in a White House briefing in 2002.

perform consistently 24/7. However, in tasks that involve empathy, emotional and social intelligence and creativity human beings can bring, in the words of ChatGPT 'a level of intuition and contextual understanding' that algorithms may lack.[10]

Writing over 20 years ago, the decision researcher Robin Hogarth, whose work we've met already, remarked that there's no shame in us admitting that computers can do numerical calculations infinitely better than we can.[11] After all, for at least the past 3,000 years, humans have been outsourcing calculations to 'machines' of one kind or another in efforts to augment the analytical mind's limited computational capacity and free up mental space for other more important and/or rewarding tasks.

Takeaway

Machines are adept at following the rules that humans make for them. Algorithmic decisions made by machines are quicker, more consistent, more scalable and less prone to bias and fatigue than those made by a human.

Stable versus unstable worlds

The stable-world principle is an idea put forward by the German psychologist Gerd Gigerenzer in his book *How to Stay Smart in a Smart World* (2022). He explained his stable-world idea using the contrasting examples of playing chess and finding a romantic partner by online dating:

- *Stable world:* the game of chess is a stable world; all the positions on the board can be specified in advance because the arena in which the action takes place is defined (it's an 8 × 8 board) and all the pieces are known (from pawn through to queen and king). To specify what's likely to occur is a matter of sheer computing power (human or artificial) and, as we know, computers can beat the very best humans in chess, not through intuition, but though sheer brute force calculation.

- *Unstable world:* the 'game' of finding a romantic partner in online dating is an unstable world. Although each person has an online profile that specifies various attributes, uncertainty is rife because the profile may not be 100 per cent accurate (for example some men have been known to misreport important facts about themselves), daters' preferences and circumstances may change, and a static online profile can never capture a modicum of what a potential partner really needs to know about another human being with whom they might strike up a long-term relationship.[12]

Gigerenzer also notes that, in stable worlds, such as chess, copious amounts of data are available, the rules are well defined, and they do not change. In unstable worlds, such as online dating, what data there is can be ambiguous, the rules are fluid and people can be both fickle and fake. Predictions can be made more confidently in stable worlds. It may boil down to a matter of computational complexity and the cleverness of the algorithms in the assessment of risk. In unstable worlds, making predictions is much harder if not impossible because of their inherent uncertainty and sheer unknowableness.

Big thinker
Gerd Gigerenzer

The eminent decision scientist Gerd Gigerenzer is a professor of psychology at the University of Potsdam and at the Max Planck Institute in Munich. Gigerenzer is a critic of the heuristics and biases research (see Step 6) and the two minds model. He's famous for, among other things, the idea of 'fast and frugal' heuristics. These are mental shortcuts that can be employed

➤

to take accurate decisions with minimal cognitive effort; for example the 'recognition' fast-and-frugal heuristic goes as follows: 'If one of two objects is recognised then we should infer that the recognised object has the higher value.'

A classic example of the recognition heuristic in action is the question Gigerenzer put to two groups of Germans and Americans: 'Which has the higher population, Detroit or Milwaukee?' The answer is in the footnote.[†]

Most Germans got the correct answer and usually beat Americans on this test because they've probably heard of Detroit, but not of Milwaukee. Americans, on the other hand, have heard of both cities and consequently get befuddled. Gigerenzer calls this a 'beneficial degree of ignorance' on the part of the Germans; it's an example of where 'less can be more' and where an intuitive response gets it right with minimal cognitive effort. Gigerenzer and his colleagues have discovered a whole suite of fast-and-frugal heuristics, including the 'take the best' heuristic: this is routinely used by humans in employee selection decisions where the most important criterion, such as previous experience, is used as the 'best' criterion rather than considering all the available information.

On the topic of intuition, Gigerenzer says that 'it's a judgement that appears quickly in consciousness whose reasons we're not fully aware of and which is strong enough to act on'. He adds that the real question is 'not *if* but *when* can we trust our gut.'[13]

Gigerenzer has used his stable-world principle to spell out where he thinks algorithms and humans can each add their own unique value.

Whether it's in baking a cake or in a complex neural network, Gigerenzer points out that algorithms need data and rules in order to be able to function. They work supremely well in well-defined, stable situations where there are copious amounts of data and where

---

[†] Detroit.

outcomes can be specified in advance. In the detection of recognised types of online financial fraud, for example, there are vast amounts of data, and the potential outcomes (fraudulent or not fraudulent behaviour) are known in advance.

According to Gigerenzer, human intelligence evolved to deal with uncertainty in a world in which data may or may not be available and in which the rules are ambiguous and fluid. As a result, human intuitive intelligence evolved to be able to spot connections and sense patterns in the things that make up our everyday world. In hiring an employee or dating someone, for example, it's impossible to specify what might happen in advance, since any number of outcomes are possible, let alone assign a probability to it, but the connections that the intuitive mind spots and the patterns that it senses can be an invaluable, and sometimes the only, guide to how things *might* turn out.

In terms of Gigerenzer's stable and unstable worlds, machines are good at *solving* and perform well in situations of risk (*stable worlds*), whereas humans are good at *sensing* and perform well in situations of uncertainty (*unstable worlds*). This fits nicely with Frank Knight's idea of risk versus uncertainty (see Step 3). Our analytical mind evolved to have a passable solving capability but this has been far outstripped by that of the machines that we've invented. That's one reason why we've quite rightly outsourced calculations to machines. Whether we can or should do so with intuition is an altogether different question.

Takeaway

Computers are adept in helping humans to take decisions by *solving* in stable worlds; humans are adept in taking decisions by *sensing* in unstable worlds.

Adding value with creative intuition

IBM describes creativity as the 'ultimate moonshot for artificial intelligence'. Creative AI claims, for example, to be able to emulate the work of famous artists. Open AI's Dall-E is an AI system that can create realistic images and art from a textual description. It's been used to create bizarre images such as 'Kermit the Frog in the Style of Edvard Munch' or 'Sea Otter in the Style of Johannes Vermeer'.[14]

The process works by feeding the AI images of paintings by an artist, such as the Norwegian expressionist Munch or the Dutch Baroque master Vermeer, which are the 'training data'. AI needs a lot of these, for example it's estimated that ChatGPT has been trained on approximately 175 billion parameters. The algorithm behind the AI then generates images similar to those it's been trained on. Incidentally, this makes out-Vermeering Vermeer a challenge as there are thought to be only 34 paintings that can be authentically attributed to Johannes Vermeer.

When it works, it can give AI the appearance of being able to carry out creative tasks; but is AI really being creative?

Creativity is the use of imagination to create something that is original, significant and meaningful; it's an unstable arena where uncertainty reigns supreme. Creativity is uncertain because it's concerned with producing things that are novel; if the outcome can be specified in advance, it's not creative.[15]

In asking OpenAI's image generator Dall-E to generate a painting of Kermit the Frog in the style of Edvard Munch, the outcome is predetermined: it will be a painting of Kermit the Frog (known) in the style of Munch (also known). The output can be judged as successful or not in terms of how well it fits the pre-specified outcome: is it a 'Kermit' and is it 'Munch-like'? Generative AI can produce an image that *mimics* the style of Munch or Vermeer. However, generative AI can't innovate the *style* of Munch or Vermeer as an original means of expressing how Munch or Vermeer *saw* and *felt* about the world through their uniquely human eyes.

Mimicry is not creativity in art or in music, nor in business. Computers have, for some years, been able to compose in the style of various classical composers, such as J. S. Bach. For example, the so-called DeepBach algorithm can produce passable replicas of music in the style of Bach. Even people who enjoy listening to Bach's music sometimes have difficulty in telling real Bach from the replica robo-Bach.[16]

But DeepBach isn't being creative because the outcome is predetermined in advance: music in the style of the composer Bach. Incidentally, Bach is low-hanging fruit for AI for two reasons. First, Bach's music is readily codifiable because of the sheer volume of music he wrote and from which the AI can learn. The 'training data' for robo-Bach is over 1,000 musical compositions. Second, the patterns Bach used in his compositions can be expressed as rules because his music is somewhat 'mathematical', and even formulaic, and therefore similar patterns can be recognised and mimicked by the AI.

Writing a six-hour opera in the style of the German romantic composer Richard Wagner – DeepWagner – might be a more exacting challenge for AI.

Getting AI to mimic an object such as a painting, poem or musical score that's been created by a human is one thing, but asking AI to create a work of art from scratch is, according to IBM, 'a more distant and challenging frontier'.[17]

Art is about looking closely at the world and responding intuitively to the human experience of being in the world. For example, Picasso 'invented' cubism as a new way of representing three dimensional objects (such as people, guitars or bowls of fruit) on a flat surface. In a cubist painting, frontal and side views of an object are captured simultaneously in the same plane. Picasso didn't set out to achieve this aim explicitly; the process was intuitive and organic and we connect intuitively and emotionally with the outcome. Before Picasso innovated this breakthrough – which amounted to a new 'rule' for how to represent things on canvas – it wasn't possible to see the front and the side of an object simultaneously in a work of art. However, by inventing cubism as a new way of seeing things in the world, Picasso invented new rules for visual composition. This speaks to a wider point about 'creativity' and 'rules' that applies beyond the confines of fine art.

Spotlight on intuition

Algorithmic creativity versus human creativity

'Algorithmic creativity' is where a computer observes and analyses data (for example images of works by Edvard Munch, or musical scores by J. S. Bach) from which it learns and then produces works (this is the training data).[18]

Even though algorithms can generate art by mimicking certain styles using algorithmic creativity, the ability to create truly novel art that connects intuitively with human emotions and says something about the human experience is, by definition, unique to human beings. This makes humans irreplaceable in the creative process and intuition an invaluable skill in the age of AI.

The fact that AI is good at mimicking gives us a pointer to a fundamental difference between human creativity and machine creativity: human creativity is about *creating* new rules, not following old rules; machine creativity is about *following* old rules, not creating new rules.[19]

If algorithmic creativity and the 'art' works that it creates could ever give us an insight into what it's like to 'be' a machine, that might be a different matter.

Entrepreneur and CEO Margaret Heffernan has noticed that it's become fashionable to try to define formulas for creative success. She sees this as a fool's errand because, for Heffernan, 'one of the deep rewards of art [and creativity in general] lies in it not being formulaic'. Attempts to capture it in an algorithm are always going to fail because in creativity 'there are no rules that always work and no rules that are never broken'. Which rules should be followed and which ones should be broken is a matter of intuitive judgement. That's in the nature of creativity itself.[20]

Human beings produce the new rules through creative intuitions and insights. The analogy of creativity in art helps us to acknowledge and appreciate the indispensable role of human creativity more generally across the piece from music to management. Radical innovations in any field that are the product of human intuitions that break old rules and help to write new rules: Netflix wrote new rules about home entertainment which broke the old rules about on-demand viewing having to involve renting DVDs; Amazon wrote new rules about home shopping which broke the old rules about the retail experience having to be on the high street or in shopping malls; Tesla wrote new rules about personal transportation which broke the old rules about cars having to be fuelled by hydrocarbons.

In all of these cases, the world was changed irreversibly because of new rules created by Reed Hastings, Jeff Bezos and Elon Musk. They're products of human creative intuitions. This makes creative intuition in the workplace a unique selling point (USP) for human beings in the age of generative AI.

Takeaway

Human beings are more creative than algorithms. Humans produce novel ideas for creative self-expression, invention and innovation, while algorithms follow rules created by humans to generate outcomes based on those rules.

Adding value with social intuition

Human beings are, by nature, intuitive judges of other humans and, for better or for worse, they evaluate other people on 'thin slices' of behaviour based on a lifetime's experience of social interactions. The topic of thin slicing was first studied by psychologists in the 1990s. A typical thin slice experiment goes as follows.

Participants are provided with short ten-second silent video clips (thin slices) of people in social situations and then asked to make various judgements about them based on what they've seen. One experiment involved three ten-second clips of college teachers; participants were asked to rate them on how 'active', 'confident', 'enthusiastic' and 'optimistic' they were. The remarkable discovery was that the participants' ratings, based on nothing more than three lots of ten-second silent videos, matched closely the actual evaluations of the teachers by their actual students.

Not content with this finding, the researchers raised the bar and made the challenge even more exacting by reducing the video clips to three two-second clips. The results were essentially the same.

As well as reducing the size of the thin slices, the researchers extended their experiments to other areas including sales people, surgeons and therapists. Again, the results confirmed the potency of thin slices in our ability to make intuitive predictions about other people, for example:

- Doctors whose tone of voice was rated as 'domineering' were more likely to have been sued for malpractice.

- The patients of therapists who were rated as using 'distancing' behaviours were more likely to experience long-term decline.

- Thin slice ratings of sales people's interpersonal skills were strongly correlated with supervisors' ratings of their actual job performance.[21]

The conclusion was that on little more than a six-second thin slice of behaviours, humans are able to make accurate social judgements of other humans on a number of important aspects of personality and social behaviour.

Big thinker

Nalini Ambady

Nalini Ambady (1959–2013) was a professor of social psychology at Stanford University. Her work on thin slices demonstrated that human beings are able to make fast, automatic, accurate judgements of other people's personalities, skills and capabilities on the briefest of snapshots of their non-verbal behaviour (which she called 'thin slices'). Ambady described intuition as essential for effective social and interpersonal interactions and referred to it as the basis of an 'elaborate and secret code that is written nowhere, known by none, and *understood by all'*. In addition to the findings discussed above, she also discovered that:

- Tasks that take up brain space, such as rehearsing a series of numbers, don't impede the speed and accuracy of thin slice judgements, which suggests that the processing of thin slices and of analytical processing are undertaken by different brain systems.

- Thin-slice judgements do seem to suffer when people have to produce reasons and justifications for their evaluations; this suggests that in such situations the first option that comes to mind may often be the best.

One of the conclusions that she drew from her own work was that 'sometimes it is dangerous to think too much'.[22]

Thin slice judgements happen automatically and the reasons behind them are outside of conscious awareness. We experience them as gut feelings, hunches or vibes. They're an efficient, but not infallible, way to arrive at social judgements because they don't require the use of the brain's scarce conscious processing capacity. An article in the US business magazine *Inc.* puts it like this: 'meeting someone and within a few minutes deciding whether they're smart [or not]' which may of course simply reflect bias or prejudice.[23]

We're skilled in social judgements because we've all had a lifetime's experience of trying to fathom other people's capabilities, motives and intentions. That's not to say that it's 100 per cent correct or that we're all equally good at it. Some people are definitely better at social intuition than others.

The jury is out on why, but some people associate these differences in social intuition with gender and explain them in terms of the stereotype of female intuition. Research suggests that females might be better than men at reading facial expressions, it's even been suggested that females may also be able to intuit whether a man is likely to be a good caretaker. On the other hand, attributing intuition to women and rationality to men might also be a way to 'deride women' and give men a monopoly over rational thought, which traditionally is seen as being superior to intuition but, as I've argued in this book, are better seen as equal partners.[24]

Spotlight on intuition

'You can take the person out of the Stone Age ... '

Some psychologists speculate that the ability to learn how to make intuitive thin slice judgements has been 'wired' into human beings by evolution (note: it's the ability to learn them that's wired in, not the judgements themselves). It could have been useful, for example in detecting cheating behaviours, and gossip would have been an efficient way to spread such information among other tribe members. The psychologist David Myers, author of *Intuition: Its Powers and Perils* (2002), described social intuition as 'an ancient biological wisdom' acquired over hundreds of thousands of years so that we can respond quickly to a 'stranger in the forest' who needs to be assessed immediately as either 'friend or foe'.[25] The evolutionist argument is that the ability to make these kinds of decision accurately, for example whether someone is likely to cheat on you, was selected for in our ancestors and that's why we have it, while those who didn't have not survived to pass on their genes and aren't here to write or read about it.

Taken at face value, the evolutionists' arguments suggest that social intuition operates on a 'better to be safe than sorry principle'. In other words, it's better to misjudge as a potential threat because

> this is a more effective way to avoid danger. It works as a kind of psychological 'precautionary principle'. As a result, intuitions err of the side of caution, especially if there's a potential threat. In our dim and distant past, it was better to err on the side of caution than be eaten by a predator or duped by a cheater.

The trouble with evolutionists' arguments for social intuitions is that this principle most likely worked well in our ancestral environment of the African savannahs where nature was 'red in tooth and claw'. That's why we're here. But, in the modern world, social intuitions, which spring to mind with very little effort, may not be appropriate or accurate, added to which they're sticky. Consequently, they may lead us into misjudging some people. There's an old saying that, 'You can take the person out of the Stone Age, but you can't take the Stone Age out of the person.' The challenge for us is to manage the Stone Age features of our mind, including our intuitions, so that they're fit for purpose in the modern world.

It goes without saying that, as with other intuitions, thin-slice judgement of another person's behaviour, performance or personality aren't infallible; they can be a source of bias, discrimination and prejudice if arrived at and used in the wrong way (see Step 6). Could computers help to overcome these?

In a study published in 2015, it was reported that computers can judge personality traits better than humans can. The research compared computer predictions of participants' personality based on Facebook 'likes' with predictions made by participants' Facebook friends who filled out a personality questionnaire about them. The computer predicted participants' personality traits more accurately that the humans did.

The researchers suggest that computer-based personality assessment using 'digital footprints' could be used, among other things, to tailor marketing messages and match candidates with jobs. They also suggested that, in the future, computers could even be used to help with consequential life decisions such as choosing career paths and romantic partners.[26] This is an ambitious undertaking.

A more invidious side to using computers to predict people's personalities and preferences has to do with privacy and manipulation. In the Facebook–Cambridge Analytica scandal, personal data belonging to millions of users was collected without their knowledge and used in political advertising campaigns.

One reason why human beings are adept at social intuition is because we're able to infer at a distance, i.e. from the outside, what might be going on inside some else's head (the technical term for this is 'theory of mind'). Theory of mind (ToM) develops in childhood. It's not mind reading as such. ToM is one of the reasons we're able to intuit what another person might be thinking or feeling, and what their motives and intentions might be. Evolutionary psychologists think ToM evolved in humans as a result of the need to cooperate in group tasks such as hunting, gathering and preparing food as well as in child rearing. In the distant past, the need to cooperate was with other members of the tribe to which we belonged. In the modern world, cooperation happens in all sorts of social groups, from families to firms, for example ToM can help managers to understand the mental states of their followers and vice versa, and effective negotiation would be impossible with being able to intuit the mental states of the other party. Social intuitions oil the wheels of cooperation, collaboration and teamworking.

If computers are capable of predicting something as basic to interpersonal relations as personality, does this mean that true love and a life of married bliss is 'just a click away'? Gerd Gigerenzer, whose work we met earlier, thinks not: in his view, the judgements that an algorithm makes about a potential partner's suitability are based on a very impoverished data set because the essence of a human being can't be captured in an online profile. Besides, online profiles also have the potential to be inaccurate because, as we know, some people are prone to exaggerations, cover ups and lying.

The judgements we've evolved to be able to make about a potential partner are based on a much richer, more embodied (they're felt in a body that a computer does not possess) and, ultimately, more authentic 'data' set. In Gigerenzer's words: 'a smile and gesture, the humour reflected in someone's eyes, the tone of voice, the way the other asks questions, intentionality or superficiality with which a person listens' not to mention 'touch and scent' are all crucial in deciding whether two people are compatible.[27]

Computer dating platforms aren't a miraculous method for matching two people in a way that trumps human intuition; they're simply a modern means of accessing a wider pool of potential mates that wouldn't be possible otherwise. They might provide a rough first cut; after that, intuition takes over. Also, other more traditional and 'embodied' methods of meeting people are still available through work, leisure and family connections as well as pure serendipity and luck.

As we know by now, making predictions about whether or not computers might be able to out-compete humans is a hostage to fortune. But in the social arena in which we live our lives, human intuition still trumps algorithms when it comes to empathy, emotional and social intelligence.

This means that, alongside creative occupations where genuine out-of-the-box thinking as opposed to mimicry is required, other AI-proof jobs are likely to be those that involve subtle and sophisticated social intuitions, for example mental health and social workers; coaches and therapists; clinical psychologists and psychiatrists; teachers and trainers; customer- and client-facing staff across the service sector; nurses, paramedics and doctors; and supervisors, managers and leaders across the board.

Takeaway

Human beings have evolved to be able to make accurate, intuitive social judgements of other humans based on the briefest of snapshots of non-verbal and verbal behaviours.

Hybrid intelligence

Even jobs that are AI-proof have changed and will continue to change as technology develops; for example AI may have become better than doctors at detecting illnesses, but the diagnosis and treatment of diseases still are better delivered by a skilled human who's able to understand the prognosis and communicate with the patient empathetically. The principle of machines augmenting human intelligences is likely to apply to most jobs.

The future of intelligence in the workplace, and in society more generally, is likely to be 'hybrid' (Figure 16). In a world of hybrid intelligence where machines are used to empower humans and humans don't concede power to machines, human intuitive intelligence will *sense* solutions to problems, human analytical intelligence will *solve* those problems that it can't delegate to machines; artificial intelligence will *augment* human intelligences in both sensing and solving.[28]

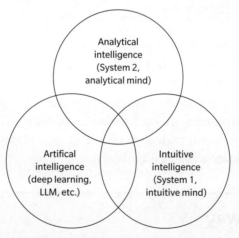

Figure 16 Hybrid intelligence

As far as the viability of human intuition is concerned, the main threat is whether it'll ever be possible to have 'artificial intuition', perhaps as the ultimate form of AI that can outperform humans in the creative and social arenas. To explore this, I asked ChatGPT the question from Step 2, 'What happens when you intuit?' to see if it thought AI could be intuitive. It replied:

> 'As a language model I don't have the ability to intuit. I am a machine learning-based algorithm that is designed to understand and generate human language. I can understand and process information provided to me, but I don't have the ability to have intuition or feelings.'[29]

For the foreseeable future, human creative intuition and social intuition will continue to add value as they have done throughout history. Until machines can create and empathise as adroitly as a human being can, the idea of an artificial intuition is a science fiction that remains in the realms of the radically uncertain.

Takeaway

The secret of success in the age of AI is to strike the right balance between human intuitive intelligence, human analytical intelligence and machine artificial intelligence.

Last words

My last words on intuition, which is a curious passion that has absorbed much of my attention for the best part of 20 years, is that it's a *sensing* system (the 'intuitive mind') that complements our *solving* system (the 'analytical mind') and reveals, often in the fullness of time, things to us that are quite unknowable by any other means. This is why I believe that, armed with the requisite level of intuitive intelligence, you will be able to decide if, when and how to trust your gut for better decision making in your personal and professional life.

Each chapter of this book began with a power quote; my favourite intuition power quote with which to end comes from the works of the English poet and spiritual writer Thomas Traherne (1637–74) that were nearly lost to the world but were saved serendipitously when they were found by chance in a barrow of books that were about to be trashed in a London bookstall in the 1890s. Traherne described intuition as 'a seeming somewhat more than view; That doth instruct the mind In things that lie behind, And many secrets to us show which afterwards we come to know' (from *Shadows in the Water*).

Dig deeper

In *How to Stay Smart in a Smart World*, Gerd Gigerenzer shows why it's a myth that algorithms and robots will soon be able to do everything better than humans, and how to use AI to augment human beings' intuitive and analytical intelligences.

If you want to find out more about intuition in general and especially if you want to dig deeper into the four different types of intuition (expert, moral, social and creative), you might like to take a look at one of my other intuition books, *Intuition in Business* (2023).

In a nutshell, add value with intuition in the age of AI

Computers are adept at solving by following rules that humans create for them; humans are more adept at sensing, which makes creativity and social judgement USPs for humans in the age of AI.

Workout 1: Integrating intuition and analysis

1 Intuition and analysis complement each other. As we know from the two minds model, intuition is fast, unconscious and effortless, whereas analysis is slower, conscious and effortful. The analytical

mind can impose a discipline on the intuitive mind's hunches; the intuitive mind can notice subtle patterns and connections that the analytical mind is unaware of. They work best together.

2 Think of a consequential decision that you're currently faced with. Ask yourself:

- What does intuition tell me to do?
- What does analysis tell me to do?

3 If they agree, it's a no-brainer; if they disagree, there's more work to be done.

4 If intuition says 'yes' and analysis says 'no', then your analysis might have spotted something that your intuitive mind hasn't noticed. In this situation, it's probably best to check out your intuition using devil's advocacy, pre-morteming, etc.

5 If analysis says 'yes' but intuition says 'no', then your intuition might have spotted something that your analytical mind isn't aware of. In this situation, it's probably best to check out your analysis, for example by going over the figures again with a fine-tooth comb, etc.

6 The 'traffic light' model (Figure 17) will help you to get the best out of both minds and avoid being sabotaged by either of them.[30]

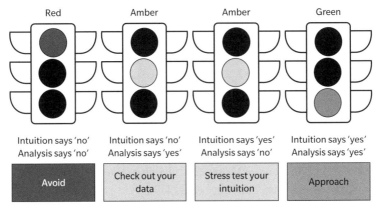

Red	Amber	Amber	Green
Intuition says 'no' Analysis says 'no'	Intuition says 'no' Analysis says 'yes'	Intuition says 'yes' Analysis says 'no'	Intuition says 'yes' Analysis says 'yes'
Avoid	Check out your data	Stress test your intuition	Approach

Figure 17 Traffic light model for integrating intuition and analysis

(Source: Care Quality Commission (2023) *Role of Intuition in Professional Judgement*. London: CQC.).

Workout 2: Building hybrid intelligence

1 Which aspects of your decision making do you think could be outsourced to a computer?

2 Which aspects of your decision making do you think can only be accomplished by you, a human being?

3 How can you, or your organisation, get the best of both worlds, the artificial and the human, in the age of artificial intelligence and use them to support better decision making in both your professional and your personal life?

Notes

1 Marr, B. (2017) '28 best quotes about artificial intelligence'. *Forbes*, 25 July. Available online at: https://www.forbes.com/sites/bernardmarr/2017/07/25/28-best-quotes-about-artificial-intelligence/.

2 Oakridge (no date) 'Direction of discovery', *Frontier*. Oakridge National Laboratory. Available online at: https://www.olcf.ornl.gov/frontier/ (accessed May 2024).

3 The Physics of the Universe (no date) *The Universe by Numbers*. Available online at: https://www.physicsoftheuniverse.com/numbers.html (accessed May 2024).

4 Dawes, R. M., Faust, D. and Meehl, P. E. (1993) 'Statistical prediction versus clinical prediction: Improving what works', in Keren, G. and Lewis, C. (eds) *A Handbook for Data Analysis in the Behavioral Sciences: Methodological Issues*, pp. 351–67.

5 Kleinman, Z. (2024) 'NHS AI test spots tiny cancers missed by doctors', *BBC News*, 20 March. Available online at: https://www.bbc.co.uk/news/technology-68607059.

6 Larkin, C. (2022) 'AI won't replace human intuition', *Forbes*, 27 September. Available online at: https://www.forbes.com/

sites/forbestechcouncil/2022/09/27/ai-wont-replace-human-intuition/.

7 Lawson, A., Lobo, M. S. and Puranam, P. (2024) 'Leave intuition to the machines', *INSEAD Knowledge*. Available online at: https://knowledge.insead.edu/strategy/leave-intuition-machines.

8 Theta Ray (no date) 'The start-up that reveals the hackers of today's accounts'. Available online at: https://www.thetaray.com/press-releases/the-start-up-that-reveals-the-hackers-of-todays-accounts/ (accessed May 2024).

9 Theta Ray (no date).

10 Prompt to ChatGPT 'When do human beings outperform algorithms?' (I'm thinking of the studies conducted by Meehl in the 1950s on clinical versus statistical prediction and where statistical prediction won each time.) Based on its answer I then asked, 'When you say, "algorithms are better than humans at recognising complex patterns within large data sets" could you give an example please?' It gave its answer but qualified it with this remark about intuition. (Accessed April 2024.)

11 Hogarth, R. (2002) *Educating Intuition*. Chicago: University of Chicago Press, p. 147.

12 Gigerenzer, G. (2022) *How to Stay Smart in a Smart World: Why Human Intelligence Still Beats Algorithms*. London: Allen Lane, p. 38.

13 Gigerenzer, G. (2008) *Gut Feelings*. London: Penguin, pp. 16–17.

14 Clarke, L. (2022) 'When AI can make art – what does it mean for creativity?', *The Guardian*, 12 November. Available online at: https://www.theguardian.com/technology/2022/nov/12/when-ai-can-make-art-what-does-it-mean-for-creativity-dall-e-midjourney.

15 Marr, B. (2023) 'The intersection of AI and human creativity: Can machines really be creative?', *Forbes*, 27 May. Available online at: https://www.forbes.com/sites/bernardmarr/2023/03/27/the-intersection-of-ai-and-human-creativity-can-machines-really-be-creative/.

16 Vincent, J. (2016) 'Can you tell the difference between Bach and RoboBach?', *The Verge*, 23 December. Available online at: https://www.theverge.com/2016/12/23/14069382/ ai-music-creativity-bach-deepbach-csl.

17 IBM (no date).

18 Bonadio, E. and McDonagh, L. (2020) 'Artificial intelligence as producer and consumer of copyright works: Evaluating the consequences of algorithmic creativity', *Intellectual Property Quarterly*, 2, 112–37.

19 Based on a quote attributed to the French 'impressionist' composer Claude Debussy (1862–1918).

20 Heffernan, M. (2020) *Uncharted*. London: Simon & Schuster, p. 178.

21 Ambady, N., Krabbenhoft, M. A. and Hogan, D. (2006) 'The 30-sec sale: Using thin-slice judgments to evaluate sales effectiveness', *Journal of Consumer Psychology*, 16(1), 4–13.

22 Ambady, N. (2010) 'The perils of pondering: Intuition and thin slice judgments', *Psychological Inquiry*, 21(4), 271–8, p. 276. The 'understood by all' quote is Ambady citing the great US anthropologist Edward Sapir (1884–1939).

23 Haden, J. (2022) 'How Jeff Bezos and a Nobel prize-winning economist use intuition to make better decisions', *Inc.*, 14 November. Available online at: https://www.inc.com/jeff-haden/how-jeff-bezos-a-nobel-prize-winning-economist-use-intuition-to-make-better-decisions.html.

24 Sciortino, C. (2014) 'What is so "female" about female intuition?', *Vogue*, 20 February. Available online at: https://www.vogue.com/article/female-intuition-breathless-karley-sciortino-slutever; Gigerenzer, G. (2023) *The Intelligence of Intuition*. Cambridge: Cambridge University Press.

25 Myers, D. (2002) *Intuition: Its Powers and Perils*. Yale: Yale University Press, p. 33.

26 Youyou, W., Kosinski, M. and Stillwell, D. (2015) 'Computer-based personality judgments are more accurate than those made by humans', *Proceedings of the National Academy of Sciences*, 112(4), 1036–40.

27 Gigerenzer (2022), p. 26.

28 Paydas Turan, C. and Sadler-Smith, E. (2023) 'A dual-process model of hybrid intelligence for improved managerial decision making'. Paper presented at Annual Academy of Management Meeting, August, Boston, MA. doi: 10.5465/AMPROC.2023.12866.

29 Prompt to ChatGPT 'What happens when you intuit?' (accessed April 2024).

30 This is an application of the traffic light model from *Inside Intuition* (Sadler-Smith, 2008, p. 264) in 'Role of Intuition in Professional Judgement' (a report for the UK Government's Care Quality Commission, 2023).

Index